# HONUS

## *The Life and Times of a Baseball Hero*

---

*William Hageman*

SAGAMORE PUBLISHING
Champaign, IL

Book design: Susan M. McKinney
Dustjacket and photo insert design: Michelle R. Dressen
Editors: Susan M. McKinney, Russ Lake
Proofreader: Phyllis L. Bannon

ISBN: 1-57167-042-4
Library of Congress Catalog Card Number: 96-68630

Printed in the United States.

*To my father, who taught me that baseball*
*was a game to be enjoyed.*

———————————————————

# Contents

# *Foreword*

Honus Wagner may be the most underappreciated player in the history of baseball.

Unlike contemporaries such as Ty Cobb and Babe Ruth, the man who came to be known as the Flying Dutchman did not promote himself. A reticent man who kept to himself on and off the field, Wagner simply played the game without the fanfare that Cobb and Wagner generated throughout their careers. He let his accomplishments speak for him: eight National League batting titles, a 17-year stretch in which he hit better than .300 every season, a .329 career batting average. All of that and more earned him charter membership in the Baseball Hall of Fame in 1936 as well as consensus acclaim as the greatest shortstop to ever play the game.

To have known him, though, as I did for six of my seasons as a player with the Pirates while he was a coach, was not to know him or any of what he accomplished at all. A loner, he rarely socialized with any of the players, his fellow coaches, or the manager, preferring his own company after hours when he would sometimes walk into a tavern, plunk a silver dollar down on the bar, drink a beer, then move on to another tavern, where he'd do the same thing.

At times on the overnight train trips that we took between cities in those days, he might adjourn to a washroom or vestibule with several players or coaches and tell stories—he was a terrific storyteller. Never, though, would he do so in a more public place, because that would call attention to himself and that was not him.

Few, though, saw the humorous side of Wagner. Those who saw him play—which I didn't—remembered a ham-handed, bow-legged man far unlike the mold from which shortstops come these days. Unlike Cobb, though, he never slid into a base with his spikes high, nor did he taunt an opponent. Calling his shot, as legend has it that Ruth did during the 1932 World Series, was not his style, either.

His style was to go about his business as a player and later as a coach. That is why, while the legends of Ruth, Cobb and other players of his era live on today on film and paper, Wagner is nothing more than several lines in a record book and a plaque on the Hall of Fame wall in Cooperstown, N.Y.

Until now. Bill Hageman's book has Wagner down cold, his personality, his accomplishments, his life. This book tells the story of a man few people alive today ever saw play, and even fewer people knew.

This book tells the story of someone who was a tough SOB as a player who never projected that image anywhere else. This book tells about a man who preferred talking about hunting and fishing, rather than baseball, when he talked at all.

This book offers terrific insight into someone who might've been the greatest player to ever play the game.

—Ralph Kiner

*Ralph Kiner was a Hall-of-Fame outfielder who hit 369 career homers with Pittsburgh, the Chicago Cubs and Cleveland from 1946-55. He is currently in his 35th season as a New York Mets broadcaster. As told to Steve Adamek, baseball writer for The Record in Hackensack, N.J.*

# *Preface*

Honus Wagner took his lead off first base and stared at the Boston pitcher. One step, then another, all the while sizing up Bob Dresser, a 23-year-old left-hander who was making his major-league debut. As Dresser went into his windup, Wagner broke for second base.

Instantly, the Boston crowd, about 3,000 on this beautiful 78-degree August afternoon, came alive at the sight of the great Wagner in full gallop. Not a cheer, not a roar, but the sound of anticipation. Hunched over as he ran, his bowed legs pumping, Wagner arrived at second well ahead of catcher Pat Moran's throw. The Braves fans settled back, another confrontation won by the Pittsburgh star.

Wagner dusted himself off, then took another measured lead from second, all the while watching Dresser. Again, as the Boston pitcher threw home, Wagner set off for third. And once more, the sound of anticipation arose from the crowd, building quickly to a grudging cheer of appreciation as Wagner slid into third with his second stolen base.

Dresser and Wagner knew what was coming. And so did the Boston fans, their partisanship momentarily put aside. Wagner slowly walked down the baseline toward home. As Dresser went into his windup, Wagner broke for the plate. The runner and the ball arrived at the same time, but Wagner slid across with the run ahead of Moran's tag.

Wagner jumped to his feet and trotted to the Pirates bench, accompanied by a cheer that was as hearty and sincere as any he had ever heard in Pittsburgh. Dresser wouldn't have to worry about dealing with Wagner again. Not on this August afternoon, not ever. He never pitched another game in the major leagues.

Bob Dresser wasn't the first pitcher victimized by Honus Wagner, nor would he be the last. And he certainly wasn't the best pitcher to be roughed up by Wagner. Honus batted .324 against the legendary Christy Mathewson; .343 against Cy Young; and .352 versus Kid Nichols. Wagner was the greatest hitter of his day. Also the greatest baserunner. And the greatest shortstop. He was popular with fans—he was cheered in every city around the league and revered as a baseball god in Pittsburgh. He was the National League's biggest star, its top drawing card.

But John Peter Wagner was a reluctant hero, a victim, in a way, of his remarkable athletic skills. For most of his 21-year National League career, the shy Wagner had little to say to newspaper reporters. He was cordial, but he didn't want to talk about his personal life. And only rarely would he discuss baseball at length. It was baseball. It was just a game. He was playing because he loved it, not to be famous, not to make a fortune.

Throughout Wagner's life, recognition and popularity came in cycles. He started at the bottom, a relative unknown playing semipro ball in Pennsylvania and Ohio. He moved to faster company—minor-league teams in Ohio, Michigan, Pennsylvania and New Jersey—before finally arriving in the National League and quickly earning a reputation as one of the sport's greatest stars.

But after his storied career ended and the cheering stopped, Honus Wagner was largely forgotten. He accepted that, even welcomed it to a degree. The hills of western Pennsylvania afforded him the peace and privacy he always sought. But his love for baseball, and financial hardships caused by the Depression, brought him back to the game as a Pirates coach in 1933. His return resulted in another wave of popularity as a new generation of fans who had never seen him play—but who had heard the stories—discovered the great Honus.

He left the public eye again with his 1952 retirement, and following his 1955 death was largely relegated to baseball's dusty back shelves. Now, though, more than 40 years later, Honus Wagner is being rediscovered. Again.

# *Acknowledgments*

When I began chasing the legend of Honus Wagner in the fall of 1991, I had no idea how long or complicated the journey would be. Three and a half years of my life. More than 100 interviews. Several hundred hours in front of microfilm machines. More than 12,000 miles traveled. Through it all, through the years it took me to complete this project, one thing that kept me going was the encouragement and cooperation I received from dozens of people, without whom this book would not have been possible.

People like Mabel Thornhill, as sweet and as wonderful a person as I have ever encountered, whose stories fascinated me for hours, and whose recollections were an invaluable help.

And Leslie Blair, Honus' granddaughter, who shared with me not only his scrapbooks, but her memories and family stories about "Buck," as well.

Then there was Sally O'Leary of the Pittsburgh Pirates' front office, who was always there to answer my questions, provide information, send me in the right direction or just chat.

And Gordie Volkman, a true sports fan and your basic good guy, who opened his personal library to a stranger. And who didn't call every six months wondering when I would be returning the boxes of books I borrowed.

I'm also deeply indebted to Rick Kogan of the *Chicago Tribune,* a classic Chicago journalist in every sense of the word, a great boss and an inspiration. I hope to grow up to be just like him someday.

There are so many other people to thank: Dr. Harold "Jack" Snyder, whose tales of his father, uncle and Honus held me spellbound; Dan and Marcella McGrogan of the Historical Society of Carnegie (Pennsylvania), always there to answer my questions and provide guidance; Frank and Sylvia Sgro, who like so many others shared their warm memories; and Steve Adamek, who, whether he realized it or not, provided the spark that made this thing happen.

Also: Ken Yorko, Eleanor McKelvey, Richard Esch, Michael Murphy of the Prothonotary's Office in Pittsburgh, John and June Swete, Dr. James Ross, former Pirates Pete Castiglione, Lee Howard, Ralph Kiner, Al Lopez and Xavier Rescigno, and, of course, my man, Jim Binkley.

The institutions and organizations that helped included: the Society for American Baseball Research, the Center for Research Libraries in Chicago, the Aurora (Illinois) Public Library, the Carnegie (Pennsylvania) Free Library, The Carnegie in Pittsburgh, the National Baseball Hall of Fame and Museum and the Pittsburgh Pirates.

Finally, my family. To my mother, Estelle, and my aunts, Fran and Ann, I wish to express my gratitude for their encouragement. To my daughters, Julie, Kelly and Kathryn, hugs, kisses and thanks for their interest and help. And to my wife, Dona, whose support and good spirits kept me going, and without whose understanding this would not have been possible. At times, it may have seemed that I had abandoned you; but believe me, you were never forgotten.

# *Introduction*

When Bill Hageman initially approached me with the idea of writing this book about Buck—a nickname for my grandfather—my first question was, "What can you possibly write that hasn't been written before?" There have been newspaper articles, magazine articles and whole chapters in books about Buck, how would this be different?

Bill said yes, those things were out there, but that wasn't what he was looking for. He wanted to do more. He wanted to do the story of the man, not the ballplayer, not the athlete. The man.

I think that anyone who reads this book will get a real sense of who and what Buck was. Material things didn't mean much to him. What he cared about most in life were his wife, his daughters, his granddaughter and all the people he loved. It was love of family, love of what was really important, that made him so special.

The other love in his life, of course, was baseball. That's where he gained his fame, and that's the Honus Wagner everyone knows. But to me he was my grandfather, Buck, the man who'd share his chocolate bars with me as I sat in his lap. And that's the person— not only a gentleman, but a gentle man—Bill has tried to capture.

I hope people can feel Buck coming out, explaining his life through Bill's words. I'm excited about this book. Yes, I have Buck's scrapbooks, his photos and things, but now I've gotten a chance to learn so much more about my grandfather.

It has been almost 80 years since Buck last played, more than 40 since he passed away. Yet people still remember him. To me, it's such an honor having his memory kept alive. I'm so proud of my grandfather—I only wish I'd had a chance to be with him a little longer—and I'm so proud of Bill for writing this book. I'm sure there were times when he could have put his pen down or shut off the computer, and said, I've done all I can; I know all there is to know. But for some reason, he kept going. It was something he had to do, and he did it. And I'm glad.

—Leslie Blair

*"Even if he hadn't been a famous ballplayer at all, anyone who ever knew him would have bragged about it."*

—Charles L. Smith,
in the Pittsburgh Press,
after the death of
Honus Wagner

# One

John Wagner quietly slipped out the front door of his house, careful not to awaken the other members of his family who were still asleep. In the predawn darkness, he could barely make out the outline of the First Ward Public School across the street from his home. But instead of walking in the direction of the school, the boy—a gangly, bowlegged teenager—was going to work.

It was 1888, and 14-year-old John was making his daily trek from the Wagner family home on Railroad Avenue in Mansfield, Pennsylvania, to the coal mines where he labored with his father.

The region was part of the richest coal-producing area in the world, and Mansfield and Chartiers, two small, adjoining western Pennsylvania towns separated by Chartiers Creek, bustled with mines. The Grant Mine, a short walk east from the Wagner home and where John and his father worked, was the biggest mine in a town that also had Bell's Coal Works, Camp Hill Coal Works, McConnell's Coal Mines, Cherry Mines, Glendale Mines and Fort Pitt Mines, among others. For many in Mansfield and Chartiers, coal mining was the family business. Immigrant fathers—Germans, Hungarians, Swedes and Slovenians—came to America and went directly into the mines; their sons followed. As difficult and dangerous as the work was, it was still preferable to the region's other industry, the steel mills. The miners worked in a country setting; they had homes with gardens and chicken coops, and lived a rural existence. Just 10 miles to the east, in Pittsburgh, was a dirty, crowded, urban environment with its equally difficult and dangerous work in the mills.

It was into this setting that Peter John Wagner arrived in 1866. Wagner had been born in Dirmingen, on the Rhine River in Germany, in June 1838. After settling in the Chartiers-Mansfield area and finding work as a miner, he sent for his 28-year-old wife, Catherine.

Peter and Catherine had six children who survived past infancy: Charles, born in November 1869; Albert, September 1871; Louis, January 1873; John, February 1874; Carrie, May 1878; and William, April 1880.[1] Three other children died shortly after birth.

The Wagners first lived in a small house on Chartiers Street, just off the main street in Chartiers. It was in that house that their fourth son was born on February 24, 1874,[2] christened John Peter Wagner.[3] The family soon outgrew the home on Chartiers and moved to a larger frame house on Railroad Avenue.

The Wagner children attended both public and private schools, initially enrolling at the First Ward Public School, but later transferring to the German Lutheran school, where they could receive the religious education that Peter and Catherine considered important. The Wagners were good parents; strict and loving, teaching their children the importance of family, of loyalty and of discipline. Peter was a believer in physical activity and "coached" his boys in track. Catherine assigned each of the boys chores around the house.

At the German Lutheran school, John became the teacher's pet. The Rev. E.F.A. Dittmer, the Wagners' minister and the instructor at the school,[4] took a liking to the well-behaved, studious Wagner boy. Dittmer even thought that John might have a religious calling, and talked to Peter and Catherine about their son going into the ministry. It was a career path that didn't interest John, however. John's schooling lasted only until he was 12, when he followed his father into the mines. At first he worked in the tipple, sorting slate, rock and small pieces of coal from the larger chunks, which were then loaded into railroad cars. Later he loaded the coal into the cars.

"I seldom saw daylight except on Sundays and holidays," Wagner once reminisced when he was well into his 70s. "I'd start for work very early in the morning when it was still dark, and return home in the dusk and darkness of the evening. I worked on what was known as a 'boy car.' I loaded a ton of coal a day in one of those cars for 70 cents a ton. That's why it was called a 'boy car,' because it was all a boy my age could handle. My pay averaged about $3.50 a week."[5]

The little spare time John did have was devoted to sports. The two main athletic pursuits in the Chartiers-Mansfield area were baseball, America's game, and soccer, a bit of the old country that many of the immigrants held onto. For most of the boys in the region, baseball was the game of choice. What better way to show you belonged in your new homeland than by taking up its national game? As the local paper put it, "Baseball is all the go among our sport loving boys. The commons swarm with them every evening."[6]

Al and Luke Wagner played on several of the local teams, and both were regarded as talented players. Brother Charley, being the oldest and expected to take on more family responsibility, ran a barber shop in Mansfield. Shortly after John turned 16, he escaped the mines for good—it was a happy day; throughout his life, his memories of his days in the mines were almost uniformly unpleasant[7]—and began working in Charley's shop as an apprentice, holding customers' coats, brushing off their jackets, sweeping up and, of course, learning the trade. "On Saturday afternoon and night I was allowed to do a little shaving," Wagner once recalled. "Many a big miner has suffered at my hands. There weren't many tips in those days."[8]

The job not only allowed John to stay out of the mines, it gave him time to do something he really loved: play baseball. He always managed to find time for baseball, whether it was in a pickup game or just tossing a ball in the air and catching it, well into the night under the Chartiers streetlights. Around the time John was 15, he had started hanging around with Al's sandlot team, which played in the Allegheny County League. He went from being regarded as Al's kid brother who carried equipment to a full-fledged member of the team—and a good one. He was good enough, in fact, that in the fall of 1889, when the local Braddock Blues wanted to beef up their roster for a postseason exhibition game against the National League Pittsburgh Alleghenies, they called on John, who was more than willing to leave the mines behind for a day of baseball. Playing against a Pittsburgh team that was managed by Ned Hanlon and had future evangelist Billy Sunday in left field, Wagner banged out three hits—one a home run—in a 4-2 loss.

By the summer of 1890, John was a regular for St. Luke's, a local Catholic team regarded as the best ballclub in the region. He was a natural athlete. He wasn't big—around 5 feet, 10 inches and 160 pounds—but he was fast (despite his bowed legs) and strong (the result of his years in the mines). He had learned early to play more than one position, and was comfortable in the infield or outfield. As good as he was in the field, he was even more impressive with a bat. On the sandlots of Mansfield, he had adopted a cross-handed hitting style. Al corrected that; soon John began holding his hands a couple of inches apart on the handle.

John began spending more time on the baseball fields—playing for St. Luke's and the Carnegie[9] Athletic Club, both in the Allegheny County League—and less time in Charley's shop. "I had as much fun in the Allegheny County League as a kid in my teens as I had in my 19 [sic] years of big league stardom," he recalled in 1930. "All I lived for was baseball. I played from the end of March until the end of each October."[10]

In the summer of 1894, he and Al played not only for the Carnegie Athletic Club, but also for a semipro team in Dennison, Ohio, about 65 miles west of Carnegie. After the 1894 season in Dennison, John and Al returned to Carnegie, where they spent the winter doing what they loved best, next to baseball—hunting. John no longer had to worry about having to go back to work in Charley's barber shop—in February 1895, it went on the block in a constable's sale. That left John, to his mind, with only one career path: baseball.

The Wagner brothers' performances in Dennison had earned them a reputation as solid ballplayers, and as spring approached they received offers of better jobs for 1895. The one they accepted was from George Moreland, owner and manager of the Steubenville club in the Inter State League. Both Al and John were under contract to Steubenville by the first week of February 1895. They, along with James "Toots" Barrett, a local pitcher, left Carnegie on April 10, taking the train to Ohio. It was newsworthy enough that their departure made Page 1 of the April 12 edition of the *Carnegie Union*.[11]

Curiously, John signed his Steubenville contract "William Wagner," and was known as "Will" during most of his time in the Inter State League. At various points in his life, Wagner said he signed his brother's name to the contract because he thought William was the Wagner Moreland really wanted (although Bill was only 15 at the time), or because "Will Wagner" sounded better than "John Wagner."

The Wagner brothers' stay in Steubenville was short.[12] John played in only seven games, making his debut on April 20 in an exhibition victory over Holy Ghost College. Playing right field, he had two hits. Steubenville opened its league season on May 2, with John—still going by "Will"—hitting a home run in a 29-11 victory over Canton. Wagner split his time with Steubenville between the outfield and the pitcher's mound. Included in his work was a complete-game seven-hitter in a rain-shortened five-inning victory over Kenton, and a couple of relief appearances.

The team, though, was failing to attract enough fans to stay afloat, so Moreland pulled up stakes and moved the ballclub to Akron, where the Wagners' 1895 odyssey continued, though briefly. The Akron team played its first game on May 13, but disbanded after less than a week, the clinching blow being Moreland's inability to meet his payroll on May 18.

The Wagners weren't idle for long after the demise of Steubenville-Akron. Al, who had hit a combined .464 with the two teams, was snapped up by Canton, and "Will" was signed by Mansfield (Ohio). John's first game with Mansfield was on May 20, when he played shortstop and was listed as "J. Wagner" in the box score.

John's stay in Mansfield lasted just three weeks, until the Inter State League crumbled. Canton folded, with Al moving on to Warren of the Iron & Oil League, and Mansfield soon followed suit, ceasing operations on June 14. It didn't take long for John, who had hit .387 in 17 games at Mansfield, to find work. On June 20, he made his debut with the Adrian Demons of the Michigan State League, playing second base and getting two hits in a 12-11 victory over Owosso.

Wagner's career in Adrian was brief, however. He batted .386 in 16 games, and during that time the Demons lost only twice and climbed into a first-place tie with Lansing. Despite those successes—and not having been around long enough to form any close friendships—he quit the team on July 6, resurfacing five days later as the first baseman on Al's Warren team.

Why did he leave? A contemporary newspaper account alluded to a lack of harmony in the organization, and blamed Wagner's departure on it. In an article that ran in the *Adrian Daily Telegram* in 1930, Rolla Taylor, who had been Wagner's manager with the Demons in 1895, said that Wagner "never hitched" with the team, and that he didn't get along with pitcher George Wilson and catcher Vasco Graham, two players Adrian had obtained from the Page Fence Giants, a black team that barnstormed through southern Michigan in the late 19th Century. The real reason Wagner quit was simple: He was just 21 and was experiencing his first extended separation from his family. Out on his own for the first time in his life, shy and not adept at forming new friendships quickly, he missed the familiar surroundings and family back in Carnegie. "I got homesick after a few weeks," Wagner told the *New York Evening Telegram* in a 1917 interview. "Most of the boys from home were playing with the Warren team in the old Iron & Oil League, and I joined the same team."

Joining Warren reunited him with Al, as well as Claude Ritchey (another old acquaintance from western Pennsylvania) and hometown pal Toots Barrett. Why Wagner left Adrian wasn't as important as what happened as a result of his departure. Jumping to the Iron & Oil League enabled him to be seen by the man who would change his life: Edward Barrow.

Wagner appeared in 26 games for Warren, splitting time between third base and right field and hitting over .300 despite having to sit out three weeks because of a freak accident. Running for a train in Titusville, Pennsylvania, he fell and suffered a severe cut under his right arm. Several stitches were required, according to an account in the July 29 *Warren Evening Democrat*. The *Warren Ledger* reported, "He fell against a picket fence and received quite a gash under his right arm-pit, which is quite painful but not serious, as none of the muscles were injured. This is hard luck as it will break up our stone wall infield and then the team will miss his batting." [13]

The opposite turned out to be true. During Wagner's absence, Warren won 12 in a row to move into first place. But it soon became obvious that there were two races in the league—one for first place, the other to survive. A week after Wagner returned to the lineup, the Iron & Oil League began falling apart, losing four of its eight teams.

It was decided that first-place Warren and second-place Wheeling, managed by Barrow, would meet for a seven-game postseason series to determine the league champion. Wheeling won four of the games, which, if nothing else, gave Barrow a good look at the Wagner boys, whose long, strange 1895 season finally ended when Warren closed up shop on September 12, nearly two weeks after the players received their last paychecks.

Wagner headed home to Carnegie, planning to spend the fall and winter hunting and fishing and seeing the family and friends he had missed all summer. But soon he was visited by George Moreland, his manager at Steubenville. Moreland was there as a favor to William Kerr, owner of the Pittsburgh Pirates, who wanted to sign Wagner for 1896. Wagner was just as interested, and went to Pittsburgh to discuss contract terms with Kerr. The Pirates offered $100 a month, and Wagner at first agreed to sign. But the deal fell through. Kerr wanted to farm Wagner out to Kansas City of the Western League. And Wagner, who had gotten homesick in Michigan, was in no mind to play ball even farther from Pennsylvania. "I'd much rather stay here at home with my dogs and go hunting than to go way out there and be lost," Wagner said he told Kerr. "Unless I went to Kansas City, Mr. Kerr didn't want me. So that ended that. I went home and hunted and fished some more."[14]

# *Two*

The train ride from Pittsburgh to Carnegie was a short one, taking only a few minutes. But Ed Barrow didn't need a lot of time on that February 1896 afternoon to work on his spiel. His powers of persuasion were considerable—he had started his career as a soap salesman in Pittsburgh— and now he was preparing to make his biggest pitch yet: to talk Honus Wagner into playing ball for him.

Barrow had escaped the financially insecure Iron & Oil League by selling his interest in the Wheeling ballclub after the 1895 season and buying into the Paterson, New Jersey, team of the Atlantic League. Barrow and his partner, Charles McKee, were looking for players to fill out their roster, and two of the best, the Wagner boys, were on their shopping list. Barrow and McKee met with Shad Gwilliam, a local entrepreneur-gambler-semipro manager who knew the Wagner family. Gwilliam suggested they talk to John Wagner, Al having already signed a contract for 1896 with Toronto of the Eastern League.

After Barrow arrived in Carnegie, the legend goes, he found John beating all comers in a rock-throwing contest in a train yard outside town. The contest probably never occurred,[1] but Barrow did meet with Wagner in Carnegie that February day. "I asked him if he wanted to play ball for me in Paterson," Barrow recalled in his 1951 autobiography.[2] "Wagner was diffident. He didn't know. He didn't know whether he wanted to play ball at all." But Barrow was persistent, and after he offered Wagner $125 a month, the deal was sealed.

"I thought it was pretty good pay for a young player of 22," Wagner later recalled.[3] "It was the beginning of a great friendship with Barrow and a lucky break for me."

Paterson's regular season opened April 23, with Wilmington visiting Paterson's Olympic Park. A pregame parade featured players from both teams driven around in an electric streetcar, a marching band and musical entertainment in the grandstand. With 1,500 fans in the ballpark and another estimated thousand watching from a hill outside Olympic Park, Paterson fell to the visitors 7-2. "Hannis" Wagner, as the papers were calling him,[4] who had impressed fans and the press with his hitting, baserunning and hustle in 2 1/2 weeks of exhibition games, was at first base for the opener, contributing a double in three at-bats.

Wagner was an immediate success. His hitting—he went 8 for 13 in the three-game series with Wilmington that opened the season—helped keep Paterson near the top of the standings. The team moved into first place on May 10 with a victory over Hartford, in which Wagner contributed three hits. For the rest of May, Paterson and the New York Metropolitans took turns atop the standings. But as was the case the year before in Warren, an injury would sidetrack Wagner's season.

On June 11, he collided with catcher Bert Eltom while chasing a pop foul and hurt his kneecap. The painful injury sidelined him more than three weeks, during which time Paterson maintained its hold on first place. Although still bothersome, the knee was sufficiently healed after his return to the lineup that Barrow was able to shift him to the more strenuous position of second base.

By the end of July, Paterson had fallen into second, a game and a half behind Newark in the Atlantic League race. A week later, the situation was reversed, with Paterson in the lead by 1 1/2 games, and by mid-August it was Hartford with a 1 1/2 -game lead over Paterson, with Newark third, two games back. Wagner was splitting time between first, second, third and the outfield—and even pitched in relief in an 8-5 loss to Newark on August 20. His hitting picked up toward the end of August as Paterson moved back into first place.

The pennant race went down to the last series of the season against Hartford. In the first game of the series, on September 8, Hartford scored two unearned runs in the ninth, thanks in part to an error by third baseman Wagner, and beat Paterson 2-0. The visitors also won the next day to move into first, and widened their lead to 1 1/2 games by winning on September 10 in a contest that featured Wagner's ejection in the third inning for disputing a call.

The series—and the season—came down to the last two games. With 2,000 fans crammed into Olympic Park, Paterson routed the visitors on consecutive days, 10-2 and 10-4, to win the pennant.

Wagner's contribution was minimal, one single in the two games. But his .349 average for the season, as well as his performance in postseason games, including contests against Brooklyn and Boston of the National League, clearly marked him as too good for the Atlantic League.

Paterson co-owner McKee realized that, so he wanted to get Wagner under contract for 1897 as quickly as possible. Within weeks of his return home to Carnegie, Wagner was visited by McKee, who signed him for the next season. While in town, McKee also made arrangements— at Honus' urging—to add another of Carnegie's baseball talents, pitcher Patsy Flaherty, to the Paterson roster.

If nothing else, Wagner's 1897 season should be remembered for his hitting. It started in the spring: a three-run homer on April 6 tied an exhibition game against Newark 12-12; the next day he had two more home runs in a victory over Newark. He had a single and a double in the regular-season opener, a 9-5 victory April 26 in Hartford. And he had two triples and a double in a victory over Lancaster on May 5 that left Paterson in first place with a 5-1 record. But Wagner's most significant hitting came against Norfolk, and it had little to do with the Atlantic League race.

Claude McFarlan was a rookie pitcher and outfielder for Norfolk, a team that Wagner had amazing success against. In a three-game series from May 10 through 12, Wagner went 4 for 10, including a home run. A little over a week later, he had a single, triple and homer in a 14-1 victory over Norfolk. McFarlan was clearly impressed. So much so that the next time Norfolk visited Newark, he decided to spread the word about Honus Wagner.

On June 2, McFarlan made the short trip into New York, where his hometown Louisville Colonels of the National League were playing the Giants. He went to the Sturtevant Hotel, where the Colonels stayed. Owner Barney Dreyfuss and team president Harry Pulliam were out on a scouting mission,[5] but McFarlan was able to get a meeting with manager Fred Clarke. He told Clarke about Paterson's great third baseman, and urged him to scout Wagner.[6]

When Dreyfuss and Pulliam returned, Clarke filled them in on Wagner. Pulliam took off the next morning to see Wagner for himself. Wagner, who was playing right field for the first time that season because of a hand injury that limited his effectiveness at third base, hammered out two doubles and a single in a 10-4 loss to the Athletics. The next day, Wagner, playing first base, went hitless in another loss. On June 5, with Pulliam, Clarke and Dreyfuss watching, he was in left field and contributed two singles and a stolen base in a 3-2 victory over Hartford. In the final game scouted by the Louisville brain trust, Paterson was a 4-3 winner, with Wagner's triple sparking a three-run sixth inning. He also had a stolen base and made several nice running catches in left field. But Dreyfuss, Pulliam and Clarke weren't convinced. Dreyfuss, usually a good judge of talent, was unsure. Clarke thought Wagner was too slow-footed to play in the National League. And he didn't have the appearance of a ballplayer. Bowlegged and huge-chested, with long arms and massive hands, he had the appearance of a coal miner or wagon driver. There was no fluidity of motion, no grace, when he went after a ball. Pulliam, though, saw a baseball player, and became a Wagner fan immediately. But even he thought McKee's asking price was too high.

"The [Louisville] club and the Philadelphia club of the National League were after him," Pulliam told a banquet audience in 1907. "[McKee] told me he could get $2,500 from Pittsburgh, which was a big price to pay for the release of a player in those days."[7]

The $2,500 price tag was just so much bluster on McKee's part. He could be had for less. On June 12 while the Pirates were in Brooklyn, their manager, Patsy Donovan, visited Paterson, not to scout Wagner but to purchase his contract. He offered McKee only $1,500 and was turned down.[8]

Wagner, meanwhile, did nothing to diminish his value. He was a crowd favorite in Paterson—fans presented him with an inscribed gold watch before a game on June 20—he hit a pair of home runs in a July 1 loss to Richmond, and he reached July 4 with a .387 average. But he saved his biggest heroics for Sunday, July 11, when he had a phenomenal day that made national headlines[9]: three home runs, two triples and a double—20 total bases—in an 11-5 victory over Norfolk.

And watching it all from center field was Claude McFarlan.

Despite Wagner's efforts, the ballcub was struggling. Paterson had flirted with first place early in the season but had fallen into the second division, fifth place at 34-36, at the time of Wagner's big day. The sale of Wagner was an opportunity for McKee and Barrow to pick up some needed cash—as the team fell in the standings, amateur games had begun outdrawing contests at Olympic Park—as well as pick up a player or two in exchange. And in the back of McKee's mind was the knowledge that Wagner was too good for the Atlantic League, and would probably want to go elsewhere for 1898. So on July 15, with his team in fifth place at 36-38, McKee agreed to send John Peter Wagner to Louisville for $2,100 and two players, third baseman Irvin Hock and second baseman Abbie Johnson.

# Three

Barney Dreyfuss must have wondered what he'd gotten himself into. A Prussian immigrant who had made his fortune in the whiskey business in Kentucky, Dreyfuss bought a substantial interest in the Louisville Colonels before the 1897 season. But this was not one of the National League's showcase franchises. The Colonels had finished last the three previous seasons, 54, 52, and 53 games behind the first-place Baltimore Orioles. And never did they win more than 38 games in a season. Prospects for 1897, even with the infusion of Dreyfuss' capital, weren't great.

The Colonels started quickly and were in second place with a 9-4 record on May 13. But then a string of injuries struck: Shortstop Joe Dolan and first baseman Perry Werden hurt their arms. Manager and second baseman Jimmy Rogers was in and out of the lineup with a leg injury; and when he did play, he struggled in the field and at bat. Louisville traded for shortstop Bob Stafford, but he ended up being sent to left field when Fred Clarke got hurt. Outfielder-catcher Charlie Dexter was given a turn at short, but had so much trouble there he vowed never to play the position again.

As the injuries mounted, the Colonels fell in the standings. They lost six in a row and were 15-15 and in seventh place by the end of May. Finally, Dreyfuss and team president Harry Pulliam decided that Rogers had to go. On June 16, after 45 games—and only 17 victories—Rogers lost his job as manager as well as his spot as the starting second baseman.[1]

Taking over as manager was Clarke, the Colonels' 24-year-old left-fielder. A native of Des Moines, Iowa, he was a natural ballplayer with a feisty disposition. Clarke had attended Drake College and started his professional career with Hastings of the Nebraska State

League. After a stint in the Southern League, he came to the Colonels during the 1894 season and hit .275, .354 and .327 in his first three years in the National League.

He inherited a ninth-place team that was decimated by injuries: Catcher Bill Wilson was out with a broken finger; second baseman Abbie Johnson took a bad-hop grounder in the eye and was sidelined; third baseman Billy Clingman suffered a hand injury; Dexter pulled up lame. It all added up to disasters like a 7-19 road trip that included a 36-7 loss to the Chicago Colts on June 29. Pulliam thought he had solved his infield problems by bringing William Winfield "Bill" Clark to Louisville. A second baseman, Clark was signed on July 9 and debuted July 12. But he wasn't the answer— he struck out three times in his first game, made four errors in a double-header the next day, and committed two more errors the following afternoon before being benched. Making matters worse, the Colonels lost third baseman Dexter with a broken leg on July 12. Dreyfuss realized that his team needed to be strengthened and took up negotiations with Paterson officials in an effort to land Honus Wagner.

Suddenly, the asking price for Wagner didn't seem so steep, and the skidding Colonels couldn't let him slip away. Pulliam offered $2,100 and two players, third baseman Irvin Hock and second baseman Johnson. That clinched the deal, and Louisville secured Wagner on the evening of Thursday, July 15.

On July 19, Wagner made his big-league debut, starting in center field against Washington. In his first at-bat in the National League, his sacrifice moved along a pair of runners, both of whom scored in a four-run first inning that helped carry Louisville to a 6-2 victory. Wagner added a walk in the second inning and an RBI single in the seventh, all off curveball expert Doc McJames.

Wagner made a smooth adjustment to the National League, hitting safely in his first nine games and carrying a .430 average after a week with the Colonels. He wasn't as quick to adapt to his new position. Wagner, who had been playing third base for Paterson, made three errors in his first week in center, and had several mixups with teammates while chasing fly balls.

As if getting to the National League wasn't exciting enough, Wagner's first week with Louisville also afforded him one of the biggest thrills of his baseball career: the opportunity to face one of his heroes, Chicago's Cap Anson, on the playing field. Anson, in what would be his final season as a player, had long been admired by Wagner. As a boy, he closely watched Anson when Chicago visited Recreation Park and Exposition Park in Pittsburgh, and he would mimic Anson's on-field mannerisms when he himself played.

Wagner was able to face Anson on the field on July 25, when Louisville went to Chicago for a one-game visit. Anson and his Colts beat the Colonels 1-0 in a game shortened to 6 ½ innings by rain. Wagner—referred to as "Hans" by the Chicago newspapers—had two singles in a loss to Chicago, which moved past Louisville into eighth place with the victory.

Despite reaching the National League and achieving immediate success, Wagner found some aspects of his new life difficult. "In those days the veteran players looked down on a rookie as though he were a worm," he once reminisced. "During practice I tried to take my turn at the plate, but one of the players threatened to hit me on the head with a bat. A rookie get batting practice? I should say not, not if the veterans had anything to say about it. After two or three days, however, Fred Clarke insisted I get my turn.

"My first job at Louisville was to carry in beer for the other players at lunch time. And how they could drink it! Clarke ordered morning practice, and the boys usually remained in the park and sent out for lunch. The rookies always were dispatched for large buckets of beer."[2]

Honus found much to like in Louisville. One of the ballplayers' favorite hangouts was the American restaurant, known for the chicken, duck and quail dishes on its menu. The city had numerous beer gardens—offering 5-cent beers, beef sandwiches, pickled eel and sour rabbit. For entertainment, he and teammates would take long buggy rides, or, occasionally, the shy Wagner would be talked into joining some of his teammates at a square dance.

On August 14, Wagner made an emotional return to Pittsburgh with the Colonels. Dozens of relatives and friends from Carnegie turned out to see him, sitting behind the Colonels' bench and loudly voicing their support for the visitors from Kentucky. Wagner, on his first trip to the plate, was presented with a diamond pin by his appreciative followers. He failed to get a hit in the game, a 6-3 Pirate victory, but did throw out two runners from center field.

In 61 games with Louisville, 52 as an outfielder, nine as a second baseman, Wagner hit .344, finishing 18th in the final league stats. He also stole 22 bases. And the .379 batting average that he left behind in Paterson stood up, giving him the Atlantic League's batting championship in absentia. Still, he couldn't prevent Louisville from being an 11th-place team with a dismal 52-78 record.

Again, changes were in order, and it didn't take long before rumors started circulating in Louisville newspapers and national publications. One had Wagner being moved to shortstop; another had him replacing the dependable Clingman at third. Still another had him being traded.

That third scenario would have been the least likely. Having given up $2,100 and two players for Wagner, Dreyfuss would not have been eager to trade a young, promising .344 hitter. But Wagner obviously was aware of—and maybe concerned about—the rumors.

"I would hate to leave Louisville," he said in the January 15, 1898 edition of *The Sporting News*, "as I have many good friends in that city, and the kindly treatment I have received makes me have a warm spot in my heart ... but I suppose if the club people want to chase me away I will have to go. If I can benefit the team any by being traded, I am perfectly willing."

As for the possibility of supplanting Clingman at third, he said: "There is but one man in the business who can fill Billy's shoes, and that is Jimmy Collins.[3] Of course, if I am ordered to take the position I will, like a good soldier, obey, but I hope that day never comes."

Dreyfuss' plans were to move Charlie Dexter to third base and keep Wagner at second.[4] And that's what Clarke was aiming for when spring training began in March 1898.

The reporting date for the Colonels was March 18. The next morning they left Louisville for West Baden Springs, an Indiana resort town that featured handball courts, swimming pools and cycling tracks. Wagner, however, didn't accompany the team. Unsigned for 1898, he didn't report to Louisville, but came directly to West Baden Springs, arriving on the 21st. Not only was he late, he was also overweight, reporting at 185 pounds, the heaviest of all the Colonels and some 10 pounds over his playing weight of the previous season.

In every other way, though, he was still the Honus Wagner of 1897. Quiet, shy, he wasn't a clubhouse leader—he was still, after all, only a few months away from being the rookie told to fetch beer for the older players. But his performance, his earnestness, had earned him a modicum of respect from the other Colonels, and for Wagner, that was good enough for now.

The team's stay in Indiana was cut short by rain, cold and wet grounds. The Colonels got little accomplished as workouts were restricted to running sprints on a covered bicycle track or taking long walks through the nearby hills. Much of the time, the players were stuck in their hotel rooms. A disappointed Clarke packed up his ballclub and returned home March 25. That night, there was a team dinner at the Galt House, the Colonels' headquarters. The following day, the players went to the Hillerich Bat Co. factory, where they each picked out two new bats for the coming season. That evening, they went to the theater, then returned to the Galt House.

The Colonels played their first intrasquad game on March 29—Wagner and the other veterans beating the subs 17-6. The next day, Wagner finally got around to signing his contract.[5] Wagner's hitting that spring was a continuation of the success he had had in 1897. He had a double, a triple and a home run in an intrasquad game, and a homer and two singles in a 16-10 victory over Detroit. His play at second base was also steady (in one game, against Milwaukee, he handled 11 chances flawlessly, making two outstanding plays, much to the delight of some 3,000 Louisville fans in the stands).

The third base job, which had been up in the air during the off-season, remained Clingman's. Wagner was doing good work at second; and Dexter, Dreyfuss' choice to play third, injured a finger while catching during an intrasquad game and was sidelined. There were new faces in the lineup, however.

President Pulliam pulled off a big trade in preparation for the 1898 season. In early February, he sent pitcher Bill Hill to Cincinnati in exchange for outfielder William "Dummy" Hoy, shortstop Claude Ritchey and pitcher Red Ehret. It was a blockbuster, especially for the Colonels. Hoy, a 10-year veteran, had hit .292 as Cincinnati's regular center-fielder in 1897; Ritchey, Wagner's old teammate from Warren in 1895 and a .282 hitter as a rookie in 1897, was to become a mainstay at second base, first for Louisville then for the Pittsburgh Pirates during their glory years in the early part of the 1900s; Ehret, 8-10 for Cincinnati the year before, played only one season for Louisville before retiring. Hill was coming off a 7-17 season (in itself a big improvement over 1896, when he was 9-28). Bothered by arm and drinking problems, he would be out of the majors by 1900.

The addition of Hoy and Ritchey gave the Colonels two solid starters; Clarke and Hoy were assured spots in the outfield. The manager told *The Sporting News* that although no positions were locked up, it appeared that the only uncertainties were at second base and in right field, and that unless another player came into the picture, the second base job was Wagner's.[6]

Wagner worked hard to justify his manager's faith in him, going to great lengths to get himself in shape and lose most of the extra weight he had gained in the off-season. Early in the spring, teammates Doc Nance and Bob Stafford had bet Wagner he wouldn't be able to get back to his playing weight in time for the April 15 opener. On the afternoon of April 14, the players visited League Park to stow their equipment in preparation for the season. Still 2 1/2 pounds away from winning his wager with Nance and Stafford, Wagner donned his uniform and began running sprints in the muddy outfield. He kept running until he had sweated away the 2 1/2 pounds—and then pocketed his winnings, $2.

The season began with a 10-3 victory over Pittsburgh, Wagner contributing two hits and playing errorless ball at second base. But most of the rest of April was a disaster, with the Colonels winning only two of nine games. A lack of hitting was to blame. Wagner's average was just .182 through the first two weeks of the season, and his teammates were also struggling, with Ritchey at .194, Dexter at .100, Clingman at .200 and Clarke at .250.

Clarke started shuffling his lineup, moving Wagner to first base in place of George Carey (.187) and putting Heine Smith at second. It didn't help. After the first week of May, the Colonels were a solid last in the league at 5-16. A 3-11 western trip followed, and Clarke was starting to feel the heat from fans and the press.

Wagner's slump continued for most of May. He was hitless in a four-game spell from May 22-24, ending the drought with three hits and a stolen base in an 8-4 victory over the Giants on May 25. By the end of May, Wagner was at .252, slightly better than the team average, but still nearly 100 points under his final figure for 1897. Wagner's average was down, but he was contributing to the team by showing the kind of spark and feistiness that Clarke admired, a spirit that also enhanced his standing with his teammates. On April 25 against Cleveland, Wagner went from first to third on a single by Smith. While the umpires weren't looking, Wagner snatched the ball from the hand of Cleveland third baseman Bobby Wallace, threw it away and ran home. A huge argument ensued, the result being that Wagner was ejected—the first Colonel to be tossed from a game that season—and the run disallowed.

June was tough for Wagner and his teammates. The Colonels were in last place, drawing only 700 or 800 fans a game, and Pulliam was cutting players—Clarke's brother Josh, among them—to save money. There was even talk in the papers that the team might be sold and moved. A brief flurry got Louisville out of last place, but the Colonels fell back into the cellar by the end of the month. To add insult to injury, the team's clubhouse was burglarized for the fifth time in the young season. Wagner was among the victims, losing a pair of shoes and a belt.

As summer approached, Wagner started showing flashes of his hitting skills once again. His two-run homer on June 12 beat Cincinnati 5-4; he had an inside-the-park home run the next day in a loss to the Reds; a 3-for-4 afternoon helped beat Washington on June 20 (he was 8 for 16 in the series); and his two doubles helped the Colonels knock off fourth-place Baltimore on June 29.

And with warmer weather, business started picking up. But with the team seemingly destined to finish near the bottom of the standings, Pulliam announced he would use the rest of the season to experiment. He obtained catcher Mal Kittridge from Chicago and signed pitcher Nick Altrock. His most important move, however, was obtaining first baseman Harry Davis from Pittsburgh. On July 20, Clarke put Davis at first and moved Wagner to third, Clingman to short and Ritchey to second. And the Colonels, who had moved past St. Louis and out of last place a week earlier, were a new team.

# *Four*

H onus Wagner had balked at replacing Billy Clingman at third when asked about such a move during the 1898 off-season, but change was imperative for manager Fred Clarke by mid-July. Clingman was hitting .265—15 points higher than Wagner—but his fielding percentage at third was a miserable .896.

Wagner wasn't meant to be a first baseman: His .970 fielding percentage was 11th in the league. He continued to struggle at the plate, hitting just .251. So Clarke's shakeup of July 20—an infield of Wagner at third, Clingman at short, Claude Ritchey at second and Harry Davis at first—made sense. It also paid immediate dividends as the Colonels swept a four-game series in Brooklyn.

The new infield lineup coincided with the return of Wagner's batting eye. In the first week after being shifted to third, he had a double and two singles in a game against Brooklyn, a 3-for-4 day against Philadelphia, and another 3-for-4 afternoon, featuring a grand slam and five runs batted in, against New York.

And Wagner settled in quickly at his fifth position with the Colonels, even making a dazzling play July 24 to help beat St. Louis. Louisville led the visiting Cardinals 1-0 in the top of the eighth, but St. Louis' Jim Hughey was on second with two outs. Tommy Dowd lashed a liner down the third-base line that hit Wagner in the knee and bounced toward the seats. As Hughey dashed for home with the tying run, Wagner recovered, picked up the ball about 20 feet behind the bag and turned and fired while outstretched, both feet off the ground. His throw beat Hughey, and catcher Mal Kittridge made the tag.

Louisville climbed to 10th place by August 9, and had moved from 11th place to eighth in the league fielding statistics. All four infielders began coming around at the plate—Wagner climbed to .268, Clingman to .266, Ritchey to .264 and Davis to .262—and, more important to Barney Dreyfuss and Harry Pulliam, attendance was strong.

The Colonels gave their fans plenty to cheer. They won three of four games from Philadelphia and swept three from Washington early in September, climbing into ninth place. The team won 26 of 41 games following Clarke's infield shakeup, and between July 20 and September 4 the Colonels played .632 ball, the best in the league.[1] "Things have been coming our way ever since the change was made," Clarke said in explaining the Colonels' revival. "Every club in the league that we have met since then will tell you that we played as fast as anybody. Wagner will yet play third as good as Clingman, and that's saying a great deal."[2]

The Louisville sportswriters were also full of praise for Wagner. Wrote the *Courier-Journal*: "Hans Wagner is the most awkward third baseman in the league. Yet he plays his position excellently, and does better at the third corner than any place he has played since joining the Colonels."[3]

Clarke, Dummy Hoy and Charlie Dexter had all raised their batting averages near .300. Wagner was up to .296 by early September and was among the league leaders in doubles and home runs.

Louisville stayed hot in September, winning three of four from Cincinnati, and followed that by winning three of four from first-place Baltimore. When the team returned to Louisville on September 28 after an 11-2 trip, a large crowd was waiting at the 7th Street depot. The fans and the team went to the Galt House, where a big meal, a band and speeches awaited the players, who also received floral arrangements before heading to the ballpark for a game with Chicago's Orphans.

The fans were rewarded for their support with another strong finish by the Colonels. They went 18-6 in September and 6-6 in October, ending up in ninth place at 70-81. Wagner likewise finished the season with a rush, despite being bothered by a leg injury suffered in an October 4 collision with Chicago's Frank Chance. He went 6 for 11 in his last three games and completed the season with a .305 average. He also settled down defensively toward the end of the season, finishing third among National League third basemen.

One of the last orders of business for the Colonels was a field day on October 16 at League Park. A crowd of some 4,000 fans saw

Wagner and his teammates participate in various contests, then clown their way through an exhibition game. Wagner was, without a doubt, the star of the day.

He won the long-distance throw with a toss—labeled a world record in the press[4]—of 403 feet 8 inches. He also placed second to Tommy Leach in the 100-yard dash and was the only Colonel able to throw a ball from home to second under a bar placed seven feet off the ground at the pitcher's mound. The day also featured a greased-pig contest and pitcher Bert Cunningham's dog performing tricks with its master.

But the most entertaining feature of the day was the baseball game. The players donned costumes and makeup for a contest pitting the "Comedians" against the "Tragedians." Wagner was a member of the former, decked out as an old Dutchman. He wore a red waistcoat, oversized pants and a coat that was several sizes too small. He smoked a large cigar and played first with a glass of beer in his hand for much of the game, and had the crowd roaring.

After the game, the Colonels were feted at a huge banquet at the Galt House. They got their final paychecks, received their share of the field day receipts—$60.40 a man—and said their goodbyes before heading to their respective homes for the winter.

Despite the Colonels' good finish and the fans' continued support (5,000 turned out for an October 12 double-header against Cincinnati), overall attendance was down in Louisville, and the team lost a substantial amount of money. At first the loss was put at $6,000, but Dreyfuss later claimed the figure was closer to $14,000 for the season.

Attendance also dropped in Baltimore, Cleveland, Brooklyn, St. Louis and Washington, and some teams were on the brink of financial disaster. Brooklyn lost a reported $15,000 (Dreyfuss claimed the Colonels' gate receipts for one three-game series in Brooklyn totaled $70). Baltimore lost between $8,000 and $10,000, and the owners in Cleveland and Baltimore were considering relocating their teams.

In December, Dreyfuss headed for a Florida vacation. Along the way he made a stop in Thomasville, Georgia, a resort town the Colonels were considering as a site for spring training in 1899.

Among the players, the bad weather in West Baden Springs had become an alibi for the Colonels' flat start of 1898. A new spring training home wasn't the only thing bothering Dreyfuss that winter.

Detroit papers reported that the Colonels might be bought by George A. Van Derbeck and moved to Detroit, a rumor Louisville management denied immediately. Another newspaper story, this one out of New York, had the Giants offering five players for Clarke and Dexter. Dreyfuss admitted that teams were making offers for his players, Wagner included. Philadelphia proposed deals for Wagner, Dexter, Clingman and Pete Dowling. But Dreyfuss said he wasn't interested in peddling talent to pay bills.

So he looked for other ways to erase his team's $30,000 debt. He asked for a contribution from the Louisville Street Railway Company, claiming it made $10,000 a year from fans going to and from the ballpark. And he offered $10,000 in Colonels stock for sale.

The league's winter meetings that year dealt largely with financial matters. Among the issues discussed was the proposed consolidation of teams (Baltimore and Brooklyn, for example). Rumors circulated that the league might buy out the Louisville club and disperse its players, and that Washington, which had sold slugging outfielder Kip Selbach to Cincinnati to raise some money, was ready to drop out of the league.

But the biggest bombshell to come out of the January meeting was a report by *New York Sun* writer Joe Vila that Wagner, Clarke, Hoy, Dexter, Kittridge, Cunningham and Bill Magee, the best Louisville players, would be going to Pittsburgh in a consolidation of the Colonels and Pirates. There obviously was something to the rumor—it came to pass a year later—but it was denied by all parties.

Besides, before he could make such a move, Dreyfuss would need to firm up his control of the Colonels. He bought up much of the new stock offering himself, and also purchased 3,800 shares from the estate of a deceased stockholder and a block of shares owned by Billy Barnie, the Colonels' manager from 1893 and '94. The maneuvers gave Dreyfuss controlling interest in the ballclub, and he began making changes; he reorganized the front office, making himself president and Pulliam club secretary and treasurer.

The league announced on February 6 that it would stick with 12 teams in 1899. Within a week, the Brooklyn and Baltimore teams and Cleveland and St. Louis clubs finalized plans to form "syndicates."

The result was the best players ended up in Brooklyn and St. Louis, with the Cleveland Spiders particularly gutted of talent, and Baltimore losing players such as Willie Keeler and Hughie Jennings and manager Ned Hanlon to Brooklyn.

While the future of the Colonels and the rest of the league was being determined in Louisville and New York, Wagner was relaxing at home in Carnegie. Still living with his parents and several siblings in the small frame house on Railroad Avenue, he spent the off-season doing what he loved—hunting, fishing and attending races at the Carnegie Fair and Trotting Association track in Heidelburg, just outside of Carnegie—and anxiously anticipating spring.

As had become his custom, Wagner waited until the last minute to show up for spring training. The players, with a March 17 reporting deadline, began arriving in Louisville the week before. Wagner didn't get into town until the evening of the 17th; he went to League Park, where he picked up his old uniform and his equipment for the next day's trip to Thomasville, Georgia.

Dreyfuss was busy putting his imprint on the Colonels. He ordered new uniforms. He trimmed expenses, eliminating unnecessary jobs at the ballpark. He cut back on the number of free passes the team handed out. He, Pulliam and Clarke each got offices at the ballpark, which also was given a new look—a two-story entrance, more seats and longer benches in the bleachers, which added room for 1,500 people.

Dreyfuss also let the players know who was boss. He called the team together at the Galt House on the eve of their departure for Thomasville. He laid out a team code of conduct and what was expected of his athletes. Finally, Dreyfuss saw to it that each player was given a pair of slippers so they wouldn't tromp through the hotel in their spikes.

Dreyfuss probably should have paid less attention to free passes and slippers and more to the politics of the league. On March 24, while Dreyfuss and the Colonels were in Thomasville, owners gathered at the Fifth Avenue Hotel in New York for a special meeting to approve the final version of the 1899 schedule. Dreyfuss was satisfied with the Colonels' dates, and authorized Boston owner A.H. Soden to give the Louisville approval of the schedule. But at the meeting at which the vote was taken, Soden either wasn't paying attention or was misinformed—depending on who was telling the story—and a revised schedule was approved, one that would have all but put the Colonels out of business.

The schedule became public when Vila, the same writer who had first reported the proposed Louisville-Pittsburgh merger, lifted a copy from the pocket of one of the owners and it was published April 1 in the *New York Sun*.

Originally, Louisville had been given 18 Sunday dates, 12 at home and six on the road. But the final schedule gave the Colonels only seven Sunday dates. Over the years, Dreyfuss had managed to alienate powerful people—Cincinnati's John Brush, St. Louis-Cincinnati owners Frank and Stanley Robison, and Chicago's James A. Hart. A year before, Dreyfuss tried to cut back on their power by trimming the National League board of directors from six to three. He also got into a dispute with Brush over a player contract and vowed to block every move that Brush would ever try to make. The opposing owners saw a chance for revenge and took the opportunity to hit Dreyfuss where it counted the most, in the wallet. The Colonels' fortunes were further diminished by a new rule that forbade in-season exhibition games, which effectively prevented Dreyfuss from recouping some of his lost Sunday revenue with exhibitions.

In Georgia, meanwhile, the players were more concerned with getting ready for the season. In his year and a half with the Colonels, Wagner had earned the respect of his teammates with his play. He still mostly kept to himself, in the locker room as well as away from the ballpark. He was friendly with the other players, and close to a few—particularly Deacon Phillippe and Claude Ritchey. But all the players acknowledged and appreciated his skills. The public, too, had come to discover Wagner. The press praised him, the fans cheered him, and although he avoided contact with both, his reputation was growing.

The Colonels took the field for their first spring game on March 29, beating a team of locals 25-0. In the crowd was Kentucky Sen. Mark Hanna, who left his carriage and took a seat on the grass near third base where he could watch Wagner, his favorite player, more closely. The Colonels also found time to play a local women's team, the Bloomer Girls, on April 5. Wagner flattened the opposing third baseman with a line drive the first time up. The inequality—and danger—of the situation was soon obvious, and they stopped keeping score with Louisville leading by 30 runs.

Wagner had reported to spring training in better shape this year. He was a few pounds overweight, but he was still below his finishing weight for the 1898 season. Early in the Colonels' stay in Georgia he hurt his leg, and the injury slowed him all spring.

While Wagner and the Colonels prepared for the 1899 season, Dreyfuss and Pulliam began laying the groundwork for the team's future. They visited Pittsburgh on March 27 to talk to Pirates owner Kerr. Ostensibly the meeting was to thank him for backing Louisville's interests at the recent league meetings. More likely, the discussions involved the possibility of him taking options on several Louisville players, as well as the rumored consolidation of the two teams.

Hart and Brush met with Louisville officials on April 10 to rework the schedule. The Colonels got some Sunday games, but mostly on the road. Only one new Sunday game was added, April 20 against lowly Cleveland. In six of the eight schedule changes, the opponent was Cleveland and games were in neutral cities (Chicago and Cincinnati, for example, where a third team would get a cut of the gate).

The Colonels left Georgia for home on April 7 and opened their season April 14 at home against Chicago before a League Park crowd put at 10,000 by Louisville papers and more than 11,000 by Chicago writers. Charles P. Weaver, the mayor of Louisville, threw out the ceremonial first pitch. But his aim was off and Wagner was unable to catch the ball, not an auspicious start for the season. Chicago went on to a 15-1 victory, and about the only highlight for the Colonels was Wagner's RBI double and three singles.

Louisville's first victory of 1899 came on April 17, an 8-0 win over Chicago. The first month of the season was rough. The Colonels drew an estimated 33,000 for a double-header in St. Louis, but came home to a crowd of 300 for an April 26 game with the Pirates—a game Louisville lost 7-3 when Pittsburgh scored four runs on four hits and two errors in the ninth. Even the pathetic Cleveland Spiders, a team that would go on to win only 20 games all season, played the Colonels tough, winning two of four games in Louisville. By the end of April, the Colonels had sunk to ninth place, hovering around the .500 mark.

Wagner's season was off to a better start. Playing third base, he had several big games in addition to the opener, and was hitting .432 at the end of April.

This season, perhaps more than any other, would be noteworthy for the building of the Honus Wagner legend. It began in spring training. At about 1:30 in the morning on March 23, a smoky fire broke out in the Colonels' hotel, the Piney Woods, and Wagner and several other players helped evacuate panicky guests. Wagner found a distraught woman trying to save her Saratoga trunk from the fire. He calmed her, grabbed the 200-pound trunk, and told the woman to follow him out of the building. He led her down three flights of stairs to safety. Dexter later said that once all parties were out in the street, the grateful woman mistakenly began hugging the Colonels' Bill Magee. "Wagner got so mad that he threatened to carry the trunk back upstairs," Dexter said.[5]

A month later, on April 25 during a game against Pittsburgh in Louisville, Wagner had another of those days that would become part of his myth. With the Colonels trailing 1-0 in the fourth, Wagner homered off Jesse Tannehill to tie the game. In the ninth he came up with the score still tied. What happened next wasn't in dispute: He homered over the fence in left for a 2-1 victory. The next day, the papers reported that Clarke had given Wagner the bunt sign, but that he had ignored it and hit the homer.[6]

In May, Wagner again added to his growing legend. For the second time in less than two  months, he displayed off-field heroism that may have saved a life. The Colonels were in Chicago for a series with the Cubs. After a 5-4 loss on Saturday, May 13, Wagner was returning to the Leland Hotel, where the Colonels were staying.  A young man, later identified as Alfred Bierlien, tried to cross the intersection of Madison and Wabash ahead of a turning cable car. He misjudged the speed of the oncoming vehicle and was knocked down, ending up underneath it. Wagner, who had stopped to let the cable car pass, rushed to where the man was trapped, grabbed the running board of the car, and lifted and shoved it back enough so that Bierlien could get to his feet. Wagner made sure the young man wasn't injured—a newspaper account said he was more frightened than hurt[7]—and went on his way.

Characteristically, Wagner told no one of his deed. The heroics would have gone unreported had not Bierlien showed up at the Leland Hotel the following morning to thank Wagner again. It was then that the other players found out.

Wagner had won the respect of teammates and the press by his clubhouse demeanor, his actions away from the ballpark and his baseball skills. Fans, too, were in his corner.  But he found little satisfaction during the early going in 1899 as he and the Colonels struggled.  Defending champion Boston visited Louisville in late May. Wagner was a combined 0 for 8 in 6-0 and 13-4 losses that dropped the Colonels into 10th place at 10-20. By June 1, their record had slipped to 12-26, and not long after that  they fell into 11th place, ahead of only hapless Cleveland.

Injuries and Clarke's search for a winning combination caused Wagner to shuttle between third  and first for the first two months of the season. His hitting cooled off only slightly—down to .343 by the end of May, still good enough for 16th place in the league.

With the Colonels' lack of success, the team began breaking down into cliques—Dexter wasn't talking to several of his teammates, Topsy Hartsel and Phillippe were mad at Leach, Ritchey was angry at several teammates. Players were blaming each other for the losses; Wagner's fairly steady performance and the respect he had earned from teammates kept him out of the sniping. But the clubhouse wasn't a happy place, and it would be only a matter of time before it erupted.

Louisville started coming around in late June, one of the most tumultuous months in the team's history. A four-game sweep of Washington moved the Colonels past the Senators into 10th place. And they weren't just winning—they were winning in thrilling fashion. On June 15 against St. Louis, Louisville trailed 12-6 with two outs and none on in the bottom of the ninth. The Colonels reeled off eight consecutive hits to tie the game at 12. In the next inning, Wagner led off with a single, stole second with a fancy slide, and two outs later scored from second when Cardinals second baseman Cupid Childs bobbled a grounder. Wagner's totals for the day: 5 for 6, all singles, a stolen base and four runs scored.

But instead of falling in line behind their suddenly successful team, the Louisville fans began to turn on the ballclub. And it wasn't just because of the team's spot in the NL standings. On June 18, during a 7-2 loss to Baltimore, the Colonels drew the wrath of a tough home crowd of 4,000 fans. "The players were jeered and hissed throughout yesterday's contest," reported the *Louisville Courier-Journal*. "About the only member of the nine receiving any sympathy being Wagner, to whom the bleachers sang a German song." Dreyfuss was also surprised at the fans' reaction. "I never saw a crowd act so ugly," he told the *Courier-Journal*. "It was enough to dishearten and rattle any player."[8]

The reason for the fans' discontent was complaints in the press from several unnamed players who claimed they had not been paid on the 15th. Dreyfuss responded by saying he wasn't holding out on them; they had been advanced money and were overdrawn on their salaries. He also said that he had fined two players for excessive drinking. Magee, one of the two, told the newspapers that he wanted out of Louisville, and said several of his teammates were contemplating a strike. Dreyfuss responded by saying that he was ready to release some players. It was no wonder fans were turning against the Colonels.

By the end of the month, Dreyfuss made good on his threat of a shakeup. Catcher Kittridge and first baseman George Decker were released. Outfielder Hartsel was sold to Indianapolis of the Western League, and Magee was sent to the Philadelphia Phillies. Injuries added to the team's difficulties. Clingman, who had been hit in the head by a pitch on May 8 and didn't return until June 11, was felled by what was diagnosed as a case of malaria. Leach, who had been sent to the minors when Clingman returned, was hastily brought back to play shortstop. Clarke shuffled his lineup and did what he could to plug the gaps, even sticking himself at short for three games. The Colonels signed 23-year-old Burley Bayer to play shortstop, but he lasted only one game, chased from the field—and the majors—by jeering fans after an 0-for-3, two-error performance in a 7-0 loss to St. Louis. Dreyfuss picked up first baseman Dave Wills. He lasted just 24 games before the Colonels realized he had a vision problem that ended his big-league career.

Despite the revolving door and the injuries, the team was able to stay headed in the right direction. A four-game sweep of Cincinnati at home during the first week in July—Wagner going 6 for 15 in the series to raise his league-leading average over .375— helped put the Colonels within striking distance of ninth-place New York.

The Colonels' problems weren't unnoticed by other teams, which hoped to take advantage of the situation. Brooklyn manager Ned Hanlon offered to trade infielder Hughie Jennings for Wagner. Dreyfuss rejected the idea; Clarke, when informed of Hanlon's offer, told the press that Wagner would not be traded under any circumstances.[9] Even Jennings threw cold water on the idea, telling the *Washington Post* that he had a sore arm that was going to sideline him for the rest of the season, and that such a trade was impossible.[10]

Louisville made its move the last week in July—part of the time without Wagner. He missed two games against Brooklyn July 22 and 23 with a sore knee, and rested the next two days with a rainout and a scheduled day off. After he came back, Louisville chalked up two victories over Cleveland and two more over the Giants to move into ninth place, having won 20 of its last 26 games. But then came an event that was a watershed in Wagner's career.

Early on the morning of August 12, with the Colonels in the midst of a three-week trip, the Louisville grandstand at 28th and Broadway was struck by lightning during an electrical storm and burned down.

Dreyfuss announced plans to build temporary bleachers that would be ready for the team's next home game on August 22. Others around the league weren't so sure the team could withstand the financial repercussions of the fire. New York papers, for example, resurrected stories that to improve their cash situation, the Colonels were going to sell Wagner. Brooklyn manager Hanlon again hinted that Wagner would be sold to his team, which was battling Boston and Philadelphia for first place.

Dreyfuss could have commanded a bundle for his star, who had already built a national following. But Wagner meant too much to the Colonels, on the field and at the gate. As the August 19, 1899 edition of *The Sporting News* pointed out, "Wagner is without a doubt the most popular member of the Louisville club. He is mayor of the bleachers and the idol of rooter's row, and the management could part with any player save Clarke with greater safety."

But Dreyfuss knew that. He had a player who was among the league's best hitters—he was over .350 at the start of August—who was splitting time between third base, first base and the outfield, and doing an excellent job wherever his manager put him, and who was popular with his teammates as well as fans. "You can not put it too strongly," Dreyfuss told *The Sporting News.* "Wagner has not nor will not be sold as long as I have anything to do with the Louisville club."[11]

By the time the Colonels returned home on August 21, Dreyfuss had had a temporary grandstand built. But the new seats offered no protection from the summer sun, and with the team stuck in ninth place, some games drew only 200 fans, and Dreyfuss claimed he was losing $200 every time the Colonels took the field. "The accommodations at the park are not very good," the *Louisville Courier-Journal* reported following the Colonels' first home game after the fire, a 15-6 win over Cleveland. "But they are the best that are possible for a short time."[12] Dreyfuss finally decided he had had enough, and got permission from the league to take the team on the road for the last month of the season, a loss of 14 home games.

What turned out to be the Colonels' final game in Louisville came on Saturday, September 2, a 25-4 victory over Washington that ended after eight innings so the visitors could catch a train. Wagner, his average up over .360 again, had two hits in his Louisville finale, a game witnessed by an estimated 500 fans.

The following Monday in St. Louis, the Colonels won a doubleheader but lost Wagner to a bruised wrist. He wouldn't return to the lineup until September 13, an absence of eight games (the Colonels went 6-1-1 without him). Wagner may not have been contributing on the field, but he was still able to help the team while he was sidelined—and help a friend in the bargain. The Colonels paid a visit to Pittsburgh during the time Wagner was injured, and he took advantage of the opportunity to get his old Carnegie buddy Patsy Flaherty a tryout. Flaherty, whom Wagner had gotten a spot on the Paterson roster[13] in 1897, had been living at home in Carnegie when Wagner convinced Dreyfuss and Pulliam to sign him. He debuted on September 8 in right field, making an error and misplaying another ball in a 5-3 victory over the Pirates. But he managed to hang on with the Colonels for the rest of the season, playing  one more game in the outfield and pitching in five other contests, going 2-3 with a 2.31 ERA.

The road agreed with Wagner and his teammates. They won 18 of 24 games in one stretch, including a nine-game winning streak, and he hit over .370 for the month, which ended with the Colonels climbing into eighth place. Three victories in Chicago from September 30 to October 3 moved Louisville past the Cubs and into a seventh-place tie with Pittsburgh at 72-72. The Colonels couldn't continue at a pace that had seen them go 21-8 since hitting the road in early September. A month on the road finally got to the players and they tailed off, losing four of their last five games and winding up in ninth place at 75-77, a half-game behind Pittsburgh. Wagner, like the rest of the Colonels, faded over the last two weeks, finishing at .345, 10th in the league.

Financially, the season was a disappointment, though not a disaster. The team had passed the break-even point before the fire, so anything Dreyfuss made after that would have been profit. But 200  fans paying 50-cent admissions hardly justified keeping the ballpark open. Home attendance was only 109,319, third worst in the league. The team drew more than twice that number (222,145) on the road.

Even without the loss of 14 post-fire home games, the attendance figures disappointed Dreyfuss, especially in light of large attendance gains elsewhere around the league.

Dreyfuss knew the end was at hand for baseball in Louisville. Consolidation from 12 teams to eight was coming, and the anti-Dreyfuss faction would have liked nothing better than to add Louisville to the list of teams to be eliminated, along with big money-losers Cleveland, Washington and Baltimore. Rebuilding the Louisville grandstand would have been an expensive project, especially in a town where support was only lukewarm. So he put other plans in motion.

Less than a month after the season ended, Dreyfuss admitted that he was negotiating with Philip Auten and Kerr for a share of the Pittsburgh Pirates. His competition was William Watkins, a former Pirates team president and manager who also was interested in buying the team. But Watkins let his option expire, giving Dreyfuss the opportunity he needed. In a meeting in the Arbuckle Building in Pittsburgh, Dreyfuss agreed to purchase the Pirates and consolidate them with the best players from Louisville.

During Dreyfuss' negotiations to buy the Pirates, he had a visitor at the Monongahela House, the hotel where he was staying. It was Wagner, eager to give his boss a tour of Pittsburgh. "I invited him up to dinner, and he agreed to return the compliment by calling for me the next morning and showing me the town," Dreyfuss told *The Sporting News.*

The next day, Wagner showed up, they had breakfast, and after a brief look around the city, they returned to Dreyfuss' hotel, where they discussed the team's move to Pittsburgh. "He cast sheep's eyes at a case of whiskey shipped to me from my Louisville distillery," Dreyfuss recounted. "I ordered the case to my room, and when the porters shunted it on the elevator, Honus saw his opening. He told me that he and his brother Al had planned a hunting trip of a month. 'Hunting withoud [sic] a little toddy now and then is like eating soup with a fork, or using a crowbar to bat Rube Waddell's curves,' was the little joke that Honus cracked. He was feeling me out for a present of a bunch of that booze. I ordered a demijohn shipped to his home in Carnegie."[14]

The Colonels' uncertain future brought more rumors about Wagner. Stories in Chicago and Cincinnati had him being sold to teams in those cities to help Dreyfuss recoup some of his money. After Dreyfuss bought into the Pirates, St. Louis owner Frank Robison claimed his team had an option on Wagner, an assertion that led to a public shouting match between Robison and Dreyfuss at a league meeting at New York's Waldorf-Astoria.

On December 13 in New Jersey, Pittsburgh club executives met and elected Dreyfuss president, Auten vice president, Kerr treasurer and Pulliam secretary, putting the final touches on the deal that consolidated the Colonels and Pirates—and brought Honus Wagner back home to Pittsburgh.

# *Five*

It was a quiet winter morning for Honus Wagner. He had no plans for the day—it was too cold to go hunting, and with Christmas still two weeks away, he would have plenty of time for shopping. But as he relaxed at his home on this December morning, he got the news he had been waiting for. The morning paper reported that the Louisville Colonels would be merged with the Pittsburgh Pirates—he was coming home.

Within hours of learning that the merger had been finalized, Wagner and Patsy Flaherty, another Carnegie native who pitched for Louisville, traveled to Pittsburgh. They tracked down Barney Dreyfuss at the team offices, congratulated the new Pirates owner, and signed their 1900 contracts.

In addition to Wagner and Flaherty, Dreyfuss brought the best of the Colonels to Pittsburgh—Fred Clarke, Charlie Dexter, Dummy Hoy, Fred Ketchum (who was later released), Mike Kelley (he also failed to stick), Claude Ritchey, Billy Clingman, Tommy Leach, Chief Zimmer, Tacks Latimer, George Merritt, Ernie Diehl, Bert Cunningham, Deacon Phillippe, Rube Waddell, Harry Wilhelm and Pete Dowling. Recouping some of his added expenses, Dreyfuss soon shipped Dexter, Clingman and Cunningham to Chicago.

Dreyfuss set up a permanent office in Pittsburgh in early January. One of the first people to contact him was Clarke. With training camp set to open in Thomasville, Georgia, in a little more than a month, Clarke asked Dreyfuss to get in touch with Wagner to suggest he start light workouts. But Wagner, who made frequent trips between Carnegie and Pittsburgh, got wind of Clarke's request and began ducking Dreyfuss. Clarke himself arrived in Pittsburgh on January 22, and one of his first orders of business was to set up an appointment with Wagner. But Honus, overweight and with no interest in beginning to work out with the start of the season still more than a month away, avoided him too.

The team departed for Georgia on March 14. Wagner, "looking as big as the side of a barn" according to the *Pittsburgh Commercial Gazette,* and Flaherty arrived in Pittsburgh from Carnegie on the 13th, decked out in their finest—matching white hats and yellow shoes.[1]

It wasn't a pleasant trip south for Wagner. He became ill on the way down and suffered through a miserable 34 hours on the rails. Weakened by the flu, he had to take things slowly at first. His training was further affected by a case of poison ivy that he caught from Phillippe. Phillippe came down with the rash after tromping through the woods during a round of golf on March 18, shortly after arriving in Thomasville. The club, wanting to make sure he didn't infect any teammates, quarantined him in his room in an abandoned Baptist church that the Colonels had had remodeled and turned into living quarters. The other players steered clear of Phillippe, but Wagner moved in with him, keeping him company, playing cards and sharing meals. He also did some doctoring.

"He took care of me better'n a nurse," Phillippe later recalled, "smearing me three times a day with some black ointment. He got the poison ivy on his hands doin' it, but he kept right on playin' ball with his hands all swole up and nobody but me knew he had it."[2]

Wagner played sparingly that spring, a combination of his ailments, rainy weather that caused several postponements, and the fact that Clarke had some three dozen players fighting for spots on the new Pirates. When he did play, it was at whatever position Clarke needed help that day. When the manager couldn't take his usual spot in left field because of a bad cold, Wagner got the call. He also spent time in right field and around the infield.

After Georgia, the Pirates began wending their way north, eventually passing through Louisville for a series of exhibitions. Dreyfuss, charging 25 cents for the games, was hardly welcomed back to the town he had abandoned. Split squad and exhibition games drew poorly—crowds at city league games outdrew contests featuring Louisville's former heroes—even with Wagner and the other ex-Colonels in the lineup. Dreyfuss was glad to get out of town—again—and to get the regular season started.

The Pirates opened April 19 in St. Louis, a 3-0 loss before 12,000 fans. Wagner and Co. won three of the six games in their season-opening trip to St. Louis and Cincinnati. And Wagner started quickly on his way to his greatest season at the plate, going 11 for 23 (four of the hits doubles) on the trip.

The Pirates were scheduled to open their home season on Saturday, April 28. But Dreyfuss, ever the businessman, talked the Reds into moving the opener up to Thursday the 26th. "Saturday is always a good day for Pittsburgh," Dreyfuss reasoned. "We need no special attraction for that day."[3]

He was right. The Pirates drew a record crowd of some 11,000 for the opener, a 12-11 loss. Wagner's return home was hardly auspicious. Splitting time between first and third, he went 5 for 12 in the three-game series against Cincinnati. Pittsburgh lost all three games (in the second game of the series, the Reds won with five runs in the 10th inning, a rally helped along by third baseman Wagner's second error of the day). But the important thing was, he was home. "I am going to be a Pirate all my life," he told newspapermen after his first home game in Pittsburgh. "This is where I belong."[4]

An injury to regular third baseman Jimmy Williams kept Wagner at third for the first month of the season. His fielding was adequate; his hitting was spectacular. Three hits against St. Louis; three more in a game against Chicago; another 3-for-4 day against the Cubs; a single, double and triple against Brooklyn, followed the next day by a 3-for-5 performance against the Superbas. By mid-June he was hitting .437, with 17 doubles and 12 triples. The Pirates, meanwhile, were in third place, chasing Philadelphia and Brooklyn and averaging 5,000 fans a game. They won nine out of 10 during a late June-early July stretch, and reached the halfway point of their season on July 14 at 37-32. Financially, they were one of only two teams (Philadelphia was the other) in the black.

Wagner, though, was unable to fully enjoy his or the team's success. His mind was occupied with thoughts of his mother, who had been stricken with typhoid fever early in the season. As Catherine's health deteriorated, she was unable to leave the Wagner home on Railroad Avenue; outings to Exposition Park to see her beloved John play became impossible; and she could only follow her son's progress through the newspapers or by listening to his tales when he came home each night.

The Pirates' game of July 13 marked a first in Wagner's major-league career: he pitched. In a 28-8 loss to Philadelphia, he worked three innings, allowing no earned runs, three hits and four walks and striking out one, relying mostly on a blooper pitch. Clarke had learned early on that if he had a hole in his lineup, Wagner could fill it. By the end of July, he had already played right field, third base, second and first, as well as his one stint on the mound, for the Pirates.

The Brooklyn Superbas moved into first in late July, trailed by Philadelphia and the Pirates, who ended June eight games below .500. But Pittsburgh came together in July, going 23-10 and positioning itself for a run at first place. The Pirates entered August in third place, five games over .500 and nine games behind first-place Brooklyn.

Wagner led the Pirates' charge into second place. He went 6 for 8, including three doubles and a triple, in a two-game sweep of the second-place Phillies in Philadelphia on Monday and Tuesday August 6 and 7. On the following Sunday, Pittsburgh beat the Cubs to take over second place from the Phillies. Wagner had two hits in that game, running his hitting streak to 18 games during which he batted .451. He went hitless the next two games, but then put together another 17-game streak during which he hit .441 and took a comfortable lead in the NL batting race.

Wagner spent much of early August at second base[5], filling in for the injured Ritchey. By the time the first-place Superbas came to Pittsburgh for a three-game series in mid-August, Wagner was back at his familiar right-field spot. Brooklyn jumped on Phillippe for three first-inning runs in the opener and went on to an 8-0 victory that dropped the Pirates 7½ games behind the leaders. Wagner took matters into his own hands in the second game, pounding out three hits as the Pirates won 5-3, and contributed a triple and a stolen base in the third game, an 8-4 Pirate victory in front of 8,000 fans.

The Pirates couldn't keep up the pressure. In the next week, they lost three of four at home against Cincinnati. It was a series best forgotten—Wagner was thrown out of the first game following a violent disagreement with ump Charles Snyder, who called him out for leaving third before the catch on what would have been a tying sacrifice fly (the Reds scored twice in the ninth to win 3-2); Clarke and shortstop Bones Ely had to leave Game 2, an 11-2 rout, with the flu; and the Reds won the final game 1-0. Only a 6-5, 10-inning victory in the third game prevented a Cincinnati sweep.

The Pirates righted themselves quickly though, winning two of three from St. Louis—again, Wagner was the driving force, going

7 for 11 in the series—then winning five games in three days in Boston to set up a showdown in Brooklyn.

Wagner tore into the first-place Superbas. His three hits led the Pirates to a victory in the opener of the series on September 6. He went 1 for 3 in the second game, which ended in a 6-6 tie, and had six hits in a double-header split on September 8 that raised his average to .394 and left the Pirates four games out.

But then came a personal tragedy. Just before the Pirates-Brooklyn game of September 10, Wagner got shocking news: His mother had died back in Carnegie. His brother Luke had found her dead in bed that morning as he was preparing to leave for work. Honus was stunned; his mother, only 63, had seemed to be recovering from her bout of typhoid. Doctors thought her progress was good. But she developed symptoms of dropsy—edema—a week earlier, and that, not typhoid, was listed as Catherine's cause of death.

While the team went on to Philadelphia to pursue the pennant, Wagner caught the first train back to Pittsburgh, reaching home in the 97-degree heat of Tuesday, September 11. Upon his arrival, he purchased a large plot in Chartiers Cemetery, where his mother—and eventually his father, sister, three brothers and newborn daughter—would be buried. Catherine's funeral was the next day. Wagner, though devastated by her death, at first intended to rejoin the team in Philadelphia. But his grief and his desire to spend time with his father and siblings kept him in Carnegie for almost a week.

Wagner rejoined the Pirates in New York on September 17. Putting aside his mourning—perhaps, in a way, dedicating his play to his mother's memory—he threw himself into the game as never before. In his first game he went 4 for 5 and scored a pair of runs in a 12-3 victory over the Giants. In his first week back he had 14 hits in 27 at-bats, a .519 average. That raised his mark for the season to .401. The heroics helped push Pittsburgh into the thick of the pennant race with Brooklyn. The Pirates wrapped up their eastern trip on September 19, beating the Giants 5-2. It was their 13th victory in 16 games on the trip, moving them within 3½ games of first-place Brooklyn, and fueling pennant fever in Pittsburgh.

When the Pirates and Cardinals arrived in Pittsburgh's Union Station the morning of September 20, several thousand people turned out to cheer their heroes. Carriages awaited the players, who were driven along a parade route downtown to a hotel for a breakfast celebration. After their meal and several speeches, another parade took the Pirates to the ballpark, where a crowd of more than 6,000 awaited.

Wagner continued to block out everything else, playing with a single-minded dedication. In the three games in Pittsburgh, two of which the Pirates won, he had 7 hits in 11 at-bats and stole six bases. The victories—and two Brooklyn losses in New York—let the Pirates close within 2½ games.

The teams traveled to St. Louis for a two-game series, where Wagner continued his onslaught. In the first game, the Pirates managed only four hits, but they beat the Cardinals 3-1 behind Wagner. With the Cards ahead 1-0 in the fourth inning and teammate Tom McCreery on second, Wagner ripped a triple to tie the score. Tom O'Brien then walked, putting men on the corners. When O'Brien broke for second and drew a throw, Wagner took off from third. He slid in safely with the steal of home to put Pittsburgh up 2-1. But Wagner wasn't done. In the seventh, he beat out an infield single. St. Louis catcher Lou Criger, already having seen Wagner steal more than a half-dozen bases in the previous week, tried to pick him off. The throw eluded first baseman Dan McGann, and Wagner went all the way to third. Jimmy Williams' hit drove him in with the third Pirate run.

But Wagner's hot streak, and the Pirates' run at Brooklyn, had come to an end.

The next day he went 0 for 3 as Cy Young blanked the Pirates on four hits. It was the start of a 2-for-22 slump during which the Pirates lost five of six games, including a dismal series against seventh-place Cincinnati. The Pirates lost four of five against the Reds, Wagner going 2 for 19. Brooklyn, meanwhile, wrapped up the National League championship by winning five of six games against Boston, clinching with a double-header sweep of the Braves on October 3.

There was one last piece of business for Wagner, his pursuit of the NL batting title. This was to be Wagner's finest season at the plate: a .381 average, 45 doubles, 22 triples and a .572 slugging percentage—all league-leading stats. But he didn't wrap up the first of his eight NL batting championships until October 13, in the Pirates' last game of the season.

All year, Philadelphia's Elmer Flick had shadowed Wagner in the batting race. They went into the final day of the season with

Wagner at .380, Flick at .378. On that Saturday, the Pirates were home against Chicago while the Phillies hosted Boston. The Cubs' starter was Jock Menefee, who was having the best season of a mediocre nine-year career. Flick and the Phillies were opposed by 13-game winner Ted Lewis.

Unofficial figures kept by Pittsburgh baseball writers had Flick and Wagner in a dead heat going into the final games of the season. During the course of the Pirates' contest with Chicago, reporters kept Wagner updated on Flick's progress against Boston.

Wagner, who had been playing with a sprained wrist for several days, had a pair of singles in four trips in a 7-5 loss. Flick finished with two doubles in four at-bats in an 8-3 victory that was stopped by rain in the seventh inning. But even if the game had gone nine innings, Flick would have needed two more hits to win the batting race. Wagner finished at .3806, while Flick, who had been hitless the previous day while Wagner was going 2 for 4, wound up at .3784.

Wagner often recounted that last day, embellishing the story as the years went on to the point that the race went down to each player's fifth at-bat, when he got a hit and Flick failed, giving him the batting title by a single percentage point.[6] Regardless of his account, his first batting crown was his most memorable. It was dedicated to Catherine, and he often called it the biggest thrill of his career. To commemorate the feat, he gave the bat that he used on that last day to his brother Al to hang in the latter's pool hall in Carnegie.

Financially, it was a good year for Wagner and the Pirates. The team cleared a $70,000 profit. Wagner, in addition to his $300-a-month salary, picked up $129 as his cut from field day activities and another $125 from a postseason series against Brooklyn,[7] and Dreyfuss also gave each player a bonus for their second-place finish.

The off-season afforded Wagner a much-needed change of pace. His mother's death, the pennant chase and the batting race were behind him. It was time for family and friends. He used part of his earnings to purchase a $400 piano for his sister, Carrie, and he was a regular visitor to Al's pool hall. But he spent most of his time hunting. Honus, who owned 14 hunting dogs, and Al were going out five days a week. On one extended trip, they bagged more than 100 rabbits and dozens of quail, pheasant and other gamebirds that they distributed to friends in Carnegie.

The winter of 1900 wasn't as relaxing for Dreyfuss. The Pirate president won a power struggle with treasurer William Kerr and vice president Philip Auten, but it cost him the services of Pulliam, who was forced out as team secretary.

Of a bigger concern to Dreyfuss was the war between the National and American Leagues. The National League, with its internal squabbling and $2,400 annual salary limit, was ripe for the picking. The fledgling American League's owners decided to go head-to-head with the National League for 1901, and figured the best way to gain credibility would be to steal away some of the established league's top stars. Nap Lajoie, Jimmy Collins, Mike Donlin, Hugh Duffy, Dummy Hoy, Joe McGinnity, John McGraw, Wilbert Robinson, Cy Seymour and Cy Young were on the upstart league's want list. And so was Honus Wagner.

Clark Griffith, manager and pitcher for the American League's Chicago franchise, was one of the new league's main agents. He was dispatched to Pennsylvania in an effort to win over Wagner, who, as usual, was unsigned for the upcoming season. Griffith arrived in Carnegie about the same time as one of the worst blizzards of the winter. As Wagner told it:

"Griff didn't know me and I was driving along the snowy streets of Carnegie in my sleigh. I saw a man trying to buck the drifts and I stopped and asked if I could help. He said he was Clark Griffith and he was looking for Honus Wagner.

"I told him I was Wagner, but he almost didn't believe me. I finally convinced him when I stepped out of the sleigh and showed him my bowed legs, my trademark. That clinched my identity."[8]

Wagner took Griffith to his house, where the latter offered him an unheard-of $20,000 for a one-year American League contract. Wagner hesitated. Dreyfuss had always told his players that the AL agents talked big but seldom delivered. Griffith's response stunned Wagner: He pulled out 20 $1,000 bills and laid them out.

The $20,000 was about 10 times what Wagner was making. He was tempted. But he also had doubts. What if the league failed? Did he really want to leave Pittsburgh, where his family and friends were? And what about loyalty to Dreyfuss? It took Wagner only a day to consider both sides and make a decision—he would remain in Pittsburgh. By March 1, he had signed a Pirate contract for the 1901 season, doubling his salary to $600 a month.

Dreyfuss was quick to stave off damage from the American League, signing 15 of his players, including Clarke, Jack Chesbro,

Waddell, Jesse Tannehill, Ritchey, Kitty Bransfield and Leach, by March 9, just as the American League talent raids were heating up in anticipation of the start of the season.

Two weeks before the mandatory March 30 reporting date, only two NL clubs, Pittsburgh and Boston, had the majority of their players under contract for 1901. While other owners were trying to hold onto their players, Dreyfuss, who lost only Harry Smith and Jimmy Williams to the rival league, was able to make plans for spring training and the season.

Dreyfuss decided to abandon Thomasville, Georgia, and train instead in Hot Springs, Arkansas, where the old Pirates had gone each spring for more than a decade. Hot Springs was a popular destination not only for baseball teams but for tourists. Thousands visited weekly for the springs; and with that many vacationers on hand, other related business flourished—the Hot Springs Opera House, for example, attracted top New York entertainment. For the less culturally inclined, there was gambling—pool halls, horse racing, card clubs—as well as boxing matches, bicycle races and bowling.

When Wagner and 15 teammates arrived in Hot Springs, they were greeted by a big crowd. Winning the National League batting championship hadn't changed the habits of Wagner, according to a *Sporting News* report of their arrival: "Hans Wagner, carelessly attired as of yore, could not hide his personality under his mask of modesty, for that burly form would be prominent anywhere."[9]

For once, the Pirates enjoyed decent weather and had a productive spring. Things went so well that Wagner was even allowed to do some catching in a split-squad game. But the weather cooperated only until the Pirates left Hot Springs. Rain followed them on their trip north through Little Rock, Memphis, Dayton and Indianapolis.

The season was scheduled to start April 19 in Cincinnati, but wet grounds forced a one-day postponement of the opener. The next afternoon wasn't much better, but some 3,000 fans turned out on a raw spring day to see the Pirates win 4-2. Sixth-inning triples by Wagner, Bransfield and Clarke, and two Reds errors, accounted for all the Pittsburgh runs.

Two more games of the series were postponed because of wet grounds, and the cold and rainy weather that had followed the Pirates north to Cincinnati from Arkansas didn't abate as they headed to Pittsburgh for the home opener. The game, scheduled for Friday, April 26 against St. Louis, had to be postponed after spring flooding left sections of the field at Exposition Park under three feet of water. When the Pirates finally got their home opener in—a 7-2 loss to the Cardinals on April 27—Wagner was patrolling a right field that still looked like a small lake.

In the early going of the 1901 season, Wagner found himself being moved from right field to  third base to left field and finally back to right as the team suffered through an injury-filled April and May. The one constant was his hitting. Through the Pirates' first 23 games, he batted a team-high .368. The Pirates, meanwhile, overcame a slow start and climbed to third place by May 14  at 11-7.

Wagner was providing not only hitting, but the kind of fire and leadership that Clarke liked to see in his players. On May 22 he was ejected from a game against the Giants for disputing a called strike. On June 1 he showed a different kind of leadership, rescuing an embattled umpire from an angry mob. Bert Cunningham, who had been Wagner's teammate in Louisville but who hadn't been among the players brought to Pittsburgh when the Pirates and Colonels were combined in 1900, was umpiring a Pirates-Reds game in Pittsburgh. The feeling among Pirate players was that he held a grudge against  Dreyfuss and the Pirates for not including him on the merged team. On this day, he further infuriated the Pittsburgh players and fans with a couple of his calls. Twice during the game, Pirate players surrounded  him to argue. Leach, in anger, threw a ball over the grandstand. Ritchey, during another dispute, shoved Cunningham. Both were ejected. After the Reds had won 4-3, the crowd got hostile, and Cunningham's safety was in doubt as he tried to leave the field. Wagner and Clarke, however, came to his aid, and, walking him past the angry fans, escorted him out of the ballpark.[10]

The Pirates took over first place by beating the Giants 5-2 on June 12 behind Wagner's two-run homer off Bill Phyle. He also had a single and his 17th stolen base, tops in the National League, in the game, which completed a three-game sweep of New York. The teams met again a week later, each winning one and losing one. A third game ended in a tie. Wagner had three doubles and three stolen bases in the Pirate victory; and he added a homer and another stolen base in the loss.

The Pirates held first place through June, a month that saw more injuries. Third baseman Leach and shortstop Ely were out of the lineup, and Clarke shuffled Wagner between right field, second base and third.

When Ely went out, Lew Carr was purchased from Troy of the New York State League. But he, too, got hurt, and Ely was sent back into the lineup. Ely managed only 4 hits in 32 at-bats after his return, and speculation started that shortstop would be Wagner's next position. "He is not a great shortstop, but he can fill that post in creditable style," *The Sporting News* reported. [11]

Clarke had more or less made Wagner his regular third baseman, the position he played almost exclusively in July. Leach, meanwhile, replaced the struggling Ely at short. After about a week, Clarke decided he wanted Wagner and Leach to switch positions, but Wagner balked. He liked third; and he thought that Leach was doing the job at short. Clarke enlisted Leach's help. He had him complain to Wagner about having difficulties playing short. After several days of listening to Leach's gripes, Wagner relented and agreed to make the move to short, taking over the position July 27. Coincidentally, in that date's edition of *The Sporting News*, a correspondent wrote: "[Wagner] has both Ely and Carr, the other candidates for the position, so badly beaten in aggressiveness, batting base running and, in fact, everything that goes to win games, that it was easy for Clarke to make a selection."

The writer didn't know how easy. During the last week of July, Dreyfuss learned that Ely was working as an agent for the American League and was trying to recruit Pirate players—especially Wagner—for an AL team that was planned for Pittsburgh in 1902. Ely's career as a Pirate was over. An angry Dreyfuss released him on July 25. [12]

Wagner's conversion to shortstop wasn't without problems. He made seven errors in his first 11 games, including three in one game against St. Louis. On the other hand, he had 91 chances in those first 11 games, an average of more than eight a contest. Ely and Carr, by contrast, had averaged only six chances a contest, showing that if nothing else Wagner was getting to the ball more often than the other two.

The latest threat from the American League prompted Dreyfuss to begin a campaign to get his players under contract for 1902. Pulliam made a push to sign as many players as possible as quickly as possible. When a story began making the rounds that the Philadelphia Athletics were interested in Wagner, Tannehill and Sam Leever, Pirate officials called reporters to the team offices to show them copies of those players' signed contracts for the following season.

Surprisingly, all the injuries and off-field distractions didn't derail the Pirates. They had taken over first place on June 15, and except for a few hours on July 4, stayed atop the standings for the rest of the season. The Pirates all but locked up the race in early September with a 12-3 eastern swing.

These were good days for Wagner and his teammates. The National League championship was within their grasp. Dreyfuss was rewarding their loyalty not only with raises for 1902, but in other ways as well. He accompanied the team to New York and, after acquiring tickets from a scalper, took all his players to a Broadway show.

Winning three games of a four-game series with second-place Philadelphia from September 18 to 21—the teams had a day off on the 19th to observe the funeral of assassinated President William McKinley—put the Pirates on the verge of the NL championship. The series left them eight games ahead of their nearest challengers.

Fittingly, the official clincher came on September 27 against Brooklyn, the 1900 champion. Just as fittingly, Wagner was the hero. With the Pirates trailing 4-2 in the eighth inning, he doubled home Clarke and Ginger Beaumont to tie the game, then scored the winning run on Bransfield's single.

The new NL champions were feted on October 2 in Pittsburgh with a big parade and the presentation to the team of a silver cup donated by the Railroad Men's Club, a group made up of railroad companies from across the United States. Festivities were followed by a game against Boston that the Pirates won in front of 3,500 fans, a crowd padded by a large number of newsboys Dreyfuss invited to attend for free.

Wagner never came close to repeating as league batting champion. The 1901 season was the first using the "foul strike" rule. Previously, a batter could foul off pitches without having them count as strikes. Starting in 1901, the first two fouls counted as strikes. As a result, batting averages were down throughout the league (NL hitters batted .267 as compared to .279 a year earlier.) Wagner, who could no longer take advantage of his remarkable bat control to foul off pitches indefinitely, hit .353, well below his league-leading figure of .381 from a year before. The leading hitter was St. Louis' Jesse Burkett at .376.

John Wagner, (third from left, with his hands on shoulders of the two children in front of him) at about age 10, poses with his Carnegie schoolmates in a class photo. Behind him and slightly to the right is his older brother, Al. *(Photo courtesy of Big House Enterprises)*

Next to baseball, basketball was Wagner's sport of choice. Among the members of his touring team in 1902 were Patsy Flaherty (second from left in back row) and Al Wagner (far right in back row). *(Photo courtesy of Leslie Blair)*

Wagner was a serious young man when he broke in with Louisville. *(Photo courtesy of George Brace)*

When they were children, Al Wagner was more than Honus' older brother—he was also his hero and best friend. *(Photo courtesy of George Brace)*

Claude Ritchey and Wagner first teamed up with Warren of the Iron & Oil League in 1895. They remained teammates in Louisville and Pittsburgh. *(Photo courtesy of George Brace)*

Fred Clarke broke in with Louisville in 1894. He became the Colonels' manager three years later and moved to Pittsburgh with the consolidation of 1900. Clarke managed the Pirates during their glory years early in the century. *(Photo courtesy of the Pittsburgh Pirates)*

George Aston—"Chauf"—went to work for the Pirates as a clubhouse man in 1909 after his friend Wagner pulled some strings. He was the first black employed by the team, and spent more than 35 years on the job. *(Photo courtesy of George Brace)*

Second baseman John "Dots" Miller and Wagner were a formidable double-play combination from 1909-11. Off the field, they became fast friends. *(Photo courtesy of George Brace)*

Wagner puts his huge arms and shoulders to use, lashing another hit in 1910. *(Photo courtesy of the Pittsburgh Pirates)*

Honus takes a breather before a game in 1913. *(Photo courtesy of the Pittsburgh Pirates)*

Wagner waits his turn during batting practice in 1914. *(Photo courtesy of George Brace)*

John Peter Wagner and Bessie
Smith, shortly before their
wedding in 1916. *(Photo
courtesy of Leslie Blair)*

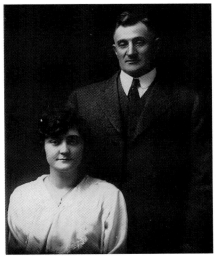

The house on
Beechwood Avenue
that Honus built in 1917
became the center of
his and Bessie's life.
*(Photo courtesy of Leslie
Blair)*

Mabel Aston Thornhill (in a
1991 photo) came to work for
the newlywed Wagners as a
teenager in 1917 and soon
became regarded as a member
of the family. *(Photo courtesy of
Elaine L. Brown)*

Patsy Flaherty was a longtime Wagner friend from Carnegie whom Wagner looked out for. He caught on with Paterson (of the Atlantic League), Louisville and Pittsburgh after being recommended to management by Wagner. *(Photo courtesy of George Brace)*

WAGNER, PITTSBURG

COBB, DETROIT

This rare, mint-condition T206 Honus Wagner baseball card (left), issued in 1910 by the Piedmont Tobacco Company, has recently been sold for as much as $450,000. A mint card of Ty Cobb (right) from that same set has a value of nearly $5,000. *(Photo of Wagner card courtesy of Treat Entertainment, Inc.)*

Tommy Leach had a 19-year major league career, playing 15 of those seasons with Wagner in Louisville and Pittsburgh. *(Photo courtesy of George Brace)*

Barney Dreyfuss: Wagner was the Pirate owner's favorite player. *(Photo courtesy of the Pittsburgh Pirates)*

Ed Barrow: Before Babe Ruth and the Yankees, his first big star was Honus Wagner. *(Photo courtesy of the Pittsburgh Pirates)*

Wagner and Detroit's Ty Cobb compare their batting grips before the start of Game 1 of the 1909 World Series—the first meeting of the two stars. *(Photo courtesy of the Pittsburgh Pirates)*

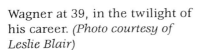

Wagner at 39, in the twilight of his career. *(Photo courtesy of Leslie Blair)*

"Honus Wagner's Young Recruits" pose with their leader in Dawson Springs, Kentucky, in 1915. *(Photo courtesy of Dawson Springs Museum and Art Center)*

Defensively, Wagner placed ninth in fielding among third basemen (.900) and ninth among shortstops (.920). Ely, the man he replaced at short, was seventh among shortstops. Wagner committed 35 errors, Ely 30, at short. Wagner also was third in fielding among outfielders (.975).

After the season, the Pirates took advantage of their popularity with a well-received barnstorming tour through western Pennsylvania. For Wagner, the highlight was a game in Dubois. Throughout the tour, Clarke had insisted that the Pirates play in their regular positions, figuring that's what the fans in the small towns wanted to see. Wagner kept asking his manager for a chance to pitch; Clarke kept refusing. In Dubois, Clarke had to leave the bench midway through the game to work the gate (Pulliam, who usually handled those duties, wasn't at the ballpark that day). After four innings, Clarke returned to the field to find that none of his players was in his regular position. The man behind the shuffle, Wagner, was pitching. His catcher was Bransfield. Wagner, in his glory, blew his fastball past the locals for two shutout innings.

After the conclusion of the tour, Dreyfuss threw a players-only banquet at the Hotel Schenley in Pittsburgh. The 1901 season had been another professional and financial success for the Pirates—their salaries were augmented by their share of a field day gate, money from the barnstorming tour and a cut of souvenir sales. And Dreyfuss, whose team had drawn more than 250,000 fans to Exposition Park and had turned a modest $50,000 profit, awarded each player a small bonus.

The players headed to their off-season pursuits—Clarke and Phillippe returned to their ranches, Chesbro went back to his job as a carpenter, Leach to his job as a machinist, Leever to his position as a teacher. Wagner went back to his favorite off-season spots: the fields and streams around Carnegie. Among his hunting partners over the winter were Dreyfuss, Clarke and Phillippe. He also visited Ritchey in Emlenton, Pennsylvania, to spend a few days in the fields, and traveled to Butler County with Phillippe for another hunting excursion. Once winter settled in, Wagner amused himself by attending basketball games, even participating in the occasional pickup contest, hanging around the house with his father and siblings, and visiting Dreyfuss at the Pirate offices.

As March drew to a close, the players began returning to Pittsburgh. They left for Hot Springs on the evening of Saturday, March 29, arriving two days later to begin preparations for what would be the greatest season in Pittsburgh Pirate history.

# *Six*

There were no big surprises in Fred Clarke's plans for the 1902 season—he had Honus Wagner at shortstop and Tommy Leach at third. The Pirates also signed Wid Conroy, who had played for Milwaukee of the American League in 1901, to back both up.

The signing of Conroy was part of the Pirates' strategy in the war with the American League. While most NL teams were losing players to the AL, the Pirates were staging their own talent raids, thanks to their $50,000 profit from the previous season and the fact that Barney Dreyfuss had the foresight to get his top players under contract early. In addition to Conroy, they signed catcher Harry Smith away from the Athletics in the off-season and added infielder-outfielder Jimmy Burke, who had spent part of the 1901 season with Milwaukee and Chicago of the AL.

Despite Clarke's plans, spring camp opened with Wagner working at third and Conroy at short. And by the time the Pirates reached Little Rock on April 8 for an exhibition against a local team, Wagner was in the outfield, splitting time between left and center. But when the season opened on April 17 in St. Louis, Wagner—who had told Clarke he would prefer to see Conroy at shortstop—was back in his familiar spot at short, and the good field-no hit Conroy was on the bench.

The Pirates got off to a phenomenal start in what would be a landmark season. They won their first five games, 14 of their first 16, and 19 of their first 22. Wagner, hitting .378 through April, was shifted to center field on May 2, replacing Ginger Beaumont, who started the season 15 pounds overweight and who was also bothered by a nagging leg injury.

Wagner settled in quickly in center field. In his first game there, he had three assists, one after making a nice running catch of a sinking liner and throwing to second to double off a runner. Wagner also played some left field after Clarke was suspended for fighting with Boston first baseman Fred Tenney. By early June, though, after Clarke had served his suspension and a healthy Beaumont—carrying a .375 average—was back in center, Wagner reluctantly returned to short, and Conroy, with his .167 average, was again relegated to the bench.

A 31-game homestand ended May 31 with the Pirates in first place at 30-6, 6½ games ahead of second-place Chicago. Pittsburgh fans were responding to the team's success. A four-game series against last-place St. Louis in early May drew more than 15,000 fans. Through the last week of the month, attendance was never below 2,500, and crowds of 5,700 were filling the ballpark on weekends. The team was such an attraction that Dreyfuss was considering a postseason tour of Europe, a grandiose dream that did nothing but increase the spotlight on the Pirates, and add to some of the resentment around the league. Said the *Baltimore Sun*: "Out in Pittsburgh they are talking of sending their prize team around the world. As a matter of fact, the team has only to turn around to accomplish the feat, for their chests already reach half way across."[1]

The swaggering Pirates took their first extended trip of the season in early June. They hit the road dressed for the occasion, each player sporting an $18 Panama hat courtesy of Dreyfuss. Again, the press from other cities took notice. And laughed. "Owing to the smallness of his stature and the immensity of his hat," wrote Charles Dryden in the *Chicago American*, "Tommy [Leach] resembles a short-stemmed toadstool. ... Hans Wagner also is a bird."[2]

The trip started June 3 and included series in Philadelphia, New York, Brooklyn and Boston, as well as exhibitions in Newark, New Jersey; Worcester, Massachusetts; and Wilmington, Delaware. That Dreyfuss would let his players participate in exhibition games during the heart of a pennant race was no surprise. The games regularly drew more than 3,500 fans—the June 17 game in Worcester was seen by 5,100—and the Pirates pocketed a tidy sum (Dreyfuss split the team's share with his players 50-50) for playing on their days off. And with the lead the Pirates had built in the standings, there was little concern about wearing themselves out.

Toward the end of the trip, rumors surfaced that Wagner, catcher Jack O'Connor and several other Pirates were on the verge of jumping to the American League for the 1903 season, supposedly to St. Louis. The stories were so widespread and persistent—the defections were to be announced June 15, the rumor went—that Harry Pulliam, with the team on its eastern trip, sent telegrams to all the Pittsburgh newspapers, denying them. June 15 came and went with no player movement, and the stories quickly faded.

But such off-field distractions were soon lost in the Pirates' phenomenally successful season. On June 30 they were 41-12, the best mark in National League history on that date, and had an 11-game lead over second-place Chicago. It seemed the only way to stop Wagner was to take him out of the lineup. And that's what happened in late July. The Pirates had run their record to 56-16 by the time they began a month-long trip to Chicago, St. Louis, New York, Brooklyn and Boston on July 20.

Wagner got the trip off on a winning note with a two-run homer in the 12th inning against Chicago, giving the Pirates an 8-6 victory. But fortunes changed three days later in St. Louis. Wagner's mood wasn't the best. He was hampered by a sore leg; early in the game he was robbed on a nice catch by the Cardinals' Jack O'Neill. The last straw was being called out by umpire Tom Brown on what Wagner considered a bad pitch. On his way back to the bench, he got into a heated argument with Brown, who had been at the center of an ugly incident with Wagner and the Pirates seven weeks earlier.

The Pirates had been in Chicago for a May 30 double-header. In the sixth inning of the second game, the Cubs' Charlie Dexter hit a grounder to Wagner at short. He hesitated for a second, holding baserunner Davey Jones at second, before throwing to first. Brown ruled Wagner's throw was late and called Dexter safe, inciting a lengthy argument. Later in the inning, Pirates catcher O'Connor threw a ball at Brown as the ump was standing near second base. It barely missed him. And later in the game, a throw by Wagner came suspiciously and frighteningly close to Brown's head.

With this latest incident, Brown figured he had had enough of the Pirates, their shortstop in particular. He reported Wagner to the league office, claiming among other things that Wagner had thrown a bat at him during the argument over the called strike. The league immediately suspended Wagner indefinitely. The announcement by John Brush, chairman of the NL's executive committee—and a longtime opponent of Dreyfuss—infuriated the Pirates owner, who speculated the real reason for the suspension was that Brush and other owners wanted to slow the Pirates and make the pennant race interesting. "I am dumbfounded in his audacity in this," Dreyfuss told reporters after hearing the news of Wagner's banishment. "Brush seems bent on ruining the game. The goose has laid golden eggs for him these many years, but now he is trying to kill this same goose."[3]

Dreyfuss had reason to suspect something was afoot. When his shortstop Conroy was involved with a scuffle with Chicago's Joe Tinker during a game on June 23, the league slapped him with a 20-game suspension, while Tinker, singled out as the instigator by umpire Hank O'Day, went unpunished. But Conroy was no Wagner, and the league could never have made such a punishment stick against the game's biggest star and gate attraction. Following a review of the incident, the league lifted the suspension after just three games, two of them Pirate losses, and Brush issued an apology.

Wagner celebrated his return to the lineup by going 4 for 5, with two doubles, three runs scored and a pair of stolen bases, in a 14-1 victory in Brooklyn on July 29. He didn't stay hot, however, going 3 for 24 over the next week against the Superbas and Giants. But the problem wasn't his timing or his leg, which was still sore. It was an off-field distraction: the American League.

Teammate O'Connor had decided to jump to the AL for 1903 and was trying to take some of his teammates with. He worked especially hard on Wagner and Leach. The AL offered both big raises, and Wagner's contract would have made him the highest-paid player in baseball. "They are fairly hounding some of my men with big offers," Clarke complained in the press.[4]

The situation exploded onto the front pages of the Pittsburgh papers on August 20. Dreyfuss suspected O'Connor was involved with the American League in some way, and had a detective follow the catcher. The detective confirmed that O'Connor had met with AL vice president Charles Somers in Somers' room at Pittsburgh's Lincoln Hotel. AL president Ban Johnson was also on hand as O'Connor brought over four players—one of them Wagner—for individual conferences. When word of the meetings reached Dreyfuss, he angrily headed for the Lincoln. Somers, tipped off that Dreyfuss was on the way, fled, catching a train to Cleveland. Johnson's exit was more ignominious. He had to sneak out via a freight elevator. A furious Dreyfuss acted quickly. He released O'Connor immediately and banned him from Exposition Park. Then he signed Wagner—increasing his salary to $5,000 a season—and Leach, not only for 1903, but 1904 as well.

Wagner was soon earning his money. A late August homestand saw him playing extensively in the outfield because of injuries to Clarke, Kitty Bransfield, Lefty Davis and Jesse Tannehill. And when Clarke left the club to return home to Kansas to nurse an injured leg, he left Wagner in charge.

On three occasions over the next two months, Wagner was made acting manager: when Clarke went home to Kansas because of his leg, when he went to Des Moines for his parents' 50th wedding anniversary on September 12, and when he was called back to Kansas because of his sister's illness a short while later.

Wagner was a moderate success in his three stints as manager. He led the Pirates to an 8-5 record, and though he didn't particularly enjoy the job, he took the responsibility seriously. After Tannehill had ignored Wagner's orders to bunt in the ninth inning of one game, the acting manager berated him in the clubhouse in front of the other players.

"In the absence of Fred Clarke, Hans Wagner is boss of the Pirates," wrote the *Pittsburgh Press*, "and he fills the position with dignity. The players say that he kicks less when he has full authority than when he was only a private. They claim he uses excellent judgment in directing the plays."[5]

August ended with the Pirates holding a 24-game lead over second-place Brooklyn. They wrapped up the National League championship by winning the first game of a double-header with Brooklyn on September 2, more than a month before the end of the season.

Three days following the clincher came another historic event, at least for Wagner. After Pirate starter Harv Cushman gave up 10 runs in $1\frac{2}{3}$ innings, Wagner came on in relief for what would prove to be his final major-league pitching appearance. He worked $5\frac{1}{3}$ shutout innings—the game was stopped after seven because of darkness—giving up four hits, striking out five, walking two and throwing five wild pitches.

Clarke's second and third absences, plus the benching of Dexter and Tannehill after disagreements with management,[6] kept Wagner shifting between the three outfield positions and first base for most of the rest of the season.

The Pirates finished with 103 victories, the most ever by a National League team. Their record-breaking 103rd win came on

October 4 in Pittsburgh and was entertaining, if not a thing of beauty. Exposition Park was barely playable because of rain, but the Pirates insisted on getting the game in in an effort to break the NL record of 102 victories set by Boston in 1898. The Reds, being forced to play what to them was a meaningless game, turned the contest into a farce. Manager Joe Kelley, third baseman Cy Seymour and shortstop Mike Donlin smoked cigarettes on the field; in addition, Seymour, Donlin and first baseman Jake Beckley did the pitching.[7] The result, not surprisingly, was an 11-2 Pirate victory and an infuriated Dreyfuss, who refunded all the money he took in that day and filed a protest with the league.

The Pirates finished 103-36[8], an amazing 27 ½ games ahead of second-place Brooklyn. They dominated the final league stats as well. Four of the National League's top 10 hitters were Pirates, starting with league-leader Beaumont at .357 (Wagner was fourth at .330). As a team, the Pirates batted .286, scored 775 runs, had 189 doubles, 94 triples, 19 homers and 222 stolen bases, all league-leading figures.

Wagner, despite playing the last month of the season with a broken hand, led the league in doubles (33), runs scored (105), runs batted in (91), stolen bases (42) and slugging percentage (.467). He was No. 1 in fielding among outfielders (.982 in parts of 59 games) and first basemen (.991 in 31 games). Among shortstops, he was only ninth (.890 in 44 games).

The team's month-by-month record showed how dominant the Pirates were: 8-2 in April, 22-4 in May, 11-6 in June, 20-8 in July, 22-8 in August, 18-7 in September and 2-1 in October. They took over first place on April 27, and went 57-15 at home, 46-21 on the road, and never lost more than two games in a row. The Pirates were equally impressive at the gate, drawing 253,725 fans to Exposition Park. Another 13 exhibitions drew 46,507 fans and brought thousands of dollars into the players' pockets.

"That was some ballclub," Wagner once recalled. "Long about the middle of August, nothin' could slow us down. We could've won the pennant with each man holdin' a couple of bags of peanuts in his hand and his glove in his hip pocket."[9]

It wasn't long, however, before the most successful team in baseball history was broken up. Davis, like Tannehill, was discovered to have been in league with O'Connor and was released late in the season; Jack Chesbro, who had led the NL with 28 victories in 1902, jumped to the American League. Most significant for Wagner was that Conroy, who had been brought to Pittsburgh a year earlier as insurance so Wagner was free to play other positions as needed, jumped back to the AL. That put Wagner back at shortstop, the position he would hold onto for the next 14 seasons.[10]

# *Seven*

The war between the National and American Leagues officially came to an end on January 22, 1903, when league representatives announced a truce. The player raids would end, the leagues would honor each other's contracts, and a board would settle the status of players who had signed with teams in both leagues. The peace between the leagues was a victory for Barney Dreyfuss. As part of the agreement, he got assurances that the American League would not put a team in Pittsburgh. What's more, his best players by and large had rejected overtures from the AL. The Pirates' biggest defections were pitchers Jack Chesbro and Jesse Tannehill, shortstop Wid Conroy and outfielder Lefty Davis, all of whom jumped to New York.

Dreyfuss also benefited from another off-season transaction. At the NL's winter meetings in December, Harry Pulliam was elected league president. It may have cost Dreyfuss his right-hand man in the Pirates' front office, but it assured him of getting a fair shake in his dealings with other owners.

There were great expectations for the Pirates in 1903. The team that had dominated a pennant race like none other before it was setting its sights on a third straight championship.

Spring training had barely started when Dreyfuss made a deal for another shortstop. Honus Wagner was going to be the Pirates' shortstop for 1903, but Dreyfuss wanted insurance in case injuries forced Fred Clarke to use his star at another position. The trade sent Jimmy Burke, a utilityman who hated playing short, to St. Louis for Otto Krueger, who had been the Cardinals' regular shortstop in 1902.

Wagner still wasn't sold on the idea of playing shortstop every day, so he was glad to see Krueger join the Pirates. He made him feel welcome—they became card-playing buddies, in fact. But Clarke wanted Wagner at short, and although he had a little time in right field during spring training, Wagner spent most of his days working out at short.

The Pirates opened their season April 16 at Cincinnati, beating the Reds 7-1 on Deacon Phillippe's two-hitter. They took the other game of the series the next day 9-2, Wagner going 3 for 4, before heading to Pittsburgh for their home opener.

A crowd estimated at 18,000 turned out as Pulliam, in his capacity as league president, presented the Pirates with the ceremonial pennant recognizing their 1902 championship. On the field, they beat St. Louis 9-8.

The Pirates held first place for only the first 10 days of the season. A loss to Chicago on April 26 enabled New York to move into the lead. May was a troublesome month. First came a series of injuries. Outfielder Jimmy Sebring came down with a fever that knocked him out of the lineup and sent Wagner into right field. Clarke was sidelined by a bad back; second baseman Claude Ritchey hurt his arm and couldn't play; Tommy Leach was called home because of a child's illness; outfielder George Merritt fractured a leg.

Wagner also found himself on the bench for three days as a result of a league suspension. On May 7 in Pittsburgh, Wagner slid in hard against Cincinnati second baseman Jack Morrissey. Morrissey accused Wagner of trying to spike him, Wagner refused to back down, and soon the two were on the verge of fisticuffs. Umpire James Holliday intervened, and Wagner grabbed him while trying to get to Morrissey. Wagner was thrown out of the game and hours later earned the distinction of becoming the first player disciplined by the new league president as Pulliam suspended him for the next three games.[1]

Wagner's suspension served to get his teammates' attention. They met on May 12 to discuss recent run-ins with umpires and what they deemed unusually strong reactions by the umps. As two-time National League champions, they were being held to a higher standard; and Pulliam was making sure no one could accuse him of showing favoritism toward his old team. After Clarke pointed that out to the Pirates, they decided it was in their best interest not to bait NL umps, and they managed to stick to their decision. In summing up the season, Francis C. Richter would later write in *Sporting Life*: "A pleasing feature of Pittsburgh's work was their season-long abstention from kicking and rowdyism—misnamed 'scrappy' playing—which had formerly been held as indispensable to pennant winning."[2]

Wagner's absence and the long list of injuries combined to help drop the Pirates into third place behind New York and Chicago by the middle of May. Clarke's back problem not only prevented him from playing, it kept him off the bench entirely. Once more, Dreyfuss and Clarke turned to a reluctant Wagner to take over, and the club went 5-2 under him. Wagner was again providing the leadership that was expected of him. And his taking the reins of the Pirates and his contributions on the field didn't go unnoticed around the league. A writer in the *Cincinnati Enquirer* proclaimed: "The game would be better off if there were more Wagners, but they are not like potatoes, and there are very few to be found in a hill."[3]

A June 1-3 series against the second-place Giants was the turning point in the Pirates' season. New York won the opener 10-2, but Pittsburgh won the next two, 7-0 on a three-hitter by Phillippe, and 5-0 on Sam Leever's one-hitter. Clarke, who was back on the bench managing when the team began the series against the Giants, returned to the field June 4 for the opener of a three-game series with Boston. Those games were like the previous two—shutout victories, this time by Kaiser Wilhelm, Ed Doheny and Phillippe. Philadelphia came to town June 8, and it was Leever's turn to throw another shutout. The stretch of consecutive scoreless innings ended at 56 the next day when the Phillies got a run in the fourth inning of a game the Pirates went on to win.

The shutout streak was over, but the Pirates' charge wasn't. They were in the midst of a 15-game winning streak that moved them past Chicago and New York. They took over first place on June 20 by beating Boston while the Giants were being rained out. Wagner, at that point leading the Pirates in hits, extra base hits, triples and stolen bases, was the hero, going 4 for 5 with a home run. The Phillies ended Pittsburgh's winning streak by taking the second game of a June 24 double-header.

Wagner and the Pirates, who had been sitting in third place in May, had taken command by the end of June. He was leading the league with a .375 average and was first in hits (87), first in triples (10), first in home runs (4) and second in runs (50); the Pirates, meanwhile, had built a 3 1/2-game lead over New York. They increased it to six games by winning three of four from the Giants in a mid-July series in Pittsburgh, and appeared on the verge of turning the race into another runaway.

But then came a series in Chicago where they lost three straight to the Cubs. It was a frustrating series for Wagner, who managed only two singles. In the second game, with teammates on second and third, he tapped back to the mound for the final out in a 3-2 loss. In the third game, a 3-1 loss, he was lustily booed by the Chicago fans[4] after colliding with a Cubs baserunner and being called for interference by umpire Hank O'Day. Still, despite the losses, the Pirates came home with a 53-26 record and a five-game lead over the second-place Giants.

The wear and tear of the race was starting to show on the Pirates. Wagner had suffered a dislocated thumb in Chicago, and was also bothered by other nagging injuries to both hands. Most days he would leave the ballpark right after the game, take the Panhandle Railroad home to Carnegie, and not be seen by his teammates until game time the next afternoon.

The other Pirates weren't in much better physical shape; Harry Smith, Kitty Bransfield, Ginger Beaumont, Tommy Leach, Phillippe, Ritchey and Sebring were all playing hurt. Clarke was again out of the lineup, this time with a shoulder injury that had been bothering him since early July. His shoulder in a cast, he left the team August 1 to recuperate on his farm in Kansas, and once more left the increasingly reluctant Wagner in charge for series in St. Louis and Chicago.

Wagner wasn't able to duplicate his managerial success of earlier in the season. His team split a double-header in St. Louis before heading to Chicago for a showdown with the second-place Cubs. Wagner's first move for the Chicago series was to get some pitching help. He wired Wilhelm, who had gone home to Ohio to recover from an injury, and asked him to rejoin the team in Chicago. Wilhelm's wife tracked the Kaiser down at a local fishing hole, gave him Wagner's telegram, and made sure he caught the next train to Chicago.[5]

The defending champions won the series opener on August 4, but played lackluster ball the next two games, losing 1-0 and 9-2. Wagner's error helped Chicago to a six-run first inning in the third game, a contest from which he was later ejected for arguing with an umpire. Errors, baserunning mistakes and a general lack of fire were noted by the Chicago newspapers. Wagner was singled out in one story after Game 3: "Many argue that Wagner is the greatest living ball player," wrote the *Chicago Tribune*, "but a man who knows no more baseball than to try to steal third in the eighth inning with his team seven runs behind looks pretty much high school."[6]

As it turned out, one of the few things Wagner did right during this stint as manager was calling Wilhelm to rejoin the team. Wilhelm pitched seven strong innings in the 9-2 loss in relief of Leever, but the game had been lost by the time Wagner brought him in, thanks to five Cub hits and four Pirate errors in the first inning.

The Pirates had the next two days off in Chicago, although they had agreed to play exhibitions on the 6th and 7th. With his pitching staff hurting and his team needing a rest, Dreyfuss suggested breaking the contracts. But Wagner insisted that the games go on. As a compromise, the game of August 6 was canceled; the Pirates traveled to Champaign, Illinois, on the 7th, where they defeated a team of college players 7-2.

Wagner's term as interim manager ended on August 8, when Clarke returned to the lineup for a 2-1 victory. But the Pirates lost the series finale 4-3 the next day. Still, they were able to maintain a comfortable lead through August, and appeared headed for another championship.

Back in July, players and team officials began discussing some sort of postseason series against the American League champ, which, it appeared, would be Boston. Dreyfuss liked the idea. He opened negotiations with Pilgrims owner Henry Killilea, and the two agreed on a best-of-nine postseason series.[7]

Wagner, meanwhile, was headed toward a second NL batting crown. He briefly lost his lead to Roger Bresnahan in early August, but by mid-month was back on top of the league statistics. In a five-game series in Philadelphia from August 22 to 25, he went 10 for 20 (the Pirates won four of the games; the other was stopped by darkness), raising his average over .350 again.

But Wagner's season was suddenly jeopardized by a knee injury early in September. He was hurt in the first game of a Labor Day double-header September 7 in Chicago. The Pirates caught Joe Tinker in a second-inning rundown. First baseman Bransfield threw the ball to Wagner, who chased Tinker back to first. Tinker went to his knees to avoid Wagner, but they collided as he made the tag, wrenching his right knee.

Wagner was examined on September 9 back in Pittsburgh. Doctors diagnosed the injury as damaged tendons and said he prob-

ably wouldn't play another game that season. They also recommended surgery. Wagner refused. He instead wanted to see Dr.
John "Bonesetter" Reese, a Youngstown specialist who had treated
Clarke, Bransfield and Leach during the season. "It's funny the way
he does it," Wagner said, describing the miracles worked by Reese.
"He just rubbed my leg a little and manipulated some of the muscles
and tendons, and I felt better right away. After I had exercised a
little more, I felt as if I had never been injured."[8] Two days later,
Wagner was able to work out with his teammates.

Although his knee was still extremely tender, Wagner was
back in the lineup on September 12 after missing five games (during which the Pirates went 2-3). He was 1 for 4 in his return, a
victory over visiting Philadelphia. Wagner limped through the final
month of the season, taking an occasional day off when the knee
became too painful, and sitting out most of the last week altogether—the Pirates had clinched the pennant on September 18—
resting in anticipation of postseason play. Even with the injury and
all the time off, he was able to finish with a .355 batting average for
his second NL batting crown. He was first in triples (19), second in
runs batted in (101) and slugging percentage (.518), third in total
bases, and tied for third in stolen bases (46).

What should have been the crowning moment of Wagner's
season, the first "World Series" as it had been dubbed by the press,
instead turned out to be one of the biggest disappointments of his
career.

Even before the first pitch of Game 1, Wagner's team was in
trouble. Leever, who had won 25 games, had a sore shoulder, leaving his effectiveness in doubt. And Doheny, a 16-game winner, had
been institutionalized late in the season for emotional problems.[9]
That left the pitching largely in the hands of Phillippe, who opposed Cy Young in Game 1.

It didn't take the Pirates long to take control of the opener, as
they scored four runs in the first inning on their way to a 7-3 victory. Wagner's leg had improved, thanks in part to the work of
Reese, who had accompanied the team to Boston and who was
being paid $500 for serving as the team doctor during the Series.[10]
Wagner singled his first time up, driving in a run, stole second, took
third on an error, and scored on another Boston miscue. He also
walked twice and popped up twice.

Boston evened the Series the next day as Bill Dinneen struck
out 11 and allowed just three hits, and Patsy Dougherty homered

twice off the sore-armed Leever. The final was 3-0. But the pitching-short Pirates came back to win Game 3  4-2 behind Phillippe, working on only one day's rest. Wagner, who had been hitless in Game 2, managed one hit in three at-bats, an eighth-inning double. But his leg was starting to bother him again.

October 4 was a travel day, and rain in Pittsburgh on October 5 postponed Game 4 for another 24 hours. Clarke gambled on Phillippe again, and he held on for a 5-4 victory that gave the Pirates a  three-games-to-one lead in the Series. By the ninth inning it was obvious that Phillippe had taken the Pirates as far as he could. The Pilgrims touched him for three runs and five hits in the inning, an omen of things to come. Game 4 was also Wagner's last productive game of the Series. He had three singles in four trips, but, in another sign of things to come, was thrown out twice on the bases as the pain in his leg worsened.

The sixth inning of Game 5 was the turning point of the Series, and Wagner was the goat. Brickyard Kennedy, a second-line pitcher who had gone 9-6 during the season, had shut out Boston on two hits through five innings. Chick Stahl hit a fly to left. It was Clarke's play, but he pulled up at the last second to avoid a collision with Wagner and dropped the ball. Clarke was given the error, the first of three in the inning. The other two were charged to Wagner— a dropped throw while covering third that loaded the bases, and a wild throw past second with the bases loaded, which allowed two runs to score. When the inning was over, Boston had a 6-0 lead as well as the momentum. The Pilgrims added four more runs off Kennedy in the seventh on their way to an 11-2 victory. Wagner's bad day extended to the plate, as he failed to get the ball out of the infield against Young, grounding out three times and striking out.[11]

The rest of the Series was all Boston. The Pilgrims tied matters at three games apiece by beating Leever in Game 6, then won Game 7 over the now-exhausted Phillippe. Still, he was all Clarke had when the decisive Game 8, October 13 in Boston, rolled around. He pitched heroically, but Boston prevailed 3-0. Wagner managed a fourth-inning single—what would be his only hit in his last 14 Series at-bats—and had the distinction of striking out in the ninth for the final out of the first World Series.

Wagner's performance in the Series—a .222 batting average and six errors—bothered him long after he had left baseball. For a player who was considered—and who considered himself—the team leader, the 1903 World Series was a major embarrassment.

The winning Pilgrims each received $1,182 as their Series cut. At a team banquet back in Pittsburgh, Dreyfuss announced he was giving his players the entire team share, raising their take to $1,316 a man.[12] It took some of the sting out of the team's disappointment.

Wagner invited Leever to stick around the city after the season to participate in some hunting. But even that ended badly. While chasing small game around Midway, Pennsylvania, with Honus, Al Wagner and Pirate groundskeeper John Murphy,[13] Leever's arm became so painful—aggravated by the recoil of his shotgun—that they had to call off their hunt so Leever could return home. Wagner's injury proved less stubborn. The knee healed quickly, and he was able to take to the fields almost daily to hunt.

Wagner also spent a lot of time during the off-season at what would become his second home: the Carnegie Elks Club. He had become a member in June, and the group's building in downtown Carnegie soon was Wagner's favorite hangout, a place where he could always find a cold beer, a waiting card game and a crowd of his friends.

Finally, with his knee healed and hunting season about over, Wagner was ready for some excitement. On the basketball court.

# *Eight*

Honus Wagner always loved basketball. He played it as a young man, and even after achieving stardom as one of the biggest names in baseball he returned to the basketball courts in the off-season.

By 1902, it had become a regular ritual: About the first of the year Wagner and pals would form a team and play around the Carnegie area. The makeup of the team varied year to year, but the nucleus was always Honus and his brother Al. Occasionally, Wagner would fill out the roster with Pirate teammates. More often, however, the team consisted of local athletes and friends. Honus played guard and served as the coach. In that capacity, he had a metal suitcase made that he would bring to the games. At halftime, when the other coaches would pass out oranges or chocolate bars to their tired players, Wagner would open the suitcase. In it, packed in ice, were bottles of beer, which he would distribute to his players. "Beer for my babies," he'd announce. "Beer for my babies."[1]

Wagner's participation in basketball was a point of friction between him and Barney Dreyfuss. The last thing the Pirates owner wanted was to have his star player and biggest drawing card injured in a meaningless basketball game. One of the reasons Dreyfuss gave his players the team's $21,000 1903 World Series share was to make sure they had enough money to last the winter—and wouldn't have to play basketball to make ends meet.[2]

But the lure was too great for Wagner, who not only loved the sport but was looking to lose 10 pounds he had gained since the end of the 1903 season. In November 1903, he formed the Pittsburgh Five, consisting of himself; Al; Deacon Phillippe, who spent almost the entire winter in Pittsburgh; Otto Jordan, an infielder for

Brooklyn who was a Pittsburgh native; and William Dickson of nearby Homestead, a local basketball star.

"I don't believe I am making any mistake, for I played [basketball] all season last year, and didn't feel any evil effects when spring rolled around," he told *The Sporting News* a month before his 30th birthday. "I decided the only thing for me to do was to get at some weight-reducing exercise, and I concluded that basketball was the best kind of winter sport."[3]

Wagner also used basketball to take his mind off baseball. Losing the World Series was bad enough; but his crucial error in Game 5 and his lack of hitting ate at him all winter.[4] The games did as Wagner had hoped, keeping him in shape until the Pirates left for spring training on March 21. Al Wagner joined Honus and the Pirates on the trip to Hot Springs. Now 34, Al was at the end of his professional baseball career, a career that had been marked by a series of contract disputes and a lackadaisical attitude that earned him the reputation as a moody athlete who never played up to his talents. He got into several split-squad games for the Pirates, playing second base for the "Yanigans," a team composed of second-stringers and tryouts. His presence in camp was more of a favor to Honus than a bid for a job, so when it came time for Fred Clarke to finalize his 1904 roster, Al returned home to Carnegie.

The Pirates opened the season April 15 in St. Louis, beating the Cardinals 5-4 in front of a chilled crowd of about 7,000. Wagner's 0-for-4 performance set the tone for the early part of the campaign. The first week of the season he was bothered by tonsillitis; then his back began acting up. Twenty games into the season, he had made 16 errors (including 14 in his first 15 contests), a couple costing the Pirates ballgames, and was being booed at home. The team wasn't doing much better, going 7-13 in those first 20 games and falling to seventh place, just 1½ games out of the cellar. And the weather didn't cooperate either, with five straight rainouts during one stretch in late April.

After a month, the Pirates were 9-15, in seventh place, and Wagner was one of only three members of the team hitting .300. The first-place Giants came to town for three games starting May 16. Wagner went 4 for 7 in the series as Pittsburgh won two of the three games to start picking up momentum. Next the Pirates swept five games from Boston, and by the end of May they were on track, owning a 16-19 record, a game and a half behind fourth-place St. Louis.

The Pirates had another successful series against the Braves in Boston June 10-13.They won the first game 8-4 with a run in the eighth and three more in the ninth; they took the second game 19-1; and they won the finale 6-4. The hero of the series was Wagner, who went 10 for 14 with six doubles and a home run. The next day in Philadelphia, he was 2 for 5 in a  win  that moved the Pirates over .500 for the first time that season. After leading the Pirates to a three-game sweep of the Phillies, Wagner's average stood at .374, best in the National League. He also led the league in total bases and doubles, and was second in steals and extra-base hits.

Not even Wagner's teammates were safe from his bat. During batting practice one day in early June, Wagner lashed a line drive that struck teammate Howie Camnitz in the knee. The injury side-lined the 22-year-old rookie right-hander—the doctors couldn't say how long he'd be out—and left the Pirates looking for a pitcher. Wagner offered a candidate: Patsy Flaherty, his longtime friend from Carnegie. Flaherty, just short of his 28th birthday, had been a me-diocre pitcher through three full previous major-league seasons. He had broken in with Louisville in 1899, after being recommended to Fred Clarke by Wagner, and went 2-3. He didn't get a decision in four appearances with the Pirates in 1900, and didn't return to the majors until 1903, when he won 11 games—and lost a league-high 25—with the Chicago Americans. After five lackluster appearances with Chicago in 1904, he was cut loose.

The Pirates signed him as a stopgap measure; they needed a pitcher, he was available, and he was local. But the reason Flaherty was signed was because he had Wagner—a longtime basketball-playing, drinking and hunting buddy—pleading his case with Clarke. Dreyfuss—or Clarke or Wagner, for that matter—never expected the season the Pirates got out of Flaherty, who ended up going 19-9 with a 2.05 ERA.

Wagner started July on another hitting tear, going 11 for 17 in four victories to open the month. That included a 6-for-9 day in a double-header sweep of Chicago on the 4th of July. But for all of Wagner's batting heroics and the Pirates' occasional spurts, they were never able to get into the thick of the National League pen-nant race, as John McGraw's Giants held tenaciously onto first place.

On July 15, during a loss to Philadelphia, Clarke hurt his back and leg making a somersaulting catch in left field. The injury kept him from the bench, and again he and Dreyfuss turned to Wagner to  serve as manager. He agreed to handle the duties, but a couple of losses to the Giants and his own slump in the field—his ninth-inning error on his first day as interim manager cost the Pirates a game—made him reconsider. Wagner knew he wasn't managerial material, and it was a lot more work than he liked. So he asked to be relieved of the responsibilities. The job was then given to Tommy Leach, who needed an hour-long talk from Dreyfuss on July 19 before agreeing to take over.

On July 20, Wagner became the first player in either league to reach the 100-hit mark, with a ninth-inning triple that beat the Giants 4-3. Still, the victory left Pittsburgh in fourth place at 42-32, 11½ games behind first-place New York. And with Clarke sidelined and star pitcher Deacon Phillippe forced to miss most of July and August because of eye trouble, the Pirates were never able to mount a serious threat to New York.

The Pirates also lost their right-fielder, Jimmy Sebring, on August 1. He had struggled at the plate all season, and the Pirates' inability to duplicate their success of 1901, '02 and '03 further added to the tension and frustration. After Sebring made a bad throw in a game in late July, Wagner took him to task on the Pirate bench. He may not have been the manager, but Wagner figured he commanded some respect. Sebring was in no mood to take Wagner's criticism. The two exchanged words and nearly got into a fight before teammates separated them. The incident may have been a contributing factor in Sebring's departure from the Pirates, but what cost him his job was a disagreement with Dreyfuss a few days later. Sebring injured his ankle in the first inning of the Pirates' July 31 game against Cincinnati. That evening, as the team prepared to catch a train to New York, Sebring told Dreyfuss that he was going home to Williamsport, Pennsylvania, to rest his badly sprained ankle. Dreyfuss insisted he accompany the Pirates to New York. But Sebring refused and jumped the team, and Dreyfuss dropped him from the squad. Even though Sebring was hitting only .269, the shorthanded Pirates could ill afford to lose him as they battled Chicago and Cincinnati for second place.

The Pirates spent most of the summer in fourth, climbing to third on a couple of occasions. After beating the Cubs twice on September 10 to move within a game of second, the Pirates headed to Chicago for a key series. The train ride was a wild one, as the Pirates and Cubs were joined by the Chicago White Stockings as well as the Cleveland Blues, who had just finished a series in Cleveland and were traveling back to Chicago. A "straw hat war" broke out, with most of the 60 players engaging in the fun, and when the train finally reached Chicago, only two hats were left intact.

The first thing on the schedule for Wagner and his teammates upon checking into the Victoria Hotel in Chicago was to purchase new headwear. The second was the Cubs. Two victories in Chicago moved the Pirates briefly into second, but by the end of the week they had dropped back to third. And new injuries and aggravation of old ones to Leach, Sam Leever, Ginger Beaumont, Roscoe Miller and Kitty Bransfield (the latter two originally got hurt when the team bus overturned August 8 in Philadelphia) kept them from seriously challenging the Giants.

Wagner, meanwhile, was coasting to his second straight National League batting championship, despite being bothered by another late-season injury. This time it was a sore arm; it had bothered him on and off for weeks, but started getting worse in early September, and by the end of the month he had to come out of the lineup, missing an entire series in Boston and making only brief appearances in series in Brooklyn and New York. An 0-for-2 effort September 24 against the Giants proved to be his final appearance of the 1904 season, as he sat out the Pirates' last 17 games, of which they lost 10.

With the pennant race over, another batting title wrapped up and his sore arm keeping him out of the lineup, Wagner left the team before the end of the season and traveled to Mt. Clemens, Michigan, which at the time was renowned as a health spa and was a favorite spot of several Pirates, including Leever and Phillippe. At Mt. Clemens, Wagner "boiled out" his arm trouble for a few days before returning to Pittsburgh.

Despite Wagner's batting title (he finished at .349, 20 points ahead of New York's Mike Donlin), it was a second straight disappointing finish for him and his teammates, who wound up 21 games over .500 (87-66) but could do no better than fourth place, 19 games behind the Giants.

The last order of business for the Pirates was a postseason series with Cleveland. Dreyfuss had angered other National League magnates by playing the champs of the upstart American League in the 1903 World Series. They were further embarrassed when Boston beat the Pirates. For that reason, plus New York manager McGraw's animosity toward the AL, there was no World Series in 1904.[4] But Dreyfuss, back in April, had agreed to the idea of a postseason series against whichever team finished in the same spot in the AL standings as his team did in the NL.

So the fourth-place Pirates and Blues opened their series October 10 in Cleveland. Wagner, his arm feeling much better, and Clarke, his leg and stomach heavily taped, were both in the lineup; Wagner hitting a home run as the teams played to a rain-shortened 5-5 tie. The five-game series saw the Pirates win one, the Blues two, and two games end in ties. Wagner went 6 for 19 for the series; Cleveland star Nap Lajoie was 5 for 19 in the five games.

Wagner wasted little time taking to the fields around Carnegie after the series ended, looking for the solitude that was becoming increasingly difficult to find. A local hero and three-time batting champion, he was a popular figure in the Pittsburgh area. But the shy Wagner tried to stay out of the spotlight as much as possible. And when he was engaged in conversation, he more often than not steered it away from baseball and declined to discuss his on-field achievements.

Others, however, were more than happy to sing his praises. A local composer, William J. Hartz, penned "Husky Hans," a march dedicated to Carnegie's favorite son. At a November concert in Braddock, Pennsylvania, the Carnegie Steel Works' 52-piece band got a rousing ovation and was called back for an encore after performing "Husky Hans" before an audience of a thousand music (and Wagner) fans.

Wagner was barely a month into the off-season when the press began reporting that Dreyfuss was considering moving him to first base for 1905. Manager Clarke had had trouble with Kitty Bransfield all season, and Bransfield's .223 batting average made him further expendable. The Pirates had found a 24-year-old prospect they thought could do the job at shortstop, George McBride, even though he had made 85 errors in 139 games and batted just .258 for St. Joseph (Missouri) of the Western League. Putting McBride at short, Dreyfuss reasoned, would allow Clarke to move Wagner to first.

A persistent story in the Pittsburgh papers claimed that the real reason Dreyfuss was trying to get rid of Bransfield was a fight he had had with Wagner, which resulted in the sore arm that sidelined Wagner for the latter part of the season. Wagner and Bransfield denied there had been a fight, as did Dreyfuss and other Pirate officials. Ralph Davis, *The Sporting News'* Pittsburgh correspondent, reported that he had seen Wagner and Bransfield playing cards the night of the alleged fight—they often hung around together—and wrote that the card game had broken up peacefully and both players returned to their respective rooms.[6]

Whatever his reason, Dreyfuss pulled the trigger in late December, and with Clarke's blessing sent Bransfield to the Philadelphia Phillies along with outfielder Moose McCormick and shortstop Otto Krueger for infielder/outfielder Del Howard.[7]

The Pirates hoped Howard would provide additional offense. Their pitching was solid, but there was a need for hitting and speed on the bases. McBride, who had stolen 57 bases in those 139 games at St. Joe, was being counted on to provide the latter. The hitting would be up to Wagner, Clarke, Beaumont and Howard.

The Pirates weren't the only team looking for hitting. Only eight National League batters hit .300 or better in 1904, and that lack of offense bothered league officials. Wagner suggested that to help hitters, owners should reduce the number of balls needed for a walk from four to three, forcing pitchers to put the ball over the plate more often. "If I were to wait for a real good strike to come over," he told *The Sporting News*, "I would never hit the ball."[8] The owners, however, failed to act on Wagner's idea—or any other proposal regarding the lack of hitting.

In addition to trading Bransfield and obtaining McBride and Howard, Dreyfuss was busy getting his players signed. By February 12, everyone but Wagner, Patsy Flaherty and Leach had signed for the 1905 season, and Leach had already agreed to terms. Wagner never cared much for salary negotiations; he always trusted Dreyfuss to treat him fairly. The Pirates' owner, with an eye on the raids being carried out by the American League, had boosted Wagner's salary to $5,000 a year for the 1903 and 1904 seasons.

But after winning the NL batting championship in both those seasons, Wagner was thinking he deserved a raise for 1905. He liked and respected Dreyfuss too much to hold out for a higher salary; besides, it wasn't Wagner's nature to ask for more money. Instead, he dragged his feet. He put off signing his contract and told the team he might be late for spring training because he had to take care of his sick father—Peter Wagner was bedridden with a serious case of bronchitis—in Carnegie. But he eventually signed again for $5,000, and he and brother Al were with the team when it left Pittsburgh on Sunday, March 12, bound for Georgia.

Most of the spring was devoted to getting into shape and playing intrasquad games. The previous year, there had been a number of exhibition games, and Clarke blamed a lack of conditioning for the team's slow start from which it never recovered. This year the emphasis was on intrasquad games—with Al Wagner getting playing time at shortstop as well as second base—before the team started wending its way north with a series of exhibitions in Georgia and Kentucky.

The 1905 season would be a tumultuous one for Wagner and the Pirates. The second game of the season, on April 15 in Cincinnati, set the tone: Clarke, trying to steal third, was called out by first-year umpire Bill Klem. Clarke argued the call so vehemently he was tossed from the game, and was later fined by league president Harry Pulliam.

The Pirates won five of their first six games, but Wagner, unlike his teammates, struggled early. He went 5 for 17 in that first week, then was forced to miss four games after being spiked in the left hand by St. Louis' Jimmy Burke on April 22. He was back in the lineup on April 28 against Chicago, going 2 for 3 and driving in one run and scoring another in a three-run eighth inning that gave the Pirates a 4-2 victory.

The Giants again jumped into first place early in the season, but unlike 1904, the Pirates stayed with them. After 20 games, New York was 14-6, with Pittsburgh just one game behind the leaders. In late May, the two teams met in a wild series in New York that saw players hurling insults at each other, several near-fights, umpire baiting and even a dispute between Dreyfuss and McGraw that went all the way to the league office.

McGraw sent Christy Mathewson against the Pirates in the opener, and Clarke countered with Leever, who threw a seven-hitter as the Pirates won 7-2. Wagner contributed a single and a double, and was on the receiving end of verbal abuse from McGraw from the bench. But Wagner and his teammates had been warned by Clarke to expect the intimidation, and kept their tempers in check.

The Giants evened the series the next day, winning 7-0 behind Dummy Taylor. The game of May 20 was the most hotly contested of the series. McGraw got into a fight with Pirates pitcher Mike Lynch and was ejected. Before leaving the field, he began yelling at Clarke, then turned his attention to Dreyfuss. He went to the Pirate owner's box and began berating him, accusing Dreyfuss of welching on horse racing bets.[9] The game ended with another Giants victory, as did Game 4, giving New York three victories in four contests and a 5½ -game lead in the standings.

The Pirates left New York in a feisty mood. After a three-game series in Boston, they moved on to Cincinnati. Pittsburgh won the opener 8-3 behind Wagner's hitting and Flaherty's pitching. On May 28, Wagner, Leever and the Reds' Miller Huggins were ejected during a 12-3 Cincinnati victory. Wagner was thrown out after a run-in with umpire Bob Emslie. He argued a call at second to earn the ejection, then was ordered out of the ballpark after walking off the field holding his nose. Wagner, who had been 5 for 5 in the series to that point, was slapped with a $30 fine and a three-game suspension by Pulliam for abusing an umpire.

By the end of May, the Giants were 7½ games ahead of the second-place Pirates. The two teams played again in early June in Pittsburgh in a series that was sedate compared to their previous meeting; no fights, no knockdowns, no intimidation. The teams split four games, leaving the Pirates in third place, eight games behind the leaders.

The Giants, though, were never able to pull away. A lackluster .500 western trip in late June cut their lead and made them appear vulnerable. Dreyfuss, looking for fresh blood for the dog days of the season, added two key players in early July. Third baseman David Brain was obtained from St. Louis, and catcher George Gibson, who was to become a lifelong friend of Wagner's, was purchased from Montreal.

The Giants and Pirates met again in mid-July, with Pittsburgh winning three of four to cut New York's lead to five games. The Giants bounced back by fattening up on Cincinnati and St. Louis and rebuilding their lead to 7½ games. Pittsburgh and New York faced off again the first week in August, and again the Pirates took the series, winning three of four. But once again they couldn't capitalize, losing three of five to lowly Boston and letting the Giants maintain a safe lead.

Wagner missed three of the games in Boston because of his second suspension of the 1905 season. On August 2 against New York, umpire George Bausewine called him out on a close play at second. Wagner protested mildly as he took his position at short between innings. As the Pirates tossed the ball around the infield, one of his throws to first baseman Howard sailed in the direction of Bausewine, who had his back turned. Howard caught the ball several feet from the umpire. Immediately, the players on the Giants bench yelled at the umpire that Wagner had thrown at him. Bausewine confronted Wagner, and, according to newspaper accounts, told him, "You great big fat head, you won't play any more today."[10] Wagner was as surprised by the ump's language as he was by the ejection.

Wagner may have been one of Pulliam's favorite people, but the National League president came down hard on him for this latest brush with an umpire, slapping Wagner with another three-game suspension. Still, there were no hard feelings between the two. During his suspension, Wagner watched the Boston games from Pulliam's box.

Wagner, meanwhile, was left to plead his case in the press. "Bausewine was at least five feet away and was not in any danger at all," he told the *Pittsburgh Press*. "He probably wouldn't have thought anything about the matter if the New York players had not shouted that I tried to hit him with the ball."[11]

After Wagner returned to the lineup, he led the Pirates on one more furious charge. In the last week of August, he went 15 for 31 as the Pirates won eight in a row, part of a stretch during which they won 19 of 21 games. But it wasn't enough to catch the Giants, who went 18-6 between August 15 and September 15. The Pirates had one last chance to go head-to-head with the leaders when the Giants visited Pittsburgh from September 25 to 27. But New York won all three games of the series despite Wagner's 6-for-11 performance at the plate, all but locking up another NL championship.

The last month of the season featured some outstanding batting duels between Wagner and Cincinnati's Cy Seymour, who was having the best year of his career. Over the last four weeks of the campaign, Seymour had 3-for-5, 4-for-5, 3-for-4 and 4-for-7 games against the Pirates. Wagner, the only player with a chance to catch him, was unable to match Seymour, who wound up hitting .377, 14 points ahead of Wagner and 74 points over his eventual lifetime average. The Pirates also had to settle for runner-up status, finishing at 96-57, nine games behind the Giants.

In the closing weeks, there had been talk of postseason play between the Pirates and Detroit Tigers, an idea put forward by Tiger manager William Armour, who challenged the Pirates to a five- or seven-game series. But Dreyfuss didn't go for it, and instead of Wagner getting his first look at a young Tiger rookie named Ty Cobb,[12] he and his teammates embarked on a short barnstorming tour around the Pittsburgh area as soon as the season ended. The Wagner-Cobb meeting would have to wait.

# *Nine*

Changes were in store for the 1906 season. The Pirates traded infielders Del Howard and David Brain and pitching prospect Vive Lindaman to Boston for pitcher Vic Willis. Looking for some offense and someone to play first after Howard's departure, Fred Clarke signed free agent Jim Nealon. And Honus Wagner lost one of his closest buddies when Patsy Flaherty, who didn't fit into the Pirates' plans following an injury-filled 9-9 season, went to Columbus of the American Association.

One thing that hadn't changed for 1906 was Wagner's foot-dragging as far as a contract was concerned. The Pirates had learned it was pointless to mail him a contract; it would just sit at his Carnegie home, unsigned. Instead, the contract was kept at the team's offices, and Wagner would sign it during one of his occasional off-season visits. By the end of January, Wagner was one of only four unsigned players, but he did come around and was under contract—at the same $5,000—well before the Pirates left for Hot Springs on March 12.

Much of spring training was hampered by cold, wet weather and the Pirates were unable to get in as much work as Clarke had hoped. Al Wagner was again in camp, and had a good spring as a fill-in infielder. Again, though, his presence was merely a favor to his younger brother, and when camp broke he again headed home instead of to St. Louis for the Pirates' season-opener.

The Pirates won two games against the Cardinals—two more were rained out—before heading to Pittsburgh for their home opener. A crowd of 17,036 saw the Pirates beat the Reds 3-2 when Wagner doubled and Nealon singled him home in the 12th inning.

New York grabbed the early lead in the standings, but Chicago went on a 10-game winning streak and moved into first. The

Pirates, meanwhile, were perched around .500 as Wagner struggled with his hitting—he batted only .266 through the first month of the season—and Ginger Beaumont was sidelined by a leg injury. Wagner began coming around in a mid-May series against the Phillies and Giants—he hit .522 from May 14 to 19—but Pirate fortunes took another bad turn when Clarke injured his shoulder against the Phillies and missed almost a week.

It was mid-June before Clarke and Beaumont both got back in the lineup, but by that time Chicago had taken control of the National League race. Wagner's hitting—he batted .472 during the first two weeks of June to get his average over .350—helped the Pirates climb into second place ahead of the slumping and injury-riddled Giants.

During July it became obvious that these Pirates weren't in the same class as Chicago. The teams met six times during the first week of the month, with the Cubs winning four of the games—all the victories coming in Pittsburgh. The Pirates slipped back into third place by the middle of the month, but won three of four from the Giants from July 21 to 25 and entered August tied with New York at 58-32, six games behind first-place Chicago. The Cubs all but locked up first place during August, when they won 14 games on a 16-game road trip. They went on to win 35 of their last 40 games to dominate the league standings with 116 victories against only 36 losses.

It was left to the Pirates and Giants to fight for second place. The teams met in a five-game series starting August 9, but it wasn't much of a contest. The Giants won all five games, dropping the Pirates back into third place. Pittsburgh made another run at second place in early September, but quickly faded to third amid press and fan complaints that the players—including Wagner—were just going through the motions.

Wagner had a league-leading .336 average on September 1, but left that day's game in Cincinnati after collecting two hits in two at-bats, complaining of a charley horse. He appeared in only one of the Pirates' eight games in the next week—and didn't return to the lineup to stay until September 15. The injury bothered Wagner for the rest of the season; even a visit from Bonesetter Reese couldn't relieve the problem. As the doctor worked on Wagner, the pain became so severe that he passed out.[1] Wagner hobbled through the rest of the month, and last played the field on October 1. He had only one more appearance during the season, as a pinch-hitter two days later.

Wagner's absence from the lineup brought rumblings in the stands and in the press that he was more interested in protecting his average than in producing for the team. *The Pittsburgh Press* hinted as much on September 23: "The Pirates have been accused of lack of interest since it became certain that the Cubs would win the National League pennant this year. The charge is certainly true in part, although maybe not to the full extent charged. ... Some of the men have actually performed as if they did not care how the games went."[2]

Even with his bad leg, Wagner finished the season at .339, comfortably ahead of Chicago's Harry Steinfeldt (.327), for his fourth batting title and 10th straight .300 season. Wagner was also first in doubles and total bases and second in hits, slugging percentage and runs scored. But despite Wagner's successes, a third-place finish 33 games over .500 and the third highest attendance in the league, the 1906 season was a disappointment in many respects. Beaumont was bothered by his bad leg early in the season, and was never able to get his game going, hitting a career-low .265 in just 80 games. Pitchers Lefty Leifield (18-13) and Deacon Phillippe (15-10) failed to live up to expectations. First baseman Nealon, expected to fill Howard's shoes, hit only .255.

Speculation began that because of three consecutive non-pennant-winning seasons, Dreyfuss planned a major shakeup. One report[3] had Beaumont, Tommy Leach, Claude Ritchey and Clarke not returning—and Wagner becoming Pirates manager.

Wagner had little interest in taking over for Clarke. He was more concerned with getting his leg taken care of. As soon as the season ended, the Pirates went on a 10-day barnstorming tour, but Wagner took off for Hot Springs, Arkansas, for treatment of what he was calling rheumatism. Shortly, he was joined in Hot Springs by his brother Al and Pirate pitcher Bert Maxwell, and the hot springs and rest—and the city's other attractions—soon eased Wagner's pain.

The Pirates' uncertain future was cleared up in early December at the league meetings in New York. Clarke showed up, signed a contract for 1907, then promptly traded Ritchey and the rights to Flaherty[4]—two of Wagner's closest friends on the team—and a player to be named later to Boston for infielder Ed Abbaticchio. As it turned out, the third Pirate in the deal was Beaumont.

Wagner knew he would miss his two friends, but he also recognized that trades were a part of baseball. And he knew it could happen to him. In fact, another story that circulated during the winter meetings had Dreyfuss, as part of the housecleaning, dealing Wagner. But the Pirates owner was quick to deny such a thing would even be considered. "When I am ready to quit baseball, then I may think of disposing of Wagner, but so long as I remain in the game he will play for me or not at all. I consider the Dutchman one of my assets, my principal asset I might say, and I would not part with him for any amount of money nor for all the players I know."[5]

Wagner did his best to stay in shape after returning home from Hot Springs. He, Flaherty and Cincinnati's Hans Lobert, who lived in the Pittsburgh area, were members of the touring Hans Wagner basketball team that winter. These weren't half-speed games Wagner had his team involved in; they were so rigorous that Flaherty called it quits after only three contests because of the exertion involved. After the basketball season ended, the Wagners, Lobert and Flaherty held almost daily workouts in a Carnegie gym.

Wagner signed his 1907 contract just before the team's departure for West Baden Springs, Indiana, where the Pirates went through their usual preliminary conditioning before heading to Hot Springs. Still, when the team left Pittsburgh on March 10, it was without the foot-dragging Wagner, who got permission to stay behind for a few days.

The Pirates opened their season on April 12, losing 4-3 to the Reds and spitballer Bob Ewing. Three rainouts and a day off kept the Pirates from the field until their home opener on April 17, when they lost 6-2 to Chicago in 35-degree weather at Exposition Park.

As in 1906, the Pirates were forced to chase Chicago as it ran away with the pennant race. April ended with the Cubs and New York Giants 1-2 at 13-2 and 12-3, respectively, and the injury-plagued Pirates (6-3) a distant third. Early on, Pittsburgh catcher Harry Smith was sidelined by stomach problems; outfielder Otis Clymer had a charley horse, then was called home to Lebanon, Pennsylvania, because his wife was ill; Nealon injured his leg sliding into third on April 18 against the Cubs; Leach went on the disabled list.

Like his teammates, Wagner started slowly, and it wasn't until June that he took over the league batting lead. A 9-for-17 series against Brooklyn raised his average to .333. The Pirates, however, weren't able to duplicate Wagner's success. On the morning of

June 12, they were in fourth place at 23-18, 10 games behind first-place Chicago.

On June 20 against Philadelphia, Wagner suffered an injury that would bother him most of the rest of the season. As he rounded first after his second hit of the day, he collided with Phillies first baseman Kid Gleason and twisted his right leg. He managed to get to third, but asked to come out of the game for a pinch-runner. Wagner was in the lineup the following day, but missed the next three games because of pain in the leg that was partially relieved by a visit from Bonesetter Reese.

Wagner was able to return for a six-games-in-five-days series with Chicago that started June 27, and despite the pain was able to contribute offensively. He went 8 for 25 as the Pirates won four games and lost one—another ended in a tie—and moved into third place.

The Pirates kept up the pressure in July, winning two of three against the Giants, then winning three of four from Boston. The surge left them a half-game out of second. For the next month, Pittsburgh and New York battled over second place, the Pirates climbing ahead of the Giants, then falling back to third, then sneaking back into second. The Giants won four of five from the Pirates early in August to regain second. Pittsburgh then won four of six from New York in a late-August series. On September 1, the Pirates were third at 69-49. Chicago pulled away in the last month, winning 35 of 40 games to finish 107-45 and capture its second consecutive NL pennant. Pittsburgh finished second, 17 games back.

The last two months of the season also saw two deals that would pay big dividends for the Pirates down the road. In early August, they obtained pitcher Babe Adams from Denver of the Western League. Adams had only an 0-2 record in four games, and was sent to Louisville in 1908. But he became Pittsburgh's ace in 1909, and went on to win 194 games in an 18-year Pirate career. The other big addition was pitcher Nick Maddox, obtained from Wheeling of the Central League in September. He made a quicker splash, striking out 11 in his September 11 major-league debut, and throwing a no-hitter against Brooklyn in his third outing, on September 20. He finished with a 5-1 record and 0.83 ERA, just a taste of what was to come in 1908.

Wagner's season again came to a premature finish—which was becoming a yearly occurrence—when he was struck by a pitch from Boston's Rube Dessau on September 27. The pitch fractured a small bone in his left hand and knocked Wagner out of the Pirates' final 12 games.

Despite the leg injury that had bothered him much of the year and the early end of his season, Wagner easily won his second consecutive NL batting championship. He finished at .350, well ahead of Philadelphia's Sherry Magee (.328) and Beaumont—the "player to be named later" in the Abbaticchio deal—who hit .322 for Boston. The American League batting championship was won by Detroit's Ty Cobb, who hit .350—though a fraction higher than Wagner—in capturing his first crown.

On October 8, Wagner and Leach took a team on a two-week barnstorming tour through western Pennsylvania, eastern Ohio and West Virginia. Wagner, his hand better, played as well as managed the squad. When the tour stopped in Carnegie on October 16, he was presented with the gold medal that went to the National League batting champion. After the tour, Wagner went back to his usual off-season pastimes, hunting and playing basketball, this time as captain of a team based in Canonsburg, Pennsylvania, that also included brother Al and Hans Lobert.

The rumor mills were working full time that October and November. There was talk of a third major league, which would put a team in Pittsburgh and name Wagner manager. And Boston Braves owner George Dovey, a Pittsburgh resident and friend of Dreyfuss, was looking for a new manager after his team's 58-90 record and seventh-place finish. His first choice: Honus Wagner.

But Wagner had big plans of his own. If two other teams were that interested in him, it was going to cost Barney Dreyfuss some money.

# *Ten*

S ince 1901, Honus Wagner had completed only one season healthy, that in 1905. In 1902, he played the last month with a broken hand; in 1903, he missed most of the last week of the season because of a knee injury; in 1904 a sore arm kept him out of the Pirates' last 17 games; in 1906 he missed much of the last week because of a sore leg; and in 1907 it was a broken bone in his left hand that ended his season 12 games prematurely. In addition, he faced the almost constant pain of rheumatism in his legs, a reminder of his days in the coal mines.

Despite the physical problems, he had continued to produce for Barney Dreyfuss. Since coming to Pittsburgh, he had won an unprecedented five batting titles (and owned a composite .352 average); he had led the Pirates to three consecutive National League championships; he had played every position except catcher for Fred Clarke and he was clearly the most valuable player on the team—as well as the top drawing card around the league.

Wagner was not, however, the highest-paid player in the league. He could have made a small fortune had he jumped to the American League in 1901, but he signed for less with the Pirates. He was on the AL's most wanted list again in 1902, but rejected overtures delivered through teammate Jack O'Connor and again re-signed with Dreyfuss, again for considerably less than what the AL was offering.

It was time, he figured, that he be paid what he was worth. But instead of publicly asking for a salary increase, he told teammates and the press that he wanted to take a year off from baseball to rest. In early December, he wrote to Dreyfuss: "I will not be with your team this season," the letter said, "but I wish you a pennant-winner and will always be plugging for Cap and the boys to win. It is certainly hard for me to lay aside the uniform I have worn since 1897, but every dog has his day and the sport has become too strenuous for me. ... I wish to thank you for your treatment of me while a member of your club and assure you that I highly appreciate the same."[1]

The contents of the letter were soon leaked to the press. Dreyfuss and Clarke knew the real story, that Wagner was looking for more money, but it would have been foolish for the team to publicize that fact. The Pirates could never win a contract fight with Honus Wagner in the press. So Dreyfuss was satisfied to feign ignorance of Wagner's intentions and negotiate behind the scenes with his star while Pittsburgh newspapers ran tales of Wagner's worn-down body and his desire to take a year's sabbatical.

When stories about Wagner's rheumatism appeared in the press, he was inundated with letters offering various folk remedies and the names of doctors and several products guaranteed to alleviate the problem. Wagner, though, didn't seem like a man nearly crippled by leg pain—he spent Christmas afternoon hitting fly balls to youngsters on a field in Carnegie. And he didn't cut back on his hunting excursions during the off-season, often spending several days a week in the field.

Dreyfuss continued to deny there was a problem. In public, at least. When he arrived in New York for the league meetings on the night of December 9, reporters asked him about Wagner's intentions to take a year off. He indicated he knew nothing of such plans. "Wagner has just returned from a hunting trip in Indiana, and when I left home he gave me no intimation that he prepared to lay off next year," Dreyfuss insisted.[2]

The next day, Wagner received an urgent telegram from his old friend, National League President Harry Pulliam. The wire instructed him to come immediately to New York, where the league meetings were being held at the Waldorf-Astoria. The summons to New York had Pittsburgh papers and fans speculating: Was Wagner in some kind of trouble with the league? Was a trade going to be announced? Was he going to be named manager in Boston as had been rumored? Or might he be taking over the Pirates from Clarke?

In truth, Pulliam had decided that the league should honor Wagner for his on-field accomplishments. (Their meeting in New York would also give Pulliam an opportunity to get the real story out of Wagner about his "retirement" plans.) Pulliam knew that Wagner would never agree to be feted at the league dinner, so he sent the urgent telegram, then had Dreyfuss and Pirate Secretary William Locke send follow-up messages. The plan worked: Honus, Al and James Orris—Honus' friend and business adviser—caught the earliest train to New York and were at the hotel on December 11 in time for the dinner.

A surprised and embarrassed Wagner was presented with a loving cup honoring his years of accomplishments and his batting titles of 1900, 1903, 1904, 1906 and 1907. In introducing the evening's guest of honor, Pulliam recounted the part he played as a member of the Louisville Colonels' front office in obtaining Wagner from Paterson in 1897.

"When my days as a baseball official are ended, I shall carry with me to my new sphere of work the fond recollection of a most valued incident of my career as a baseball official—the fact that I was, in some measure, responsible in bringing to the National League its greatest player," he told the audience.

After he secured Wagner, Pulliam reminisced how he "wired Barney Dreyfuss . . . as follows: 'I have purchased the release of the best player in America. . . .'

"This was his beginning, gentlemen, in the National League, and what he has done since then is an open book. In the long history of the National League, the oldest baseball organization in America, he has accomplished the feat never before equaled in the annals of the league, of being our leading batsman for five years. With all his success, with all his skill, with all his prowess, he has remained the same modest, unassuming fellow that he was when I first met him in Paterson many years ago."[3]

The Wagners and Orris returned to Carnegie on December 13, toting the large silver trophy, but the trip to New York did nothing to answer the questions about the 1908 season.

The uncertainty over Wagner had a ripple effect on the Pirates. The Cincinnati Reds had for months been interested in making Tommy Leach their player-manager for 1908. Dreyfuss, fearing he might not have Wagner in the lineup for the upcoming season, was reluctant to lose Leach, the Pirates' second-best hitter. He turned negotiations over to Clarke, who wanted three players in return for his center-fielder, but Reds owner August "Garry" Herrmann balked. Finally, the impasse ended on January 17 when Herrmann hired John Ganzel for the job.

The episode left Leach disappointed, and he may have held Wagner at least partly responsible. Leach had managerial aspirations, but when the Pirates needed an interim manager they always turned to Wagner first. Now, Wagner's impending absence was one reason he was unable to get a shot at managing the Reds. Leach was further perturbed by the contract he was offered for 1908. He had appeared in 149 games in 1907, hit a career-best .303 and scored 102 runs. And in trade talks with the Reds, the Pirates thought enough of Leach to demand three players in exchange. Still, all he was offered was a 15 percent raise.

Joining Leach as a holdout were catchers George Gibson and Harry Smith. By the time training camp opened, there was public speculation that Wagner's absence was nothing more than a contract dispute. But Wagner—who had been told by the Pirates' Locke to name his own terms[4]—insisted, publicly, at least, that money was not a factor. Dreyfuss continued negotiations behind the scenes, twice coming to Carnegie to increase the team's salary offer.[5] After he and Wagner met on February 20, the *Carnegie Union* reported "Honus insisted he would not play this year."[6]

Dreyfuss even tried exerting some subtle pressure in the press. "Wagner has a perfect right to retire," he told *The Sporting News*, "and I hope that the year's rest will benefit him."[7]

Despite Wagner's claims that he was serious about sitting out a year, others were less sure.

"Honus seems bent on raising chickens in preference to playing ball this year," reported the *Carnegie Union*. "His intentions are good, but his friends do not believe he can long resist the temptation to get into the game."[8]

A week later came another report: "He has received two flattering offers this week to play elsewhere but has turned them down. On Tuesday, a telegram was received offering $10,000 and a chicken farm to play independent ball with a Chicago club this year. Wagner promptly replied that he didn't want the salary, but would take the chickens ...

"Honus has plenty of good, true friends here in Carnegie, who want to see him do well, not only as a ball player, but in a financial way as well, so that when his ball playing days are over, he will be comfortably fixed for life. These friends are afraid it will be a mistake for him to pass up a year's big fat salary (which can never be regained) and take chances of getting into his old time form after being out of the game for a year."[9]

Wagner soon received yet another job offer, this one closer to home. William P. Field, the secretary of Carnegie Tech in Pittsburgh, visited Wagner on March 18. He offered him the baseball coaching job at the school. Two days later, Wagner visited the campus but wouldn't commit himself on the offer, one way or another.

Dreyfuss was getting frustrated, and not a little upset at Orris, whom he believed was responsible for Wagner's "retirement." "I've got not only Wagner, but this other fellow, Orris, holding out on me," Dreyfuss claimed.[10]

Reporting date came and went. Leach signed on March 13 for what had been originally offered; that left only Gibson, Smith and Wagner missing as the team went through spring training in Hot Springs.

The Pirates broke camp on April 2 and began a 10-day exhibition tour through Oklahoma, Kansas and Missouri. On March 31, Wagner and his brother Al had left Carnegie, headed for a rendezvous with the Pirates in Kansas. The year before, an exhibition game was scheduled in Winfield, site of Clarke's Little Pirate Ranch. Wagner had promised his manager he would participate in the game. But was his trip west merely the keeping of that promise? Or was he about to end his holdout?

"You can say positively I will not play ball this year," Wagner said as he and Al prepared to leave Carnegie. "I am firmly convinced that I need a year's rest, and am determined to have it."[11]

But two days later, when a reporter caught up with him in Wheeling, West Virginia, Wagner seemed to indicate he might play after all. "While not declaring outright that he would be in the game, he hinted so broadly that it could easily be seen that matters would be fixed up between Clarke and him when the two men meet in Kansas," the *Pittsburgh Gazette Times* reported.[12] The paper also claimed that Wagner had said he had been offered $30,000 over three years, but that he did not want to commit to a long-term contract. Still, the *Gazette Times* said, Wagner indicated he probably would be signing for 1908.

It appeared a deal was imminent. The Wagners traveled to Massillon, Ohio, where they met holdout Smith. Gibson, who had just come to terms, and Dreyfuss caught up with the Wagner party and wired ahead to Locke that they were all on their way. Dreyfuss, the Wagners, Gibson and Smith intercepted the Pirates train as it made a stop on its way to Wichita. Around 4:30 a.m. on April 5, the three missing Pirates descended on the train's sleeping car, waking their surprised teammates.

Wagner sat on the sidelines as the Pirates played exhibitions April 5 and 6 in Wichita. He huddled with Dreyfuss and Clarke on the trip to Winfield, and lived up to his promise to his manager on April 7, suiting up and playing in a split-squad game, getting three hits.

Despite the warm welcome from his teammates, the Pirates' contract offer, and his success in the exhibition game, Wagner still wasn't ready to sign. He asked Locke for a train ticket home. The Wagners and Smith, still a holdout, departed for Pittsburgh on April 10. A couple of days later, a reporter tracked down Wagner and Smith, fishing in Cambridge Springs, Pennsylvania. Wagner clearly considered the reporter's presence an intrusion. "I don't know whether I will or not. Perhaps I will, perhaps I won't," he said when asked if he would play in 1908. "Holy smoke. I came up here to get away from you fellows. I thought I was safe here.

"I'll tell you the truth, as I said before: I don't know what I will do this summer. Now I'm going to get a string of fish."[13]

Wagner was a little friendlier—but still not very forthcoming—with Ralph Davis, correspondent for *The Sporting News.* "It was just accidental that I hit and fielded well in the game I played with the Pirates in Kansas," he said. "I never felt sorer in my life than on the evening and the day following that game. It was the first hard practice I had. Heretofore I have kept in condition by playing basketball during the winter, but I did not play the game last winter. My legs are bad and I feel the need of rest, and I am going to take it."[14]

The Pirates were scheduled to start the season April 14 in St. Louis, but rain delayed the opener—a 3-1 Pittsburgh victory—until April 16. The following day, Wagner showed up at team headquarters. The Pirates were willing to meet his contract requests, but they wouldn't listen to his demands that Smith be given a big raise, something Wagner had brought up repeatedly during negotiations (Smith, in fact, was traded to Boston shortly after the season started). Wagner finally signed for $10,000, double his previous salary. By the time the deal was announced the next day by Dreyfuss, Wagner was enroute to Cincinnati, where he made his first appearance of the season on April 19 to a huge ovation from Reds fans. In his first day back on the job, he had a single in four at-bats and two runs scored in a 4-3 loss.

The Pirates started the 1908 season with several holes in their lineup. First base had been turned over to rookie Harry Swacina;

the decision of 1907's third baseman Alan Storke to attend law school meant that Clarke had to shift Leach to third and try several players in center field; another rookie, Owen "Chief" Wilson, was given the right-field job. But despite the shuffling the Pirates were in contention from Opening Day. Chicago and New York were their main competition, although Cincinnati and Philadelphia were among the challengers early in the season. Chicago moved into first on April 23 and held the lead until June 30, when a Cubs loss and Pirates day off moved Pittsburgh into first and set the stage for a big six-game series.

"Without exaggeration, this old town is just about baseball crazy now and is likely to remain so as long as the Pirates keep up the fine work," reported *The Sporting News*. "You hear nothing on the streets but baseball. The scores are being posted in every conceivable place, and no matter where it appears, it never fails to attract a crowd."[15]

A crowd announced at 18,249 attended the July 2 double-header that opened the series, and which the teams split. Wagner, who had reached the 2,000-hit milestone on June 22 in a 4-0 loss to Cincinnati, was 4 for 7 in the double-header, but he was hitless the next day as the Pirates won 7-0, and managed only one hit in seven trips as the Cubs swept a July 4 double-header to edge past the Pirates into first place. The series moved to Chicago for the final game on July 5, Wagner hitting a home run in a 10-5 victory that put the Pirates back on top. Three days later, the Cubs regained first and held it for a week before the Pirates again climbed on top on the 15th, where they stayed for the next five weeks.

Early in the season, in the afterglow of the re-signing of Wagner, the Pirates announced plans for a Honus Wagner Day July 17 at Exposition Park. Despite eight stellar seasons during which he won five batting championships and led the Pirates to three pennants, Wagner never had a "day" held in his honor in Pittsburgh. Dreyfuss told Wagner the Pirates would remedy that oversight. The day couldn't have come at a better time. Wagner was hitting over .320, but a sore hand was affecting his fielding and some in the stands were getting on him. The problem of hecklers was an old one. On several occasions during the 1907 season, he was jeered by the gamblers who populated the bleachers in Exposition Park. The betting crowd had been harassing Pirate players for years, but they were especially hard on Wagner that season. His performance never seemed to satisfy them; and the injuries that knocked him out of the lineup only made them angrier at Wagner.

Fans were invited to contribute to a fund for Wagner. There was a $1 limit, and $700 was collected. The W.M. Laird shoe company gave away 10,000 megaphones for fans to cheer Wagner. Before the game he was presented with the money as well as flowers, a watch, chain and charm and a gamecock.

"It was a laughing, froliksome [sic] holiday crowd decorated profusely with Wagner buttons and blowing through megaphones most outrageously," reported the *Pittsburgh Gazette Times*. "They shouted and cheered as soon as they had selected their seats and fairly yelled when the two teams marched toward home plate divided into two lines. ... At the rear end of the Pittsburgh string was the burly Wagner, with naked arms, bowed legs and a new shave."[16]

What should have been a glorious day for Wagner soon went sour, though. He was hitless in the game, a 4-0 Boston victory that was stopped by rain in the seventh inning. Even more disturbing, afterward he was asked about persistent stories that he was reconsidering retirement.

Giants catcher Tim Needham had been quoted in *The Sporting News* as saying Wagner had told him he would use his day to announce his retirement. "I had a long talk with Wagner, and he told me positively that after the game on Friday [July 17] he would quit the Pirates and quit ball for good," Needham said. "I thought he was joking at first, but he assured me he was in dead earnest. He is completely disgusted by the way he has been treated by the Pittsburgh fans. During the past 10 days he has been playing with a sore hand that would have put most fellows out of the business. Yet because he slipped up on a few difficult chances, he was roasted unmercifully."[17]

After the game Wagner issued a statement through the Pirates, denying he had planned to quit, ending it with "I love baseball more than anything else on earth."

Certainly, a July 24-28 series against the second-place Giants in New York did nothing to dampen his love for the game. In the opener, he had two hits as the Pirates lost 2-1. But on the 25th, in front of a crowd estimated between 25,000 and 30,000, he went 5 for 5 with two doubles to lead Pittsburgh past Christy Mathewson, who was on his way to a 37-11 season. He added another 2 for 4 day on the 26th, another Pirate victory, before the teams closed the series by playing to a 16-inning, 2-2 tie on the 27th.

Not even the enemy could ignore his 9-for-18 series. "Hans Wagner made a great hit in New York," reported *The Sporting News*. "He clouted the ball at a terrific rate, and the fans went crazy over him. On Saturday, in the presence of the biggest crowd that ever flocked to the Polo Grounds, Wagner hammered out three singles and two doubles, and this feat so delighted the fans that after the game they tried to carry the big fellow off the field on their shoulders, and one enthusiast swiped Wagner's cap to keep as a souvenir. It is seldom, indeed, that New Yorkers can see any good in anything that does not bear the Gotham trademark, but Wagner's play was so great as to demand recognition everywhere."[18]

It would have been difficult for anyone to ignore Wagner in 1908. By mid-August, he led the National League in batting average, home runs, doubles, triples, stolen bases, total bases, extra bases and runs. And the Pirates were able to maintain a narrow lead over the Giants and Cubs in what would go down as the greatest three-team race in baseball history.

The Pirates fell from first during a late-August stretch that saw them go 2-5 while the Giants were going 6-0. New York came to Pittsburgh on August 24, winning both games of a double-header to regain the lead, and held it until September 29 as the Pirates and Cubs battled for second. The race came down to the final day of the season. On October 4, the first-place Pirates (98-55) and the second-place Cubs (97-55) met in Chicago. The third-place Giants (95-55) had the day off, but were to open a three-game series against sixth-place Boston the next afternoon.

A victory in Chicago would have given the Pirates the pennant, but the Cubs, cheered by a record West Side Park crowd of 30,647, broke a 2-2 tie with single runs in the sixth, seventh and eighth for a 5-2 victory. The Giants swept the Braves in their three-game series, leaving New York and Chicago tied for first at 98-55. The Cubs beat the Giants in a one-game playoff on October 8 to win the NL championship.

In the last-day showdown with the Cubs, Wagner managed two hits. His double in the sixth drove in the first Pirate run, and he tied the game at 2 moments later when he scored on Ed Abbaticchio's single. He added a leadoff single over second in the ninth but was later forced at second. Wagner also made two errors, the first of which, in the fifth, helped the Cubs to a 2-0 lead, and the second of which came in the seventh and was partly responsible for another Cubs run. About all Wagner came away with for the day was his sixth National League batting title. But it gave him little satisfaction.

"What does it all amount to when we didn't win that game yesterday?" he said upon arriving home in Carnegie the next day. "I would gladly have given every world's record I ever had or hope to have if we could only have pulled that game out of the fire yesterday. It would have been the greatest finish to the greatest race in the world's history for us ... "[19]

As it was, he had to settle for a .354 average and third consecutive batting championship. His nearest challenger, New York's Mike Donlin, was at .334, and Wagner's mark was some 115 points higher than the league average. He was also at or near the top in almost every other statistical category: first in runs batted in (109), hits (201), doubles (39), triples (19), total bases (308), slugging average (.542) and stolen bases (53), and second in home runs (with 10) and runs scored (100, to New York's Fred Tenney's 101).

Less than a month after the season ended, the Pirates were back in the headlines. Barney Dreyfuss announced the purchase of nearly seven acres of land at the opposite end of Pittsburgh where he would build a new ballpark. It was the start of an incredibly successful 12 months for the Pirates.

# *Eleven*

The Pirates announced the building of a new stadium in late October and wasted little time getting started. The plans were drawn up by Charles W. Leavitt Jr. of New York, who had built the grandstand at Belmont Park, and the grading and foundation were started less than a month after the new ballpark was announced.

It was also a busy off-season for Honus Wagner. His big raise of 1908 had left him money for investments, but as would be the case several times later in his life, the return on those investments wasn't what he expected.

In November it was announced that Honus, Al and Luke were forming the Wagner Brothers Circus. Al and Luke were to run the show; Honus' job, aside from bankrolling the operation, was undecided. Reported *The Sporting News*: "His contract does not call for his personal presence with the company, but it has been pointed out to him that it would be a tremendous advertisement and do much to swell the box office receipts to have him lead the daily parades in his big white automobile, or better still, armed with a baseball bat, ride astride one of the huge elephants."[1]

A week later, an oil well belonging to the Geyser Oil Co., of which he owned 25 percent, came in on company land a few miles from Carnegie. And in January, Wagner entered a partnership with J. Joe Felcht, forming the Wagner and Felcht Auto Co. to sell the Regal from a garage on Mary Avenue in Carnegie.

But none of the business deals panned out. The circus never got much beyond the talking stage. Al and Luke would have been out of their element running a circus; and Honus riding an elephant? Not in a million years. The Geyser Oil Co., likewise, never made Wagner rich. For every well that came in, there were many more that came up dry. And the Wagner and Felcht Auto Co. was to last only 10 months. The two dissolved their partnership on November 5, 1909, though Wagner continued running a garage in town. But Wagner was largely unconcerned about the failure of these business ventures. Baseball, not high finance, was his area of expertise.

As usual, Wagner was one of the last Pirates to sign for 1909, reupping for the same $10,000 he received in 1908. The team left for West Baden Springs on March 11, arriving in Indiana the next day. But Wagner, with the leverage of being the league's biggest star, was excused from spring training. He claimed he needed to attend an auto show in late March; in truth, he simply wasn't interested in the rigors of spring training. His plans were to join the team in Terre Haute on April 12, a month after workouts had started and only two days before the 1909 opener. While the Pirates were in Indiana and then in Hot Springs, Wagner was getting in shape by playing basketball three nights a week around Carnegie.

When Wagner finally showed up in Hot Springs, he was accompanied by a friend, George Aston. Aston was a member of a pioneering black family from the Pittsburgh area. He and Wagner had met years before on a golf course when Aston caddied for Wagner. They hit it off immediately, and soon Aston was driving Wagner around Carnegie. When the two arrived in camp, Wagner was asked who his friend was. "My chauffeur," he replied, half kiddingly. From that day on, Aston was called "Chauf" by the players. Before camp had ended, Wagner had prevailed upon the Pirates to hire Aston as an assistant clubhouse man, a job he would hold for almost 40 years.

When the bell rang to start the season, Wagner was ready. He was teamed with a new second baseman for 1909. Jack "Dots" Miller was a handsome 22-year-old rookie from Kearney, New Jersey, who had been signed by the Pirates after a tryout in 1908. He and Wagner hit it off immediately—Miller, like Wagner, was of German heritage, both were single, and both enjoyed their beer and the relatively new pastime of automobiling. Wagner and Miller became almost inseparable, with Miller eventually moving into the Wagner family home with Honus, Honus' father Peter and brother Luke. They also made a formidable infield combination in 1909: Wagner would be a close second in fielding among NL shortstops and would lead the league in double plays at his position; Miller ended up leading all second basemen in assists and fielding percentage.

The Pirates lost three of four games in their season-opening series in Cincinnati. Still, they stayed in the hunt early before eventually taking over first place on May 5. The pennant race was in doubt only until the end of the month. On May 21, the Pirates beat Boston 6-2. It would be the start of a stretch during which they won 20 of 21 games and opened their lead to five games over second-place Chicago. Wagner was providing much of the offensive spark during the Pirates' charge, hitting .426 in the 21 games. By June 10, he was hitting .420 and leading the league in doubles, hits and stolen bases.

Between the Pirates' success and the imminent opening of the new ballpark,[2] interest in baseball in Pittsburgh was soaring. Reported *The Sporting News'* Pittsburgh correspondent: "Enthusiasm here has reached a higher point than for several years, in fact, since the pennant winning days of 1903."[3]

The last days at Exposition Park were melancholy ones for Wagner and his teammates. They were leaving the ballpark where they had won pennants in 1901, '02 and '03; where they had played the first World Series. Wagner's memories included sitting in the bleachers there as a teenager, then winning six batting championships there on the field.

President William Howard Taft paid his respects to the ballpark on May 29 when he attended a Pirates-Cubs game. Taft, a longtime Honus Wagner fan, was in Pittsburgh for several speaking engagements and a dinner. While Taft was at one event, his brother Charles was given a tour of the new ballpark by Barney Dreyfuss and Charles Murphy, owner of the Cubs. After Dreyfuss, Murphy and Charles Taft returned to the president's side, he overheard them discussing baseball and the new facility. Taft decided he wanted to see a ballgame, so preparations were hastily made for him to attend that afternoon's Cub-Pirate contest.

Wagner gave the president something to cheer in the first inning when he laced a ground-rule double. "When Wagner knocked out what looked like a home run, the President leaped to his feet, cheering with the best of the frenzied fans about him," the *Pittsburgh Press* reported. "When the ground rules deprived Wagner of two bases, Taft sat down again and slowly shook his head back and forth, laughing deprecatingly."[4]

Wagner, whose average was at .400 going into the game, added another hit and made a sparking defensive play in the ninth, but it wasn't enough to prevent the Pirates from losing 8-3.

Exposition Park bowed out on June 29, the opponent again the second-place Cubs. The Pirates won 8-1, with the curtain ringing down on the old ballpark when Lefty Leifield struck out Jimmy Archer for the final out. At that instant, a bugle sounding "Taps" was heard from center field. As 11,000 fans and two teams of ballplayers stood in silence, the flag was lowered, and Exposition Park became history.

The same two teams met the following day to christen Forbes Field. The new ballpark, billed as "the finest baseball field in the world," was situated in the Oakland section of Pittsburgh on the east side of town. "It is one of the finest structures for outdoor amusement that has been built in any part of the world," gushed the *Spalding Official Baseball Guide.* "It is all steel and concrete, and most ornate, from an architectural standpoint. With its high towering galleries it provides seats and splendid outlook in every foot of the huge structure."[5]

"A sight of the crowd was worth a journey to the park," wrote Ring Lardner in the *Chicago Tribune,*[6] "although said journey is anything but comfortable. From early in the forenoon until the game started the masses of people crowded their way into the beautiful suburb. . .

"The women came dressed as if for the greatest society event of the year, and perhaps it was for Pittsburgh's year. Gorgeous gowns, topped by still more gorgeous hats, were in evidence everywhere. Most of the gowns were white and formed a pretty combination with the prevalent green of the stands."

A crowd of 30,338 saw the Cubs beat the Pirates 3-2. Wagner had two hits, a bunt in the fourth and a liner to left in the fifth, but Chicago pitcher Ed Reulbach allowed just three other hits.

Less than a month after the opening of the new ballpark, Wagner, the Pirates and the rest of baseball were shaken by the news that National League president Harry Pulliam had shot himself in his room in the New York Athletic Club. Pulliam, the former Louisville Colonel and Pirate executive, the man who had obtained Wagner from Paterson, had recently returned to work after a five-month leave of absence he had been granted because of health problems, mental as well as physical. On the evening of July 28, he went to his room, got undressed, put a .38 caliber revolver to his right temple, and fired. He died of his injuries at 7:40 a.m. the next day.

Monday, August 2, 1909, was a day without baseball across America. The National and American Leagues, as well as most minor leagues, canceled the day's action out of respect for Pulliam.[7] Services were held in Louisville, and dozens of baseball dignitaries helped swell the crowd to more than a thousand mourners. Representing the Pirates at the services were owner Barney Dreyfuss, manager Fred Clarke and players Sam Leever and Lefty Leifield.[8] One notable absentee was Wagner, who was unable to make the trip to his old friend's funeral because of a painful injury he had incurred against Cincinnati on July 28.

Wagner had slid into home and suffered a badly strained muscle in his side. A rumor went around that the injury was actually heart trouble, but the Pirates debunked those stories. The injury was serious enough to keep Wagner, who was hitting .346 when he got hurt, out of the starting lineup until August 13. On the day of his return, he had a three-run double and a single—he was also robbed of a third hit by third baseman Eddie Grant—in a 2-1 victory over Philadelphia.

The pennant race, as it turned out, wasn't much of a race at all. From July 1 until the end of the season, only two changes occurred in the standings, and neither included first-place Pittsburgh, second-place Chicago or third-place New York. Despite having a terrific team that won 110 games, the Pirates were never able to shake Chicago. The Cubs won 104 games and finished just 6½ back. The Pirates didn't wrap up their first championship since 1903 until September 28, when the second-place Cubs were officially eliminated after a 3-2 loss to Philadelphia.

The American League race was just as tight. The Detroit Tigers, led by Ty Cobb, Sam Crawford, Donie Bush, George Mullin and Ed Willett, didn't wrap up their championship until September 30, finally finishing 3½ games ahead of Philadelphia.

To hear the newspapers tell it, this World Series was as much Wagner vs. Cobb as it was Pittsburgh vs. Detroit. Wagner had just won a fourth straight NL batting title (.339), and had led the league in runs batted in (100), doubles (39), total bases (242) and slugging average (.489). Cobb had led the AL in batting (.377), home runs (9), RBIs (107), hits (216), total bases (296), stolen bases (76), runs scored (116) and slugging average (.517).

But their confrontation involved more than statistics. It was a battle between the beloved Wagner—the fan favorite, the best player in the National League who, at 35, would soon be nearing the end of the road—and the feisty Cobb—at 22 already a three-time American League batting champion and one of the game's most feared and disliked players.

The Series, which the Pirates would go on to win in seven games, was scheduled to open on October 8 in Pittsburgh. As the two teams warmed up in Forbes Field before the opener, Wagner spotted Cobb. The Pirate star walked over and greeted Cobb with a strong handshake and big smile. Cobb returned the greeting. Members of the press, seeing the two stars talking near second base, converged on them. Photographers posed them side-by-side in batting stances, Wagner the right-handed hitter, Cobb the lefty. It was at that point that Cobb took note of a surprising fact that he recounted in his autobiography:

"We both gripped our bat in pretty much the same way—lower hand a few inches from the knob and with hands a palm-width or so apart. Only a few players used the style then, and very few have used it since.

" 'Did you pick that up yourself?' I asked Honus.

" 'Yep. How about you?'

" 'I worked it out, too.' I said. 'Good luck in the Series. I've admired you a long time.' "[9]

Cobb later cautioned reporters about making too much of their matchup in the Series.

"Oh, you mustn't compare us. He is a baseball veteran, and I am only a youngster. He has had years of experience, and is up on all the tricks of the trade. I have never seen him play, but from what I have heard of him, he must be a wonder."[10]

The press knew this meeting would result in a good story. Even if it had to be fiction. The most widely told tale to come out of the 1909 World Series involved a confrontation at second base between Wagner and Cobb. The Tiger star was perched on first, the story went, and yelled to the Pirate shortstop, "Look out, Krauthead, I'm coming down!" On the next pitch, Cobb broke for second. Wagner took catcher George Gibson's throw and smacked Cobb in the mouth, cutting his lip and necessitating three stitches. It was a tale Wagner himself often told; it was picked up and reported in many Wagner newspaper stories over the years. The only problem: It never happened.

Never during the Series was Cobb thrown out trying to steal second. He did swipe it in Game 1, and Wagner tried to make a tag, but the throw was late and off the mark, and the best Wagner could do was swipe at—and miss—the Tiger star, who made a fadeaway slide to avoid contact altogether.

While Wagner kept the story alive on the banquet circuit in his later years, Cobb did what he could to refute it.

"Wagner and I never had a cross word," he wrote in his autobiography. "And I certainly didn't stand on first base, hollering, 'Look out, Krauthead, I'm coming down!' And then get my lip split when Wagner slammed me with the ball.

"That's 100 percent concoction, and the proof of it is that, at the time it was supposed to have happened, I wasn't even the runner at first base. The press hasn't had to strain much in building the public image of Ty Cobb. But it seems to me they broke all records for manufacturing hokum when they located me on a base I didn't occupy.

"Spike Honus Wagner? It would have taken quite a foolhardy man. He wore thick felt pads under his socks to absorb any slider's cleats. And he could block off a base-runner with his huge bearlike body in a manner that made the boys very careful when they slid in his vicinity."[11]

Forbes Field was jammed with 29,577 fans for the Series opener—the biggest crowd ever to attend a postseason game—and they were not disappointed. Babe Adams stopped the Tigers on six hits, Clarke homered, and Leach made a running catch in center against Cobb with two men on in the seventh, preserving a 4-1 Pirate lead that held up for the victory.

Cobb, who was hitless in the opener, provided the spark for a Tiger victory in Game 2. The Pirates had taken a 2-0 lead off Wild Bill Donovan in the first, but Detroit tied it in the second against Howie Camnitz. Jim Delahanty's two-run single in the third made it 4-2 and left him on first and Cobb on third. On the next pitch, as Camnitz began his windup, Cobb streaked for the plate, stealing home with a fadeaway slide for a 5-2 lead. Cobb offered one more bit of flash for the Pirate fans. In the seventh, he tried to go from first to third on a grounder to Miller at second. He beat the throw to Bobby Byrne, but overslid third and was tagged out. The final score was 7-2, sending the Series to Detroit tied at one game apiece.

Wagner, held to two hits in the first two games, took his place in the spotlight in Game 3. "The duel between the two headliners,

Wagner and Cobb, raged furiously through it all," wrote Ring Lardner after the third game, "and at the end honors were with the Dutchman." [12]

He had four singles, three runs batted in and three stolen bases—he was also caught stealing once—as Nick Maddox beat the Tigers 8-6. Wagner struck quickly in the first, when the Pirates scored five runs. He singled across two runs, stole second and went to third on a bad throw on the play, then came home on a wild pitch for the third run of the inning. Cobb provided two clutch RBI hits—a single in a four-run seventh and a double in a two-run ninth—and made a spectacular diving catch on Miller's low liner in the ninth to save another run.

The Tigers again rebounded to take Game 4 5-0 on Mullin's five-hitter, sending the Series back to Pittsburgh tied.

Adams started Game 5 for the Pirates, who took a 3-1 lead after three innings. In the sixth, Wagner threw away Delahanty's grounder to help the Tigers tie the score. But the deadlock lasted only until the bottom of the seventh. Byrne and Leach singled off pitcher Ed Summers, and Clarke followed with his second home run of the Series for a 6-3 Pittsburgh lead. Summers took out his frustration on Wagner, the next man up, hitting him with a pitch. Wagner got a measure of revenge by stealing second and third, then coming home on catcher Charley Schmidt's bad throw on the second steal.

Game 6, back in Detroit, was the hardest-fought of the Series. The Pirates jumped ahead 3-0 in the first on Clarke's RBI single and Wagner's two-run double. But the Tigers chipped away against eventual loser Vic Willis and Camnitz, tying the score in the fourth and adding single runs in the fifth and sixth for a 5-3 lead. The Pirates opened the ninth inning with singles by Miller and Bill Abstein, putting men on first and second.

Chief Wilson bunted in front of the plate. Catcher Schmidt made the play, but his throw to first was up the line, and as first baseman Tom Jones reached for the ball Wilson crashed into him, knocking him unconscious. As the ball rolled away, Miller scored to make it 5-4. Tiger manager Hughie Jennings brought Crawford in from center field to play first, and he was tested quickly. Gibson hit a bouncer to first. Crawford made a nice pickup, then threw home. Spikes flying, Abstein crashed into Schmidt hard, inflicting a bloody gash on his thigh. But the Tiger catcher held onto the ball for the first out of the inning.

Clarke sent Ed Abbaticchio to bat for Deacon Phillippe, who had relieved Camnitz in the seventh. Abbaticchio worked the count full against Mullin. On the 3-2 pitch, Wilson broke for third. Abbaticchio struck out, and Schmidt's throw got Wilson, but not without a cost. Wilson's spikes tore into third baseman George Moriarty, who had to be helped to the dressing room.

After that finish, Game 7 would have been hard-pressed to provide an equal amount of excitement. As it turned out, the finale, October 16 in Detroit, wasn't much of a contest. Adams, earning his third Series victory, allowed just six hits as the Pirates won their first world championship with an 8-0 victory. They scored twice in the second against Donovan, who lived up to his nickname of "Wild Bill" by walking six in three innings. The Pirates added two more in the fourth, and Wagner tripled home two runs and scored another in the sixth. They added a final run in the eighth for good measure.

A crowd generously estimated at 50,000 welcomed the Pirates home the night of October 18. With many of the marchers carrying torches, the team paraded through downtown to Forbes Field, where dignitaries and players made speeches, and the world champions were presented with checks for $1,825 as their share of the World Series gate.

To Wagner, the money wasn't as important as the vindication this Series provided. In 1903, he hit a paltry .222 and made six errors in the Pirates' Series loss to Boston. This time, though, he was the Pirates' hero. Wagner won the matchup with Cobb going away. He outhit Cobb .333 (8 for 24) to .231 (6 for 26). He had six runs batted in and six stolen bases. Cobb also had six RBIs, but stole only two bases.

"How the wise boys are ever going to compare Cobb with Wagner, after this series, is beyond us," wrote Wagner's hometown paper. "The big German's title as King of the Diamond was not menaced in the big series. Wagner hit better, fielded better; yes, and even ran better than the terrible Tyrus."[13]

Still, after the Series, it was obvious Wagner had been impressed with the Tiger star. "Cobb is the fastest man I have ever seen," he told *The Sporting News*. "I never thought he could have that much speed. I heard a lot about Cobb, and how fast he was, but he surprised me by the speed he showed on the bases in the World Series. Cobb is what I call a perfect player. He lacks nothing.

There is not a thing a ballplayer should have that Cobb hasn't got, and he's got a bunch of things that no other ballplayer has."[14]

Wagner and Cobb found they had something in common besides baseball: a love of hunting. A month after the Series had ended, Wagner joined Cobb in the fields near Macon, Georgia. *The Sporting News* quoted Wagner as saying: "I could have had a crack at a ground squirrel or two and perhaps a barnyard chicken, but as for hunting, Georgia won't do. Mr. Cobb is one of the most genial gentlemen I have ever met, but there are two things we will never agree on—game and baseball. ... The South is all right, and Cobb's all right, too, but I wish he hadn't told me about the swell hunting in Georgia."[15]

Later in that off-season, Wagner turned down a chance to renew his acquaintance with Cobb, as part of a vaudeville act. Promoters offered Wagner, Cobb and Cleveland star Nap Lajoie several thousand dollars each to appear on stage together. Their act would have involved recitations and demonstrations of their baseball skills. But Wagner—in no need of the money and certainly not interested in the spotlight—killed the deal by declining the offer.

Another business opportunity, albeit on a much smaller scale, came Wagner's way during 1909. He also refused to participate in that transaction—a decision he's remembered for almost as much as he's remembered for his baseball career.

In the September 4, 1909 edition of *Sporting Life*, the American Tobacco Company ran an ad promoting tobacco cards of ballplayers that were being inserted in packages of Piedmont, Sweet Corporal and Sovereign cigarettes. Ten player cards were pictured in the ad—among them, one of Honus Wagner. Wagner had been approached about allowing his picture to be used, but had declined. It was speculated his refusal was tied to a dislike of tobacco products, but Wagner was a lifelong chewer and smoker.[16] In later years, he said his reason was simple: He didn't want young fans spending their money on cigarettes. Some suggested he was merely seeking a bigger check from the tobacco companies, but Wagner's lack of interest in outside income makes that doubtful. Whatever his reason, he left the American Tobacco Company, which licensed the photos to the various cigarette brands, in a bind because the Wagner cards were in production and were being inserted. The firm tried an intermediary, offering Pirates scorer John Gruber $10 if he could persuade Wagner to sign a contract. Wagner again declined, but not wanting Gruber to lose a chance to make some money, sent him a check with a note."I enclose my check for the amount promised you by the tobacco company, in case you got my picture, and hope you will excuse me if I refuse,"[17] Wagner wrote. Gruber kept the note and framed the check, which he displayed proudly in his home for years. Finally, the American Tobacco Company had no alternative but to pull the card from production, but not before several hundred got out.[18]

To a man, the Pirates were eager for the start of spring training and a chance to begin the defense of their world championship. During February, a group of players—Miller, Maddox, Abbaticchio, Gibson and Leach among them—formed a team to play in an indoor baseball (actually softball) tournament in Pittsburgh. Wagner had been invited to join, and at first agreed. But he changed his mind and backed out. It wouldn't be the only time Wagner would let his teammates down in the coming year.

The first contingent of Pirates left Pittsburgh for West Baden Springs on March 8 under the direction of Gibson. Included in the group were Maddox, Phillippe, Vic Willis, Pat O'Connor, Edward Bridges, Samuel Frock, Ralph Cuttong, W.B. Powell, Charles Webb, trainer Ed LaForce and three newspapermen. A few days later, another batch of players headed west—Adams, Leever, Leifield, Chick Brandon, Camnitz, Eugene Moore and Mike Simon. The rest of the team was to leave Pittsburgh under Clarke on the 14th, the day before the whole team was due to be on hand in West Baden Springs, from where the players would head to Hot Springs.

Wagner, as usual, was in no hurry to leave Carnegie. On the eve of Clarke's departure, not only his whereabouts but his intentions were a mystery. He still had not signed a contract for 1910—not unusual. But what was odd was the way he was avoiding contact with Pirate officials. Miller, Wagner's closest friend on the team, reported to Clarke and the newspapers that Wagner had been keeping in shape by playing basketball once a week and was spending his spare time indulging in his passion for automobiles—driving them and repairing them in the garage he operated in town.

The last group of players left Pittsburgh on the 14th without Wagner, who waited as long as he could before giving in to the inevitable. Later that day, he met with Dreyfuss and finally signed his contract, again for $10,000. Dreyfuss, Wagner and Leach left town on March 18, heading south.

Wagner had little use for spring training. He was 36 years old and he didn't think he needed the drills or the conditioning. Still, he managed to enjoy himself in Hot Springs. He and Hans Lobert of the Cincinnati Reds, who also trained there, took one afternoon off to visit a big poultry farm outside of town. He spent a lot of his time in his room playing cards with Miller. He also entertained himself at the expense of a photographer who had been hired by a Pittsburgh newspaper to take photos of the Pirate players.

The photographer had caught up with all the players except Wagner and Gibson, who had taken the day off, one afternoon at Whittington Park, where the Pirates trained. The next morning, the photographer went to the Eastman Hotel, where the team was staying, and asked the clerk to point out Wagner. The clerk pointed across the lobby where Wagner and Gibson were talking. The photographer approached Gibson and, thinking he was Wagner, asked if he would step outside to have his picture taken. Wagner prodded his teammate. "Go ahead, John," he told Gibson, and nudged him toward the door. Gibson went along with the joke and posed as Wagner. The photographer got his pictures, or so he thought, thanked "Wagner," and left. The next day he was back at the Eastman selling five-cent Pirate postcards—including one of Wagner-Gibson.[19]

The Pirates had a good spring, with nice weather and few injuries. They opened the season April 14 in St. Louis, beating the Cardinals 5-1. After winning two of three in St. Louis, the Pirates went to Cincinnati, where their fortunes abruptly changed. All three games against the Reds were rained out, and their return trip to Pittsburgh was delayed by a wreck on the Baltimore & Ohio line. Instead of a triumphant return home, the 1909 world champions arrived in Pittsburgh just two hours before the start of the opener, some of the players minus their luggage, which had gotten lost on the long ride back from Cincinnati. Opening Day ceremonies went on despite a cold, rainy afternoon that held attendance to less than 8,000.

When it came time to raise the world championship banner, both teams marched out to center field with a band. The winds got the flag twisted and it had to be lowered and untangled. It was again raised, but this time the banner was upside-down; again, it was brought down. Finally, on the third try, the banner honoring the Pirates was raised.

Wagner started the season strongly, with five hits, including two triples and a double, in his first 14 at-bats. But he soon tailed off. At one point, he went hitless in three consecutive games, his average falling below .200. He also complained of a sore arm, suffered in a collision with Brooklyn third baseman Humpy McElveen, and asked to be taken out of the lineup on May 12 against the Superbas, but Clarke refused. "Wagner wanted to lay off, fearing he would not do himself justice, but I prevailed upon him to remain at his post." [20]

Rumors began circulating there was something wrong with Wagner. At first he attributed the slump on his sore arm. Later he chalked it up to just a bad season. Clarke maintained Wagner's problem was a nagging cold. *The Sporting News* claimed the hours that Wagner and other ballplayers spent behind the wheels of their cars affected their vision and their nerves. But the truth, and what other players were talking about and what was being hinted at in some Pittsburgh papers, was more serious. Honus Wagner's drinking was getting out of hand.

# *Twelve*

**B**eer brewing and beer drinking were two of the traditions brought to this country by the German immigrants who settled in western Pennsylvania. Honus Wagner loved his beer; he had started drinking as a young man, and it was a lifelong habit. By the end of the 1909 season, however, what had been a habit had become a problem.

During the season he had drinking buddies on the Pirates—Dots Miller and Alex McCarthy were his favorites—and in the off-season he had his hunting pals and Carnegie cronies. Wagner was a genial drinker; seldom did he show his temper. But as his drinking increased during the 1910 season, his disposition as well as his performance suffered. There were disagreements with teammates—Wagner and new first baseman John Flynn had a confrontation, and his long friendship with Tommy Leach deteriorated. Wagner sulked. He missed games. Most obvious, though, his skills were dulled.

The Pirates started quickly and were in and out of first place during the early part of May. But the Cubs moved into the lead on May 25, and the Pirates soon fell back, sitting in third or fourth place and staying around the .500 mark well into July.

"Our 1910 team was my greatest disappointment in baseball," Barney Dreyfuss later said. "Never did I see a great team fold so quickly."[1]

Wagner was a big reason the team was struggling. His batting average was hovering around .250, and his sloppy and/or careless play in the field was bringing boos from the Pittsburgh crowds. His drinking also may have been a factor in two auto accidents. In the more serious of the two, Wagner's car, with Miller as his passenger, crashed into a railroad crossing gate in Carnegie on May 26. Neither Wagner nor Miller was seriously injured, but the car suffered extensive damage, and both players showed the aftereffects during the next day's game, during which Wagner made three errors and Miller one.

A Pittsburgh paper soon seconded *The Sporting News'* theory that Wagner was spending too much time behind the wheel and it was affecting his vision and reflexes.

But finally, the sore arm/nagging cold/too much driving excuses ceased. As Wagner continued to struggle, he further alienated teammates and fans. Even *The Sporting News* criticized him in print:

"The most inexcusable performances have been those by Wagner, who draws $10,000 a year from Barney Dreyfuss for delivering the goods. Wagner has been billed as the world's greatest ball player, and he deserved the title. But in those days he was 'playing ball.' Now he is performing in a manner that would not be excused in a bush leaguer. His fielding has been most erratic and so has his hitting.... He has on more than one occasion failed to run out hits and has acted often as if he did not care how matters were.

"It is difficult to understand how a man who draws $10,000 will so endanger his future. It is not easy to conceive of a man entirely lacking in ambition as to risk the hisses and the hoots that have recently greeted Wagner at the bat and on the field simply for the love of liquor."[2]

The "hisses and hoots" reached a crescendo during an early June road trip, during which Wagner "harassed by taunts from patrons and players was so distracted that he often swung at the ball ere it reached the plate."[3]

Wagner's game showed some improvement in late June, including back-to-back 3-for-4 games against Chicago, and seven consecutive hits over two days against Cincinnati. A 4-for-4 afternoon against the Reds on June 30 raised his season average 13 points to .297, and gave him a .680 mark over his last seven games. "This is a wonderful record," said the *Pittsburgh Press*, "and the loyal fans trust that he will keep it up, and that he will show similar improvement in his fielding, which to date has been a bit ragged."[4]

Soon, though, Wagner had to contend with a series of off-field distractions. His auto suffered a punctured tire and he left the car at a garage on Seventh Street in Pittsburgh. When he came to pick it up, he found the business padlocked. On the door was a notice that the contents of the building would be sold at a constable's auction for back payment of three months' rent. Wagner had to go to court to get an order allowing him to get his car back.

His next involvement with Carnegie police didn't end as satisfactorily. In early August, Wagner and his teammates were on an eastern trip. Back in Carnegie, Wagner's dog, Prince, had been ill for a few days. During his master's absence, the dog started chasing neighborhood children, growling, barking and snapping at them. Several of the children were hurt as they tried to escape the dog. Residents drove the dog back to Wagner's home on Railroad Avenue. Prince ran into the garage and stood his ground in front of his master's car. Police arrived and finally had to shoot the dog.

It was a tribute to Wagner's character that he was able to overcome the distractions and start to get his drinking under control. Or, at least, to curtail its effect on his performance. By the end of July, the Pirates were back in the National League race and Wagner's average was up over .300. "John Henry Wagner hasn't stored his autos," reported *Sporting Life*. "Chances are he will not. The renowned artist may have cut out other pleasures that detract from baseball efficiency. It is known that when the big fellow was going at his poorest, especially at defensive duty, the Pittsburgh Club management was undeniably angry over apparently finely founded reports that John was enjoying himself by too many trips to a social club where they had dark brown refreshments on tap."[5]

By the second week in August, Pittsburgh was in second place, 6 ½ games behind first-place Chicago. On August 18, the Pirates completed a four-game sweep of Boston, giving them 22 victories in their last 28 games. Wagner was a big contributor to the cause, batting over .375 for the month. The highlight was a 7-for-7 day in an August 22 sweep of two games against the Phillies at Forbes Field. In the first game, he had a homer over the left-field wall and three doubles; in the nightcap, another home run over the wall and two singles.

But the Cubs weren't going to be caught. By the end of the month, they had increased their lead to nine games. The Pirates began tailing off and were passed by the Giants in the standings. Wagner, though, continued his hot pace, raising his average above .300 by September 1. He hit .448 for the first week of September, and was soon around .330 for the season.

Still, with all the criticism he had endured, and with his team fading, the last weeks of the 1910 season were miserable for Wagner.

Flynn was released when Fred Clarke decided he wasn't the Pirates' first baseman of the future. The manager began looking for someone to play the position for 1911[6] and wanted to go with Wagner. Wagner, who had always been willing to play wherever the team needed him, wasn't as cooperative this time. When Clarke put him at first to see if he could still handle the position,[7] he told his manager that he wanted to stay at shortstop and began moping.

"A leading stockholder of the Pittsburghs was heard to intimate that Wagner seemed to sulk, except for about five weeks of the race," wrote *Sporting Life*. "This man isn't afraid to speak his mind. And why shouldn't he? Wagner may be a king-pin diamond artist, but he is as deserving of just criticism as any man." [8]

Wagner missed four games from September 20 to 23, the result of an injury suffered while sliding home in a September 17 game in Boston. His bid for a fifth consecutive National League batting championship went down to the final days of the season. With two days left, he was second in the race, only 3 percentage points behind league leader Sherry Magee of Philadelphia. But Wagner went 0 for 8 in his last two games and finished at .320, 11 points behind the champ.

In the waning days of the season, rumors began to circulate that the Pirates intended to unload Wagner. Papers in Pittsburgh, Chicago and New York all carried stories that he was on the block, most likely going to Cincinnati, which was willing to pay Dreyfuss between $15,000 and $20,000. The rumors became the talk of baseball and angered Wagner, who said he would quit rather than play elsewhere. He attributed his roller-coaster year to the fates. "Any baseball player will have a good year and then a bad year," he told *The Sporting News*. "And that's what happened to me this season. For a long time I couldn't seem to hit them safe, and that's the reason my percentage slumped."[9]

But the Pirates knew what Wagner's problem had been. Clarke sat him down at the end of the season and told him he would have to choose between alcohol and baseball. Dreyfuss took the team's temperance stand to the papers. But rather than accuse Wagner of drinking, he used pitcher Howie Camnitz as an example, saying he had broken a temperance clause in his contract. "The day of the boozer is over, so far as the Pittsburgh baseball club is concerned. ... Next year every man who signs a Pittsburgh contract will have to first sign the pledge. There will be a total abstinence clause in every document handed out by the club to the players."[10] He also said the Pirates would have repeated as champions "if two or three players had stayed on the water wagon."[11] Clearly, he was making a point with Wagner, who, despite the drinking, his uneven season and his increasing moodiness, remained Dreyfuss' favorite player.

Still, the talk of a trade persisted well into December, when league officials met in New York for the annual winter meetings. One proposed move would have sent Wagner to the Reds for 21-year-old first baseman Dick Hoblitzell; another deal, suggested by Philadelphia owner Horace Fogel to Dreyfuss at the meetings, would have sent shortstop Mickey Doolan, a career .235 hitter, to the Pirates for Wagner. Clarke denied there were plans to trade Wagner, despite the headaches his star had caused him all season.

"I will neither sell, trade nor release Wagner," he told reporters on December 14, the night before he left Pittsburgh for the meetings. "If he ever plays ball again it will be with Pittsburgh. Of course, he may not want to play, but if he does he will be throwing dust around our infield next summer."[12]

Wagner responded to the questions about his future in the January 19 edition of *The Sporting News.* "I am not ready to quit yet, and I don't know that I would want to play with any other team than Pittsburgh," he said. "A few weeks ago I noticed that some of the papers had me on the market, but all the time I knew there was nothing in these reports. I like the Pittsburgh management, and as long as Mr. Dreyfuss and Cap Clarke want me to play ball for them, I guess I'll do it. Still, you never can tell when something is going to happen. You know, I can't go on playing forever. I must quit sometime, and the time to quit is when you find you are going back."

Although Wagner told Clarke he would reform for the 1911 season, he balked at having a temperance clause in his contract. He spent the winter at home in Carnegie, living up to his promise to Clarke, watching his weight and staying in shape by playing basketball two nights a week, and tending to business at his automobile garage.

Wagner's future was the subject of much speculation, and one Pittsburgh paper wanted to do a big Sunday spread on him. After four weeks of cajoling, he agreed to sit still for an interview and pictures.

A reporter spent two hours with him one January day, but Wagner began having second thoughts when it came time to schedule the photos. Finally he agreed to pose outside a Carnegie hotel. When the reporter and photographer arrived, they saw Wagner walking down a nearby alley. He told them he was heading to his auto shop and asked them to wait. An hour later he returned, freshly shaven, in a new brown suit, yellow flannel shirt, black tie and felt hat. He had one last request before submitting to the photo session: He wanted to have a picture taken of him and his dog, named Jason Weatherby. The photographer agreed, and not only got his shots of Wagner, but one of Wagner and "Jason" shaking hands.

All eyes would be on Honus Wagner this spring, and he knew it. It seemed he would be unable to duck spring training with so much at stake. Then he got a break: He was ordered to report for jury duty in Common Pleas Court in Pittsburgh on March 6, the day the team was to leave for West Baden Springs. "Let Honus serve his country," Dreyfuss told *The Sporting News.* "We can get along very well without him on the spring trip, and perhaps he can get exercise enough trotting up and down the court house steps. Honus would probably have been racking his brain for a suitable excuse to offer to dodge the water-drinking jaunt to West Baden, and now he has it."[13]

But Wagner, after weighing playing baseball—even if it was only spring training—against spending two weeks cooped up in a courtroom, requested to be excused from jury duty. The judge acceded to Wagner's wishes, but instead of joining the team in West Baden Springs for the early phase of training, he went directly to Hot Springs, and was waiting for his teammates when they arrived on March 19.

Dreyfuss made several notable changes for 1911. Sam Leever, who had won 194 games over 13 years in Pittsburgh, was dropped. Max Carey, who had come up briefly in 1910, would be retained (early in the season he became the Pirates' regular center-fielder, supplanting Leach). Newt Hunter was anointed as Flynn's successor in the Pirates' never-ending search for a first baseman. And the team signed pitcher Claude Hendrix, whose interest in hunting and fishing quickly endeared him to Wagner, who took him under his wing.

Dreyfuss, recalling the problems of 1910, also decided he needed to get tougher with his players for 1911. On April 1, Clarke called the players together at the Eastman Hotel in Hot Springs to lay out the team rules for 1911. Not surprisingly, at the top of the list was a ban on drinking. He also barred smoking, and told players they had to be in bed by midnight and up by 8 a.m.

The Pirates opened the season April 12 in Cincinnati with a 14-0 victory. Wagner went 3 for 5, Bobby Byrne went 5 for 5, and Babe Adams allowed just four hits. Their home opener on April 20 was just as successful, a 9-1 victory over the Reds in which Wagner homered and singled.

The Pirates got off to a decent start, holding on to second place after the first month of play thanks largely to their hitting. Clarke was batting over .400, and Wagner, Dots Miller, Chief Wilson and Hunter were all well above .300.

The first big series of the season started on May 9 when the first-place Phillies, who led the Pirates by two games, hosted Pittsburgh. The Pirates won the opener 8-1 behind Adams' pitching and Wagner's hitting (two triples). But the Phillies took the next three games, and when the Pirates left town the Phils had a four-game lead. The wildest game of the series was the third, on May 11.

The Phillies scored eight runs in the eighth to go ahead 19-3, but the Pirates made it interesting with a seven-run ninth. The Pirates spent much of the day arguing with umpires William Finneran and Charles Rigler, and Wagner and Gibson eventually were ejected; Wagner for laughing at a remark Miller had directed at the umpires.

Injuries soon started taking a toll on the Pirates. Clarke went out with a sore leg in late May, Miller was sidelined after being struck in the hand by a pitch, and Wagner (leg) and Byrne (knee) were forced to play hurt. By mid-June, Clarke was scrambling to patch together a lineup each day. On June 20, a reluctant Wagner was sent to first base, replacing Hunter. Taking over shortstop temporarily was Bill McKechnie. Leach was benched so Clarke could put Carey in center. McCarthy soon replaced McKechnie at short, but he got hurt and Wagner was moved back to his natural spot. The Pirates re-signed Flynn, who had been cut the previous season, and Hunter, who had been waived only weeks earlier. That enabled Clarke to leave Wagner at short, where he wanted to stay.

Dreyfuss also made another move that would typify the season: He purchased 23-year-old pitcher Marty O'Toole from St. Paul of the American Association. The price was staggering: $22,500, more than twice what he was paying Wagner and the highest amount ever paid for a player. For good measure, Dreyfuss also purchased

O'Toole's favorite catcher, Bill Kelly, for another $7,500, and sent first baseman Flynn to St. Paul.

Dreyfuss also tried to pull off another deal that could have been nearly as big, though it wouldn't have done much to placate Wagner. He wanted to obtain shortstop Buck Herzog from Boston and install him at short, freeing up Wagner to finish his career at first base. But the Braves instead shipped Herzog to the New York Giants, and he went on to have 10 more productive seasons in the National League.

The Pirates had stumbled into fifth place by mid-July, though they were only 4½ games behind the first-place Phillies. They went 13-3 over the last two weeks of July, and by August 8 had moved into  second place, only a half-game behind Chicago. Leading the charge was Wagner, who hit .500 (9 for 18) during the first week of August to raise his average over .360. On the 13th, the Pirates were but 4 percentage points behind the first-place Cubs and seemed ready to make the move into first.

On August 16 at Brooklyn, the Pirates beat the Dodgers 9-0 but lost Wagner. He was standing near second when he tripped over the edge of the bag and fell, injuring his right leg. He was carried off  the field and taken to Methodist Episcopal Hospital, where Dr. W. D. Scanlan X-rayed the injury. Wagner was told he had torn ligaments in the ankle and a broken fibula, and his season was finished. He returned to the ballpark to catch the end of the Pirate victory, and intended to remain with the team. But the pain was so great that night that he could not sleep, and the Pirates decided to send him home. Wagner summoned his teammates to his room at the Somerset Hotel. "I'm out of it for a while," he told them. "Don't think of me, but go in there and show 'em that you can lick them anyway." [14]

Wagner's return to Pittsburgh was front-page news. Nearly 40 fans were on hand when Wagner arrived by train from New York on the morning of August 18. "I'll be back in the game in a couple of days," a smiling Wagner assured the crowd. "I'll watch the scores every day, and I believe the Pirates will keep winning." [15]

Also on hand was Pirate team physician Dr. G. S. Berg, who helped Wagner into a wheelchair and then to a waiting automobile that took Wagner home to Carnegie. There he was met by family members—and Jason Weatherby, his favorite dog, with whom he shared his breakfast. Dr. Berg was able to examine the ankle, and later tests indicated the injury wasn't as serious as Wagner had been told in Brooklyn. There was no fracture and the ligaments weren't badly damaged, and he was told that he would probably be back in the lineup within a month.

With first Leach and then McCarthy filling in at short, the Pirates went 11-13 during the four weeks that Wagner was sidelined. He returned on September 13, playing first base and contributing a single in a 5-4 victory in Cincinnati. By that time the Pirates had slipped to third place, six games behind first-place New York. They finished September 4-9—losing six in a row at one point—to fall out of the pennant race.

Clarke wrote off the last 10 days of the season. After sweeping Philadelphia on September 30, the Pirates had a day off followed by a game in New York on October 2. That was followed by four off days before a season-ending three-game series in Chicago. With his team banged up and the pennant race decided, Clarke started letting people go home. O'Toole, Dreyfuss' expensive gamble, managed only a 3-2 record because of arm trouble; he was sent to see Bonesetter Reese.[16] Miller was given the rest of the season off, as well. Wagner, with his ankle still not fully healed, could have used the time off, but he was engaged in a fierce struggle for the NL batting championship.

It was a three-man race between Wagner, Boston's Doc Miller and New York's Chief Meyers. Wagner entered the October 7-9 series in Chicago at .333. He went 1 for 4 in the first game, a 5-0 Pirate victory, but was blanked in three trips the following day, a Pittsburgh loss. That left him at .330, third behind Meyers, who was done for the season because of an injury, and Miller, both at .332. On the last day of the season, Miller went 4 for 10 in a doubleheader against Philadelphia to raise his average to .333. But Wagner wrapped up the batting crown—the eighth and what would be the last of his career—with a 3-for-4 afternoon that raised him to .334.

At 37, Wagner had made a remarkable recovery from the problems of 1910 and his ankle injury. This off-season there would be no barnstorming, no basketball, just a quiet winter in Carnegie preparing for what everyone knew would be a transitional season for the Pirates.

The team would have a new look in the outfield for 1912. Clarke, at the age of 39, had decided his playing days were over. He had patrolled left field for the Pirates since the consolidation of 1900. And for five seasons before that he had anchored the Louisville Colonels' outfield. But age, injuries—he had suffered a frightening beaning the previous July—and a desire to concentrate on managing had prompted Clarke to take himself out of the lineup.

The Pirates would need a captain to oversee matters on the field, and Clarke turned to Wagner. The only other candidate was Leach, but he and Clarke had had a falling out after Leach lost his starting job to Max Carey. In addition, Leach's wife had died during the 1911 season, and he withdrew from his teammates—he and Wagner, one-time pals, now seldom spoke. That left Wagner as the logical choice for the captaincy.

In the past he had been reluctant to assume such responsibilities. But at 38, he knew his playing days would soon be coming to an end, and perhaps he would be able to stay in the game as a manager or coach. It would be good training for the future. Also, at 38, he may have been becoming aware of his place in baseball history. He had become more open, more accessible in recent months. In late January, he uncharacteristically spent more than an hour talking baseball with Pittsburgh writers. When they asked him what he hoped to accomplish in 1912, he replied that he wanted to hit .300 again. It would be his 16th consecutive .300 season, he pointed out, breaking the record of 15 held by his old hero, Cap Anson.

Wagner also softened when it came to the subject of spring training. He still didn't enjoy it, but as captain he was expected to cooperate. So when Clarke asked him to lead a contingent of players to West Baden Springs—a place Wagner had tried to avoid for years—he agreed ... provided he had to stay there only a couple of days before heading to Hot Springs.

But some things didn't change. Wagner was one of four players who hadn't signed by mid-February. The others were Dots Miller, Lefty Leifield and Vin Campbell, all three holding out for more money. Dreyfuss solved one problem just before spring training by sending Campbell to the Boston Braves for outfielder Mike Donlin. The deal also filled the gap left by Clarke's departure, giving the Pirates an outfield of Carey in left, Chief Wilson in center and Donlin in right. The right side of the Pirate infield also had a new look, with the re-signed Miller at first and McCarthy at second.

Dreyfuss' retooled ballclub stumbled out of the gate, losing its first four games. Wagner got off to a better start, going 6 for 15 during the first week. But he, too, tailed off, and by the end of April was hitting .333, though he did lead the Pirates with 16 runs batted in. On May 2 against Chicago, he suffered a charley horse. The next day he walked in the first inning, but when he reached base he realized his leg was too sore to play on, and asked to come out of the game. Wagner and Donlin, who had missed most of the first month with a toe injury, didn't both return to the lineup until May 10, by which time the Pirates were 7-11, in fifth place, 7 ½ games behind the league-leading Giants.

With his team struggling to reach .500, Dreyfuss made another change. On May 30, he sent Leach and Leifield—his two other spring holdouts—to Chicago for outfielder Arthur "Circus Solly" Hofman and pitcher Leonard "King" Cole. It seemed to be a reasonable trade. Leach had worn out his welcome in Pittsburgh and had hit only .238 the year before; Leifield was a .500 pitcher in 1911 and had seen better days. Hofman was one year removed from a .325 batting average; and Cole had gone 18-7 and 20-4 in the previous two seasons.

The trade left Wagner and Clarke as the only two Pirates who had come to Pittsburgh in the 1900 consolidation, and only Wagner was still playing. Even though he and Leach had had their disagreements in recent years, Clarke took Leach's departure hard. The day after the deal was announced, Leach visited the Pirate clubhouse to say his goodbyes. Clarke asked his players to leave so he and Leach could have a moment in private. "Leach and I have been together so long that it is with sincere regret that I see him leave," Clarke told the Pittsburgh papers. "I would never have consented to part with him for anything less than a star."[17]

But the trades didn't have the desired impact for the Pirates. Donlin was forced to leave the team for two weeks in mid-June when his wife, the actress Mabel Hite, took ill.[18] And shortly after he returned, he took a foul off his foot that sidelined him again. And neither Hofman nor Cole contributed anything to the cause.

But even if Donlin, Wagner, and the rest of the Pirates had remained healthy, and even if the trades had panned out, it's doubtful the team could have caught the Giants, who won 16 in a row at one point in June and July, and who were led by Rube Marquard, who won 19 in a row before being beaten by the Cubs on July 8. By that time, New York had built its lead to 13 ½ games over second-place Chicago.

Any chance the Pirates had of making a move on the Giants evaporated when the two teams met in mid-July in Pittsburgh. The Giants won the opener on the 17th 10-2. The teams split a doubleheader on July 19, the Giants winning the opener despite Wagner's single, triple and homer. New York closed out the series with a 2-1 victory the next day that left the Giants at 61-21, 13 ½ games up on the third-place Pirates.

Before the season started, Wagner had set as a goal another .300 season, but by early August it appeared there might be a danger of that not happening. His average was at .314 on July 25, and continued a slow slide over the next week, down to .308 on August 2. But Wagner had bottomed out and started climbing again. He had a great series against the Giants from August 22-24, going 7 for 9 in one double-header—including hitting for the cycle against Rube Marquard on the 22nd—and was 10 for 20 in the series, raising his average to .315. New York won three of the five games in the series, and when the Giants left Pittsburgh on the 24th, their lead was at 5½ games over second-place Chicago, and 14½ games over the third-place Pirates.

The fight was for second between the Pirates and Cubs. The teams met in a showdown series starting September 29 in Chicago. O'Toole allowed the Cubs just two hits in the opener, which the Pirates won 9-0 to move into second by a half-game. Pittsburgh took Game 2 9-3, and won the next contest 4-1 behind Adams' four-hitter and Wagner's 2-for-3 day at the plate. By the time the Pirates left Chicago, they had locked up second place.

Washington, Cleveland and the Philadelphia Athletics approached Dreyfuss trying to set up a postseason series. But he was only lukewarm to the idea, and when Wagner announced he was too tired to consider extending his season, the plans were scrapped. Wagner also had an offer to "cover" the World Series between New York and Boston for a newspaper syndicate, as well as offers to barnstorm in Cuba with a team of NL stars or in Kentucky and western Pennsylvania with some teammates. But Wagner, 38 and tired after a long season, rejected all overtures. He also had an offer for off-season employment—a job as a greeter in the men's section of a Pittsburgh department store. But he wasn't interested in that, either. "Not for a million a minute," he said. "I see enough people when I'm playing baseball."[19]

The 1912 season marked the end of one phase of Wagner's career and the beginning of another. It would turn out to be the last pennant race he would be involved in as a player. He reached his preseason goal of hitting .300 again—he finished at .324—but it would be his last outstanding season as a hitter. And the Pirates of 1913 and beyond would not be Wagner's Pirates. Clarke's playing career was, for all intents and purposes, over. Leach and Leifield, the last links to the glory years, were gone.[20] Deacon Phillippe, Vic Willis, Sam Leever . . . all were out of baseball. And Wagner was wondering what his future held. Although his love for the game was as strong as ever, he knew his best days were behind him, no matter what others were saying on his behalf.

"When I see Hans Wagner scooping up grounders and hitting the ball out of the lot, I feel very young," Frank Chance told *The Sporting News* a month after the season ended. "Wagner, they tell me, is 38 years old, and as I am several years his junior, I'm going to remain in harness for some time to come."[21]

# Thirteen

*"Hans Wagner celebrated his thirty-ninth birthday recently. The 'Flying Dutchman' says he isn't a bit feeble and will try to make a safe hit now and then. Hans denies the report that he intends to dye his hair black to conceal the silvery threads."*
—*Sporting Life*, March 15, 1913

By the beginning of the 1913 season, Honus Wagner had be come baseball's elder statesman. At spring training, he was surrounded by players who weren't much more than toddlers when he broke into professional ball in 1895—Alex McCarthy was 24; Claude Hendrix and Hank Robinson were 23; Jimmy Viox just 22. Wagner's pet project that spring was Everett Booe, a 22-year-old outfielder whom he took under his wing, as he had done with Dots Miller and Hendrix in previous years.

Inevitably, age was catching up with that elder statesman. On March 28, during the fifth game of an exhibition series with the Boston Red Sox, Wagner wrenched his left knee. The injury was painful enough to keep him out of the lineup for the rest of the spring, and when the Pirates opened the season April 12 in Cincinnati, Viox was at shortstop in Wagner's place.

Wagner consulted with Bonesetter Reese, who diagnosed the injury as floating cartilage. Seeking a second opinion, he saw Pittsburgh orthopedist Dr. David Silver on April 25. X-rays showed no damage, and Silver decided the injury was just a severe bruise that needed rest.

Wagner wasn't the only Pirate absentee. Catcher George Gibson broke his ankle when he crashed into the grandstand while chasing a pop foul in St. Louis on April 20, and on April 22 manager Fred Clarke was handed a five-day suspension for an altercation with umpire Clarence Owens. It all added up to a disappointing start for the Pirates.

Wagner made his 1913 debut in a May 5 exhibition against Cleveland, lining a wicked double in his first at-bat, much to the delight of the Cleveland crowd. He played his first official game the next afternoon at Boston, going 0 for 4 with two errors in a 3-2 loss. He had missed 19 games, during which time the Pirates had tumbled to fifth place at 10-9. His return didn't improve the team's fortunes—the Pirates lost seven in a row with Wagner in the lineup and slid into seventh place.

They ended their skid on May 14 with a victory over Philadelphia, Wagner going 3 for 4. The next day he went 3 for 5, including his first home run of the season, in a win over the Giants, and was 2 for 4 the following afternoon against New York. That left the 39-year-old Wagner at .381 through his first 10 games. By the end of May, his average was .346 and the Pirates had moved into fifth place.

First-place Philadelphia came to town during the first week in June, but neither Wagner nor the Pirates had much success. He was 2 for 14 as the Phillies won three of four. And when Wagner went 0 for 7 in his next two games, the fickle fans at Forbes Field began getting on him, with numerous episodes of jeering and booing during a subsequent series against the Giants.

By the middle of the month, the Pirates, who at one point lost six straight games by one run, were back in sixth place. And Wagner found himself back on the bench, sidelined by his balky knee.

The injury was aggravated on the evening of June 19, when Wagner was shaken up in an oil well explosion near Carnegie. A four-quart can of nitroglycerin that was being lowered into a well exploded prematurely. Wagner was knocked down by the blast—as were six others in the vicinity—and had to be dragged away from the fire scene. Neither Wagner nor the other six men were injured, and he was able to play the next day, contributing a hit in a victory that moved the Pirates back into fifth. But the explosion did nothing to help his already sore knee, and his appearance June 23 in a loss to Cincinnati would be his last start for almost a month.

Wagner missed 17 games altogether and pinch-hit in seven more through the first three weeks of July. While he was out, the

Pirates began a climb in the standings, winning 12 of 13 at one point and moving into third place by beating Brooklyn on the 19th.

Wagner was back in the lineup on July 21, playing center field as a late-inning replacement. He returned to the starting short-stop spot the next day, getting two hits in nine at-bats as the Pirates swept a double-header from the Giants.

But his return was tempered by the catcalls from Forbes Field fans, who were blaming the team's failings on the 39-year-old Wagner, and who were targeting him regularly for verbal abuse. It was particularly harsh during series against Boston and Brooklyn, when his average dropped 20 points in one week and slipped below .300. Wagner, though, had his supporters. In response to the booing, another, larger group of fans began cheering and applauding every time Wagner stepped to the plate. Also coming to Wagner's defense were the nation's sportswriters.

"When a home audience can rise up and pan the hide off Hans Wagner in a batting slump, there is little to be said for the average loyalty of the fan," wrote Grantland Rice.[1]

"In the Brooklyn and Boston series Dutch was cut to the quick by the onslaught [of the booing fans]," wrote A.R. Cratty in *Sporting Life*. "Wagner was visibly affected. Actions, not words, gave unmistakable testimony to the old boy's feelings. It was plain that he swung half-heartedly at the ball, not picking out groovers as was his wont for so many years. One day his stick average dropped below the .300 class. This fact was made the subject for comment in every city paper. John didn't stay out long, but the next game scurried back into the charmed circle. However, no one gazes at the grizzled fellow covering short field for the Pirates without awakening some surmise of this sort: 'Is this Big Wag's last year?' "[2]

Wagner still showed the old spark at times, and even his toughest critics in the Forbes Field bleachers had to be impressed with his performance on August 7 against Boston. With the score tied 3-3 in the 10th inning, Wagner was on first. Miller singled to center, and Wagner decoyed Braves center-fielder Otis Clymer by coasting into second as Clymer picked up the ball. Wagner then accelerated around second and headed for third, forcing Clymer to rush his throw. It sailed over third baseman Art Devlin's head, and Wagner trotted home with the winning run.

The next day Wagner contributed two hits in a 4-2 victory over Boston that moved Pittsburgh back into third, and a week later, on the 19th, he went 4 for 5, including a home run—the first in his career off Christy Mathewson—as the Pirates beat the Giants 8-6. (He was 12 for 22 in the New York series, moving his average back above the .300 mark.)

With the Pirates' pennant chances slim at best, Clarke tinkered with his lineup over the last month of the season. He put Gil Britton at short in Wagner's place, but the 22-year-old didn't show much, going 0 for 12 with two errors in three games. Art Butler was also inserted at short for a couple of days. When Wagner did play, he was batting in the No. 3 slot in the lineup, only the second time in his career he had been removed from the cleanup spot.

Wagner got his batting average over .300 to stay during the last week of September when he went 5 for 10 in a three-game series against Chicago. He was at .300 exactly at the conclusion of the regular-season schedule, but the Pirates had two makeup games to play in Chicago on October 4 and 5. To protect his old friend's .300 average, Clarke kept Wagner on the bench for both games, both losses. One paper claimed Clarke was holding Wagner out to rest him for a postseason exhibition series against Cleveland[3]— ignoring the fact that Clarke had let Wagner play in an October 3 exhibition in Milwaukee.

What the manager was really doing was making sure Wagner's streak of consecutive .300 seasons reached 17. Wagner was back in the lineup the next day in Cleveland, when the Pirates and Naps opened a week-long best-of-seven postseason series. Wagner was a paltry 4 for 24 as the Pirates lost to Cleveland in the full complement of games.

That was just the start of a sad and turbulent off-season for Wagner. On November 12, his father died. Peter John Wagner had been able to leave the coal mines years before when Honus achieved baseball success. Through his son's efforts, he had gone to work as a ticket-taker and watchman at old Exposition Park and later at Forbes Field[4] before finally retiring to the family home on Railroad Avenue in 1911. The elder Wagner, who was 75 and who had been in ill health for two years, died of pneumonia.

A month to the day after Peter Wagner's death, Honus was shaken by the news that Dots Miller, his closest friend on the team, had been traded to St. Louis.

Dreyfuss had gone to the winter meetings looking for a first baseman. To get one, he made one of his biggest trades, one that would backfire like no other. Dreyfuss was after St. Louis first baseman Ed Konetchy, who had led the National League in fielding in 1913 and who had hit a respectable .273 for the last-place Cardinals. He also wanted third baseman Mike Mowrey and pitcher Bob Harmon. Dreyfuss gave St. Louis manager Miller Huggins a list of 12 players who were available in trade. Huggins chose five—outfielder Chief Wilson, infielders Miller and Art Butler, infielder-outfielder Cozy Dolan and pitcher Hank Robinson.

Dreyfuss and Clarke considered the five Pirates expendable. Miller had played a more than adequate first base the year before, hitting .272. But defensively he was no Konetchy; besides, he had angered Dreyfuss with his holdout in the spring of 1913. Wilson, a regular since 1908, was coming off his worst season, a .266 average. Butler had been in only 125 games over the two previous seasons, and Dolan had hit just .203 in 35 games in 1913. The only player in the deal who was coming off a quality season was Robinson, who had gone 14-7 with a 2.38 earned-run average.

"Knocks me off my feet," a stunned Wagner said of the trade. "I can't say anything as it takes time to think over a deal like this. Wonder why they don't throw me in the deal. ... [I]t seems like half the team is gone now."[5]

Wilson, Miller, Butler, Dolan and Robinson weren't the only Pirates who changed addresses over the winter. The Federal League, which had been born as a minor league, decided on August 2 it would challenge the American and National Leagues. Teams were planned for Chicago, Indianapolis, Buffalo, Baltimore, Cleveland, Brooklyn, Kansas City, St. Louis—and Pittsburgh.

Some familiar names jumped to the new league, among them ex-Pirates Harry Swacina and Kaiser Wilhelm (to Baltimore), Artie Hofman (Brooklyn), and Everett Booe (Buffalo). Other well-known players who went to the Federal League included Joe Tinker (Chicago), Edd Roush (Indianapolis) and "Three-Finger" Brown and Fielder Jones (St. Louis). Several members of the 1913 Pirates were more than willing to jump, among them pitchers Howie Camnitz (to Pittsburgh) and Claude Hendrix (Chicago) and catcher Mike Simon (St. Louis). The Pittsburgh Feds, in their search for a manager, also went after Wagner.

"When the Federal League was organized, I could have picked my team and named my own salary," Wagner told *The Sporting News* for an article marking his 75th birthday. "Six clubs were after me. Barney Dreyfuss heard about it and paid me a visit. I hadn't signed my contract with Pittsburgh, but Barney brought a blank contract with him. He told me to fill in the figures myself. I put down the same amount, $10,000, as I had received the year before. I was satisfied."[6,7]

Wagner walked into the Pirates' headquarters on March 3, bringing with him his signed contract and an eagerness for the new season. Five days later he was among the first group of Pirates to leave for Dawson Springs, and he threw himself into spring training. "No youngster is going into the practice session more strenuously than Hans Wagner," *Sporting Life* reported. "The veteran is working with the zeal of a youngster."[8]

The Pirates had invited Ervine Kantlehner, a 21-year-old left-handed pitcher from San Jose, California, to camp. Kantlehner and Wagner met for the first time on the field in Dawson Springs; within minutes, Kantlehner was asking Wagner for playing tips, and Wagner was more than happy to oblige. Kantlehner, a church organist back home who came to the Pirates with the nickname of "Peanuts," and the 40-year-old Wagner seemed an odd pairing, but they quickly formed a friendship based on their favorite pastimes, baseball and hunting. When the Pirates broke camp and began a short preseason tour, Wagner asked to have Kantlehner assigned as his roommate on the road for that season.

It didn't take long for the Pirates to be haunted by their big trade with the Cardinals. The two teams opened the season on April 14 in St. Louis, and three of the players who had been traded by Pittsburgh led the Cards to a 2-1 victory: in the first inning, Dots Miller doubled home Art Butler, and in the ninth, Chief Wilson singled Butler home with the winning run.

But the Pirates won the next three games of the series—one of the victories a four-hitter by Kantlehner. They followed that with three wins in Cincinnati for a 6-1 record that left them in first place. Wagner went 10 for 26 (.385) through the first week of the season, putting to rest, at least temporarily, the stories that he was washed up. Wrote Ren Mulford, *Sporting Life*'s Cincinnati correspondent: "Good old Hans Wagner loomed up at short in the same old familiar way—a tower of defense. On the inside, the old boy proved that his batting eye is still bright. He only hit .461 in the series and was in the thick of every victory for the Pirate colors. There was lots of applause for the veteran, and if he has 'gone back,' no one in Redland who saw him in action could notice it."[9]

Behind Wagner—who was hitting .323 with six stolen bases—Pittsburgh won 15 of its first 17 games. Two of the players obtained from St. Louis, Mowrey and Konetchy, were hitting .323 and .288, respectively; George Gibson was at .321. Pitchers Wilbur Cooper and Hugh McQuillan were 4-0; Joe Conzelman was 3-0. The Pirates were the surprise of the National League.

But then came a crucial series May 14-16 against the second-place Giants. Wagner was out of the lineup with a sore hand and the Pirates lost all three games to New York. They lost the first game of their next series, to Boston, and suddenly found the Giants just 1½ games behind them.

New York kept up the pressure, finally moving past the Pirates into first place on May 30 when the Giants beat Brooklyn twice while Pittsburgh dropped a double-header to Cincinnati. The two losses were part of a 10-game Pirate losing streak that didn't end until June 6, when they beat Philadelphia 5-2. The skid left them at 21-18, in third place.

What turned out to be the high point of Wagner's season came on June 9, when he doubled off Philadelphia's Erskine Mayer for the 3,000th hit of his career. It was typical Wagner—a long line drive to left field—and was greeted with a huge cheer from the Philadelphia fans. The hit left him with a more than respectable .316 average, but his season, and the Pirates' season, were on the wane. He hit just .138 over the next 10 days—including an 0-for-16 series against the Giants—and his average dropped to .288. The Pirates, meanwhile, were swept by Boston and lost two of four to New York, falling into a fourth-place tie with Philadelphia at 24-24. By the end of the month, they were fifth at 30-31, and Wagner's average had slipped to .279.

"There is no doubt that Big Wagner is on the decline in batting," said *Sporting Life.* "If he is driven into retirement soon it will not be by reason of a defective defense, but rather lessened offense."[10]

His batting eye may have been dimmed, but Wagner could still provide excitement. On July 17, during the sixth inning of what would be the longest game in National League history, Wagner was on first after a single. Jimmy Viox singled, and Wagner headed to third, where he collided with the Giants' Milt Stock. Somehow, the ball got into Wagner's jersey. While the New York infielders scrambled, looking for it, Wagner picked himself up and ran home. As he crossed the plate he shook the ball out of his shirt. The Giants erupted in protest, and umpire Bill Byron sided with them, calling Wagner out for interference. It was a run the Pirates could have used; they ended up losing 3-1 in 21 innings on Larry Doyle's home run.

But Wagner's days of being a hero three or four times a week were over. He had to content himself with only occasional flashes of brilliance. On August 29, for example, in the 13th inning against Brooklyn, he was safe on an error, stole second and scored the only run of the game on Alex McCarthy's hit. And on September 26, his two-run homer off Christy Mathewson helped beat the Giants 4-2 and end a 12-game Pittsburgh losing streak.

The dog days came early to Wagner and the Pirates that season. They had fallen into last place on July 19 when Boston beat Cincinnati to climb into seventh. The Braves then came to Pittsburgh and won four of five games to start one of the greatest charges in baseball history. Boston, in last place at 35-49, 14 games out, on July 18, went on to win 59 of its last 69 games, taking the National League pennant by 10 ½ games over the second-place Giants.

Wagner and his teammates were left to stumble to the finish line. They wound up seventh at 69-85, 25½ games behind the "Miracle Braves" and just nine games ahead of last-place Cincinnati. Wagner finished with a .252 average, what would be the lowest in his career, a 48-point dropoff from 1913. More remarkably, it was the first time in his 18-year major-league career that he failed to hit .300.

"Nearly all contestants for honor in the sports world have their off-seasons," wrote the *Philadelphia Public Ledger*. "They find one campaign when things simply will not 'break right' for them. Their supply of 'pep' appears to be exhausted, and they have to watch their average dwindling while they pray for a new supply.

"But Wagner was unusually consistent; his pepper was stocked up for 17 campaigns, and not once did he have to offer the excuse for an off-season. This, above all else, makes the Dutchman the baseball marvel for all time."[11]

In the closing weeks of the season, Fred Clarke shifted Wagner to third base, wanting to take a look at 23-year-old shortstop prospect Wally Gerber.[12] Clarke and Dreyfuss were once more facing a familiar problem: where to put Honus Wagner for 1915? One solution presented itself when Konetchy jumped to the Federal League shortly after the 1914 season, opening up the first base spot for Wagner.

It was obvious the Pirates needed a younger man at shortstop. Wagner again led National League shortstops in fielding (.950), but again his inability to get to balls hit in his direction was reflected in the fact that he had far fewer chances than his competition (the Reds' Buck Herzog, for example, had a .939 percentage, but had 850 chances to Wagner's 785, while playing in five fewer games). Another factor in the Pirates' search for a new shortstop: Wagner's arm was also growing weaker.

"We are going to build a new team," Clarke promised. "The old foundation won't do."[13]

It may have been obvious the Pirates needed a younger man at short, but Wagner couldn't—or wouldn't—see it. Late in the season, as he killed time waiting for a train out of Philadelphia, Wagner discussed his future with sportswriter Peter Carney.

"This is my seventeenth season," Wagner said. "I feel as good today as I ever did in my prime as a player. I used to chase after a lot of drives that I could not catch with a crab net or a clothes prop. That day is over. I am as fast as I ever was. How do I know it? I can still trim anyone on my team going around the bags. My fielding is as sure as ever. I have had a little hitting slump, but I will hit over .300 before another two weeks. I am right close to it now.[14] The team has been down in the race this season. That takes a little edge off of any fellow's playing.

"Wagner has seen shortstops come and go—and Honus is still playing the same game. I expect to play three more years of my best ball. That will make 20 years—then I may mail my glove to some good friend and retire. No bush league playing for me. When I am done as a big leaguer I will go down to Forbes Field and root for the Pirates. I may say I will sit in the bleachers too. You can say what you please out there.

"Now get out your baseball guide and see who was my rival 15 years ago. Where is he today? Take 10 years ago. Yes, five years ago. I have seen a great army of star ball players march back to the minors while I have been playing. There was Gene DeMontreville, [Jack] Glasscock, Herman Long, Mike Doolan, Joe Tinker, Monte Cross, Bill Dahlen, [Tommy] Corcoran, [Fred] Parent and a half a hundred more. It seems [Larry] Lajoie and I sort of stand alone, and I'll be back for the next three years."[15]

# *Fourteen*

The 1914 season had been one of the most frustrating and disappointing in Pittsburgh Pirates history. The seventh-place finish was a shock, and the deal that brought Ed Konetchy and Mike Mowrey to Pittsburgh from St. Louis backfired as they struggled while the players sent to the Cards prospered. Even Honus Wagner wasn't spared the embarrassment of a .252 batting average—the worst of his professional career and the first time he had failed to hit .300 in his 18 years in the National League—and the jeers of the hometown fans.

Prospects for 1915 looked even dimmer when first baseman Konetchy and third baseman Mowrey jumped from the Pirates to the Federal League after the 1914 season. That left Fred Clarke and Barney Dreyfuss with two holes in their infield. Dreyfuss was all for making Wagner his regular first baseman. "Koney's shoes are too small for Honus," Dreyfuss said. "Why, Wagner can pitch better than Koney can play first base. Wagner is the best all-around player the game has ever known, and he has several years of usefulness ahead of him."[1]

Dreyfuss, of course, knew that wasn't the case. So did Clarke, who planned to wait until spring training before making a decision. He didn't need to unsettle Wagner, who preferred staying at shortstop, and who had become respected as baseball's preeminent elder statesman.

As such, Wagner was taking his responsibilities seriously. During the off-season he corresponded extensively with pitcher Erv Kantlehner, whom Wagner had taken under his wing during Kantlehner's rookie season in 1914. The letters offered encouragement and tips for the 22-year-old pitcher, who was playing winter ball in the Imperial Valley League in southern California. Wagner also uncharacteristically consented to sit down for extensive press interviews during the off-season. They went with the job, he reasoned, although one was as a special favor to James Jerpe, a writer for the *Pittsburgh Sun-Dispatch*, who had lost his eyesight in 1913. Jerpe was able to sell the resulting story to, among other publications, *The Sporting News*.

Jerpe's profile painted a glowing picture of Wagner as a man who earned everything he had from baseball, passing up the opportunity to cash in on his fame through endorsements and vaudeville appearances. Also, he came across as one of the common people.

"Wagner is among the humblest of men," Jerpe wrote. "He abhors chance acquaintance with well-dressed folk. In his travels he makes pals of railroad men, elevator operators and quite often he will  hook up with some poor fellow and show him a time. He would rather whittle a stick with some poor farm hand than be entertained by a millionaire. On the ball club he holds aloof from the big fellows and for companions he selects the youngest and most obscure 'rookies.' "[2]

This "humblest of men" found himself the center of attention on February 24, when the Pittsburgh Stove League honored him with a 41st birthday banquet at the Colonial Annex Hotel. A crowd of 250 attended the dinner, listening to speeches and telegrams praising the guest of honor. Two of the more touching wires were from the Cubs' Johnny Evers and the Tigers' Ty Cobb.

"You hear about 'second' Cobbs, 'another' Lajoie, but you never hear about 'second Wagners,' " Evers wrote. "Why? Simply because there never will be a second Wagner. He is in a class by himself."

Cobb's telegram read: "I feel that anything I might say towards eulogizing Hans would be insufficient to show my real admiration for him. So I will just say that my heart is with him, wishing him two score more of pleasant years and that he will lead them all just as long as he wishes. I will be drinking a toast to the greatest ball player that ever lived on his forty-first birthday the night of February 24 down here in Georgia."[3]

A week after the banquet, Wagner signed his 1915 contract—again for $10,000—and three days later was on a train to Dawson Springs, Kentucky, where the players were to avail themselves of the mineral waters for a week before the trip to Hot Springs.

Clarke's plans for Wagner were a mystery. The Pirates had obtained first baseman Doc Johnston from Cleveland on February

22 and had signed him to a two-year contract. But Clarke refused to rule Wagner out of the first-base competition. Wagner had led National League shortstops in fielding the previous season, but again it wasn't an accurate gauge of his skills. He had slowed down greatly, and his high fielding percentage was merely a reflection of his inability to get a glove on balls hit in his direction. The Pirates also had a candidate for shortstop if Wagner didn't start the season there. He was Wally Gerber, who had appeared in 17 games at short for the Pirates in 1914. And Dreyfuss plugged the hole left by the defection of Mowrey to the Federal League by signing third baseman Doug Baird, who had played in the Western League in 1914.

In Dawson Springs, Wagner had more important matters—at least to him—on his mind than working out. He spent much of the week at the spa organizing "Honus Wagner's Young Recruits." His "Young Recruits" were a group of pre-teenage boys who got uniforms, equipment and coaching from Wagner during the team's stay in Dawson Springs.

After a week of hanging around with his new friends and ducking workouts—spring training was, after all, still spring training to Wagner—he and the Pirates moved on to Hot Springs. Wagner had an impressive start, getting three doubles and a single in one exhibition game, and playing well at first and second. Gerber spent much of his spring at short for the regulars, and Clarke insisted he hadn't decided who would be where when the season started. Still, when he made out his lineup on April 14 in Cincinnati, Clarke had Wagner at second base, Gerber at short and Johnston at first.

The Pirates opened with a 9-2 victory, Wagner going 1 for 5 and playing errorless ball at second. He had another flawless day in the field the following afternoon, a 4-2 Reds win. Wagner was relegated to pinch-hitting duties in his next four games after suffering a bruised left hand in the loss to Cincinnati, but returned to the field April 20 in a victory over the Cubs to which he contributed a single and a triple—and another errorless game at second.

Wagner adapted well to a position he had played only 39 times since coming to the National League, and not at all since one game in 1911. He went errorless in 12 games at second base, but Clarke's experiment ended on May 2 when Wagner, hitting just .250, was moved back to shortstop.[4] Wagner's defensive work had been adequate. But Gerber's hitting was proving to be a liability, as he dipped below the .200 mark. Clarke had decided he wanted Jimmy Viox, who had a career .284 average, in the lineup. So Viox went to second and Wagner—despite his limited range and problems throwing runners out at first—went back to short. Wagner's problems in the field were exacerbated by the fact that Viox had even less range, leaving the 41-year-old Wagner with that much more ground to cover.

The Pirates fell out of the National League pennant race early. By May 4, they were in seventh place at 5-12, though a six-game winning streak from May 4-10 moved them to 11-12 and into fifth. Wagner by that time had raised his average to .272. On May 25, they were 15-15 and in third place, though Wagner, who went almost a month without a multiple-hit game, saw his average drop back to around .250, from where it continued to drop.

Clarke began making a lot of moves trying to get some offense into the lineup. Dan Costello took over for Larry Lejeune in center, but soon the poor-field/no-hit Costello was replaced by Zip Collins. Baird was shifted from third to the outfield, and Gerber took over third. The changes worked for a while, as the Pirates went 14-7 between June 5 and July 1 to improve to 31-23, good for third place. Wagner, too, began coming around, hitting .275 (22 for 80) during the stretch to get his average to .249 (50 for 201) by the end of June.

July figured to be a make-or-break month for the Pirates. Because of earlier rainouts, they were scheduled to play 37 games in the month. They got 32 in, winning 16 and keeping pace in the pennant race. July started with a key series against the first-place Cubs. The Pirates won just two of the five games, and Wagner was an unproductive 1 for 20 in the series. And the month ended with four games against second-place Brooklyn. The Pirates won three of them, Wagner managing just four hits in the series.

July ended with the Pirates in third place, five games behind first-place Philadelphia. They played like contenders at times during August—they won three of four from the first-place Phils the first week of August, and two weeks later won two of three in Philadelphia as Wagner went 7 for 13, including two home runs. But September arrived with Pittsburgh in seventh place, 11 games out of first.

Clarke had had enough. On September 8, he announced that he would not return as Pirates manager for 1916. After four first-place finishes, one world championship, more than 2,800 games as a manager and almost 1,600 victories—he would finish at 1,602-1,179—Clarke had decided it was time to retire to his farm.

In the press and among fans, Wagner was considered the logical choice to take over as manager. His playing days were clearly numbered. As Pirate captain, he had the respect of his teammates. Also, a year earlier when the Federal League expressed interest in signing him, he had remained loyal to Dreyfuss. It would seem that the owner owed Wagner the opportunity to manage the Pirates. But all parties agreed the matter of Clarke's successor would wait until after the Pirates completed their season.

"It is too early for me to say anything," Wagner told the *Pittsburgh Press*.[5] But one of Wagner's "closest friends," quoted by the *Press*, wasn't as reluctant to talk. "I think Wagner would make a great mistake to assume managerial responsibilities," the friend told the paper. "He is rounding out in a blaze of glory one of the most remarkable careers. ... He is honored everywhere as the greatest ball player of all time. His luster as a performer will never be dimmed. He does not need the money, and why should he run the risk of having his name linked with a possible baseball failure in the role of manager? I think Honus will refuse the job if it is offered him."[6]

But such decisions would have to wait. For now, the Pirates were playing out another disappointing season. There was little for the team to laugh about during those last weeks of the campaign. One of the few diversions was an elaborate practical joke played on Wagner during a one-day visit to Marion, Indiana, on September 29.

The Pirates stopped in Marion on their way to St. Louis, to play an exhibition game against a team of local athletes. After the contest—the Pirates were easy winners—Wagner was approached by three Marion citizens, Ora Drischol, Hal Smith and Homer Gant, who invited him to go fishing at a nearby farm. What Wagner didn't know was that behind the scenes, some of his longtime friends from Marion and his teammates were conspiring against him.

Wagner fell for their offer. With Erv Kantlehner, who was unaware of the plot, in tow, Wagner met Drischol and Gant at the Spencer Hotel, where the Pirates were staying, at 7:30, and the four headed for the farm and its pond just outside town. No sooner had the four reached their destination when a man stepped out of the bushes and accused them of trespassing. He also pointed out the fishermen had a seine in their possession, which was illegal. At that moment, two alleged sheriff's deputies showed up and announced the arrest of the four.

The four tried to make a run for it. One of the "deputies" fired shots in the air—that only made Wagner run harder. After a few hundred yards, he stopped, discarded his waders, and continued his dash toward town in his stocking feet. But the deputies caught up with the four and took them to the Grant County jail, where they were told they would stay overnight until the case could be brought before a judge the next day.

An upset Wagner begged the jailers to release them so he and Kantlehner could catch the Pirates' 10:58 train to St. Louis. Drischol and Gant pleaded along the same lines, asking for an immediate trial. Finally, a night session of the court was arranged. The four were handcuffed and marched through the town square to the courthouse. A crowd of nearly 500 citizens, all aware of the joke being played on Wagner, followed, and packed the courtroom.

The state presented its case—two of Marion's better-known citizens, Gus Condo and John Browne, played prosecutor and judge, respectively—before Kantlehner and Wagner took the stand. Both denied knowing they were trespassing, or having knowledge of the illegal seine.

"Sure, I did run, but not until I heard the shots," a nervous Wagner testified. "I thought it was a joke at first, for they are always trying to get me in on something, but when the shots were fired and Kantlehner started to run, I thought it was time to beat it...

"But I didn't resist arrest. When I saw it was the real thing I got right in the automobile and tried to square the thing so I could get out of here tonight."[7] As 10 o'clock approached, "defense attorney" Sam Stricler said he would rest his case with just the testimony of Kantlehner and Wagner.

The judge lined up the four defendants. Drischol was fined $100 and given 60 days in the county jail. The judge told Gant that because he had been before the court before, he would be fined $150 and sentenced to 90 days.

Wagner and Kantlehner were next: They each were fined $100 plus court costs and given 30-day suspended sentences. Wagner was asked if he had the money to pay the fine. Before he answered, Fred Clarke, who had been enjoying the show with several other Pirates, stepped forward and said he would pay the fine.

"Mr. Wagner," the judge then said, "I believe that you told this court that at first you thought this was a joke."

Wagner nodded.

"You have now learned that this city is one in which law-breakers are not allowed. But, Mr. Wagner, I want to inform you that you have been the victim of one of the greatest jokes ever pulled off in the history of the United States to my knowledge."

As the crowd burst into laughter, Wagner broke into a big smile. He'd been had. He was persuaded to take the stand again, this time to make a speech to the courtroom full of fans. Kantlehner and Clarke followed, making brief remarks before rushing off to catch their train.

"They got me," Wagner told a *Marion Chronicle* reporter as he left the courtroom. "But, say, in your article, don't mention the seine. Just say we were going fishing."[8]

The Pirates finished the 1915 campaign in fifth place at 73-81, a half-game ahead of St. Louis and two games in front of seventh-place Cincinnati.

When the season ended on October 3, Wagner had appeared in 151 of the Pirates' 154 games, quite an accomplishment for a sore-legged 41-year-old shortstop. He finished with a .274 average, and again led National League shortstops in fielding (.948 in 131 games at short, although he had the fewest chances of any regular shortstop in the league). These weren't the Wagner stats of old, but they would have been an adequate cap on his playing career had Wagner gone on to become Pirate manager. But he had decided he did not want the job, and told Dreyfuss as much in the waning days of the season. Still, for all intents and purposes, Wagner was the Pirates' acting manager during October and November. He paid frequent visits to the team offices to discuss personnel and team matters with Dreyfuss. He helped evaluate players, suggested possible signings, and assisted in making spring training plans.

On December 16, Dreyfuss finally announced his choice as manager: James "Nixy" Callahan. The 41-year-old Callahan had served two stints as manager of the Chicago White Sox, going 308-329 over parts of five seasons. He had agreed to manage and be part owner of the Los Angeles Angels of the Pacific Coast League for 1916, but a delay in the transfer of team stock and a call from Dreyfuss changed his plans.

One of the first things Callahan was asked after being named manager was whether Wagner would still be the Pirate captain. "I am not going to make any change in the captaincy," Callahan said, "nor am I going to tell Wagner how to hit."[9]

Callahan was smart enough to have Wagner continue in his advisory capacity, the two meeting almost daily with Dreyfuss. But preparations for 1916 didn't go smoothly. The delay between Clarke's retirement and Callahan's hiring—despite Wagner's attempts to fill the gap—put the Pirates behind schedule. Things were further complicated by the departure of team business manager John Dailey, who resigned to run for the Pittsburgh city council. As late as February 10, the site for spring training had not been finalized, and no exhibition schedule had been drawn up. Largely at Wagner's suggestion, Dreyfuss agreed to train again in Hot Springs, reversing a decision he had made at the end of the 1915 season.

But before heading off to Dawson Springs and Hot Springs, Wagner had one last commitment. Pittsburgh's Stove League feted him on his 42nd birthday on February 24 at the Colonial Annex Hotel. More than 300 guests paid Wagner tribute, including Tommy Leach and Deacon Phillippe, two heroes of the championship years, and Detroit manager Hughie Jennings. In addition, telegrams in praise of Wagner were read to the crowd, including one from federal judge Kennesaw Mountain Landis, who had overseen the Federal League's lawsuit against the American and National Leagues. Other telegrams came from Callahan, George Gibson, Miller Huggins, Joe Tinker, Ed Barrow, August Herrmann and Grantland Rice.

"Perhaps never have I had a chance to publicly praise Honus," Leach said. "No more. No greater, nor square player ever lived ..."[10]

Wagner was deeply moved by the adulation. "Thanks. I feel like the fellow on third base when a run was needed and his team couldn't hit—I want to steal home," he said, unable to hold back the tears.[11]

The post-Fred Clarke Pirates left for Dawson Springs on March 6. After two weeks there, it was on to Hot Springs. Wagner spent much of the next 2 ½ weeks working out at second base; shortstop was occupied by Jimmy Smith, a Pittsburgh native who had spent the two previous seasons in the Federal League. The Pirates were plagued by minor injuries throughout the spring—catcher Gibson and pitchers Kantlehner and Al Mamaux all developing sore arms.

When the season opened April 12 in St. Louis, Wagner was penciled in as the Pirates' second baseman. But that was out of necessity. Regular second baseman Joe Schultz was out with a sore arm, so Callahan moved Wagner to second and inserted Smith at short. Wagner lasted at second only until the sixth inning, when he was moved to first base after Doc Johnston was ejected after arguing a call by umpire Mal Eason. At the plate, Wagner lined two singles off Cardinals' starter Bill Doak and added an infield single. But it wasn't enough as St. Louis won 2-1.

Callahan's first three weeks as Pirate manager were a disappointment. The team stumbled out of the gate, a combination of injuries and a lot of new faces, and was 6-8 at the end of April. Otto Knabe, another Federal League refugee, moved to second base because Schultz's arm wasn't coming around. Max Carey was slowed by a severe cold. Jimmy Viox came down with a leg infection. And Wagner had a sore instep, sore arm and a split finger, but he refused to come out of the lineup because the rest of the team was doing so badly. By May 9, when the last-place Giants came to town, the Pirates were seventh at 9-12. The Giants swept all four games of the series, the start of a 17-game winning streak. The Pirates were headed in the other direction. By mid-May they were in last place with a puny .229 team batting average.

Despite his age and injuries—Wagner was the most productive member of the Pirates. He played short, second and first, as needed. Batting third, fourth or fifth in the lineup, he kept his average around .300 all of May and June and into July. He put together a 16-game hitting streak between June 20 and July 4, hitting .387 (24 for 62) in that stretch. He also provided leadership on the field and hustling play the Pirates were lacking.

But Wagner couldn't carry the Pirates by himself. This wasn't a good team, and Dreyfuss and Callahan knew it. Over the next three months, there was a revolving door on the Pirate clubhouse. Knabe was released during the first week in June; Smith was let go a month later. Johnston was waived. So too was Viox. Wagner's pal Kantlehner was sold to Philadelphia. Utilityman Jack Farmer, outfielders Carson Bigbee, Ray O'Brien and Pete Compton and pitcher Burleigh Grimes were dealt for or signed as free agents. Alex McCarthy was re-signed. In August, Gibson and Adams were released, leaving only Wagner from the 1909 world champions.

And Wagner's age was showing. A sore thumb and charley horse knocked him out of the lineup on July 31, replaced by McCarthy. He missed the next three games, pinch-hit the following day, then returned to the lineup August 5 against Brooklyn. But he had to leave that day's game after taking a smash by Hy Myers in the hand.The ball opened a gash between two fingers, needing 10 stitches. Wagner sat out the next nine games, returning on the 19th. But again, he lasted only one game, returning to the bench for 10 more games, re-emerging only to pinch-hit on August 29 and 30. Over the next week, he saw action only three times, each as a pinch-hitter. The Pirates' elder statesman had become an old man.

"The long predicted seems to have come to pass—Hans Wagner apparently is done," *The Sporting News* said in an editorial. "But Old Father Time had to call the Jinx to his aid to put Honus out. The game's most popular figure has appeared in the lineup only two or three times in a month. First it was a bruised thumb, then a strained tendon, and this latter injury was aggravated the other day when Honus, going in as a pinch hitter, swung hard and missed.

"Such injuries do not mend rapidly in men past 40 and it is hardly likely Wagner will get into another game this season, unless perhaps to hit for some would-be successor who has yet to find his batting eye. ...

"Since it had to come, it is better by far that Honus retires as he does. Better that he should be put out by an injury while still retaining much of his greatness as a player than he should gradually slow down to the point where everybody could see it and commiserate over it."[12]

But Wagner didn't heed the advice. He returned to the lineup on September 7, playing first base and shortstop—making four nice defensive plays and throwing out the potential tying run at the plate—and adding a single and a double in a 5-4 win over Chicago. That raised his average to .322. Unfortunately for Wagner, the season had another month to go. He started 27 of the Pirates' 28 remaining games, but hit only .156 (14 for 90) to bring his final average for 1916 down to .287.

It looked like this might be the end of the line. Wagner would be 43 by Opening Day of 1917. He had missed more than 30 games in 1916 because of injuries. The Pirates' prospects for the next season weren't bright. No matter what changes Dreyfuss and Callahan made over the winter, one fact seemed certain: Honus Wagner would be at first base, not shortstop, in 1917.

Wagner could see what was coming. He thought that perhaps it was time to walk away.

Perhaps it was time to get married.

# *Fifteen*

John Garbutt Smith was well-known in Pittsburgh baseball circles. He had played professionally in Canada, and when his career ended he returned home to Crafton, outside of Pittsburgh, where he played some sandlot and semi-pro ball. Bessie Smith was his daughter, 17 years Honus Wagner's junior. And it was baseball that brought them together.

"As a kid I used to watch him play," Wagner once recalled. "Had one of the sweetest curve balls I ever saw in my life. I met her with her father one day on a street car comin' home from a ball game."[1]

As the years wore on, the friendship between Honus and Bessie turned into a romance, with the encouragement of John Smith, who would often invite Wagner to dinner. The shy Wagner began courting Bessie when she was in her early 20s, and by early 1914 they had become an item, with him bringing her flowers and candy on his visits to the Smith home, the two of them spending the evenings talking—and with Wagner diving into the boxes of chocolate he had brought.

Wagner had considered marriage,[2] but knew a baseball player's life wasn't conducive to the family situation he wanted. Besides, baseball had always been his first love. By the end of the 1916 season, however, Bessie had supplanted baseball in his heart. And she wanted him to retire and start raising a family.

Right after the 1916 season ended, rumors circulated that Honus and Bessie would be married shortly, rumors he denied. On December 30, the two took out a marriage license. Reporters found out and flocked to Wagner's home. He confirmed the impending wedding, saying the ceremony would take place on the afternoon of January 1. With the press temporarily off their trail, Honus and

Bessie moved up their wedding to the following day, Sunday the 31st. That afternoon, they drove to the parsonage occupied by Rev. E.F.A. Dittmer, pastor of St. John's Lutheran Church in Carnegie. Honus and Bessie were accompanied only by their two witnesses— best man Al Wagner and maid of honor Alice Downey, a close friend of Bessie's. Rev. Dittmer, who had taught Honus at the German Lutheran School more than 35 years before, performed the ceremony in the parsonage on Highland Avenue. The newlyweds then proceeded to Bessie's family home in Crafton, where they announced their marriage and got her parents' blessing.

The first few weeks of married life were busy. Honus moved out of his boyhood home on Railroad Avenue, and he and Bessie moved in with his sister Carrie. They began making plans for a new home, to be built high on Beechwood Avenue, the loveliest section of Carnegie. He also bought a new car—a 1917 Studebaker roadster—and the Stove League banquet marking his 43rd birthday attracted 500 people to the William Penn Hotel. And he also had to make a decision about his baseball career.

Wagner's future with the Pirates—if he had one—was as a first baseman. Manager Jimmy Callahan had made that plain to Wagner and to the newspapers. As a hedge against Wagner's possible retirement, the team also signed Warren Adams, a 22-year-old first baseman who had hit .331 for Winnipeg of the Northern League the year before. But the Pirates were still willing to have Wagner back for 1917.

What Wagner wanted to do was scout. But when management told him it would mean a big pay cut, he ruled that out as an option and considered coming back for his 18th season in Pittsburgh.

Then Barney Dreyfuss delivered more bad news: Regardless of what Wagner did for the Pirates in 1917, he would have to agree to a salary reduction. The Federal League had been dead for a year, and as the inflated two- and three-year wartime contracts that players had signed expired, American and National League owners were moving to reduce salaries to pre-Federal League days. That, plus the fact that Wagner's skills had deteriorated markedly and he no longer was the drawing card he once was, moved Dreyfuss to offer him a $5,400 contract—a $4,500 salary with a $900 option for the following season.[3]

Wagner had been receiving $10,000 a season since 1908, the year of his "retirement." A cut to $5,400 was not only financially devastating, it was also insulting. He refused to sign, but also never announced his retirement.

For 1917, the Pirates decided to abandon Hot Springs, and instead train in Columbus, Georgia. The preliminary trip to Dawson Springs was also dropped. When the team left for Georgia on March 9, it was without Wagner, who, in addition to balking at the pay cut, was in no condition to play ball after a winter of home cooking and inactivity that left him overweight and out of shape.

A week before the team's departure, Wagner and Dreyfuss met to discuss a contract. The owner was firm; Wagner again expressed an interest in a coaching job, but not at the salary the Pirates were offering. They couldn't come to an agreement, leaving Wagner in limbo as spring training started.

Wagner would soon find another reason for staying home: Bessie was pregnant. The baby wasn't due until around the first of the year, but he would have to start planning now. It was important that the work on the new house stay on schedule. On the other hand, he'd also have to consider what another year's salary— even $5,400—would mean to the growing Wagner family.

Wagner's absence from camp wasn't ignored by the press. *The Sporting News*, for one, took his side in the salary dispute with a lengthy editorial:

"As a general proposition, Barney Dreyfuss of the Pittsburg [sic] Pirates is to be commended for the firm and consistent stand he has adopted with his players in his announced plan to reduce his salary roll to a business basis, but issue is taken with him in the particular case of John Henry [sic] Wagner. Mr. Dreyfuss has made a mistake in adopting a hard and fast rule regarding salary reductions that takes no account of sentiment if baseball is still to be regarded as something more than mere commercialism.

"...Now from Mr. Dreyfuss' point of view Hans is not worth $10,000 as a player, therefore the reduction. That may sound like business logic. But Hans Wagner is more than a ball player out to earn his salary. Hans is a baseball institution around which the greatest sentiments of the game are gathered. He is an integral part of the Pittsburg Club and his connection with it should not be considered on the basis of the salary he can earn as a player or even as a gate attraction.

"The suggestion that the great Dutchman should suffer a cut in salary, as long as the Pittsburg Club is solvent, is repugnant to the fans who adore him. They feel that he has in his 20-odd years of service had too large a part in the establishment of the Pirates and baseball in general to be touched by the knife of economy, based on mere commercial calculation.

"He is, in fact, the Pittsburg Club, rather more than is Barney Dreyfuss himself, and only a most desperate situation confronting the Pirate magnate could excuse any action that would include him in a revision of the club's salary roll.

"We take it the Pittsburg Club is not in desperate condition, and baseball sentiments therefore are outraged at its action. Mr. Dreyfuss' business calculations that have ignored that sentiment will not be likely to rebound to his profit nor increase the regard for himself in particular or magnates as a class. It smacks too much of that 'commercialism' which brooks no considerations that appeal to sportsmanship."[4]

But public opinion wasn't going to change Dreyfuss' mind. The Pirates opened the season April 11 in Chicago, with Bill Hinchman, an outfielder, at first base—Adams had been a bust and was waived in spring training—and Chuck Ward at shortstop. Pittsburgh lost the opener and the next two games before finally getting its first victory. The struggling Pirates tumbled quickly into the cellar and were 4-10 after the first two weeks of the season, a spot they held well into May.

With the new season unraveling for his Pirates, Dreyfuss realized he had to have Wagner back, if only for public relations purposes. The two met again on May 26 in Dreyfuss' office. Afterward, Wagner was less than forthright with the press.

"I am through with baseball once and forever," he was quoted in *The Sporting News.* "There never was any question of salary connected with my determination to withdraw from the pastime."[5]

In truth, by the start of June he was quietly working out with his teammates, preparing for a return. And Wagner and Dreyfuss agreed on money: He would be paid $750 a month in salary, with an additional $250 a month as an option on the next year.

On June 6, Wagner finally signed his 1917 contract. There was one final formality, petitioning August Herrmann, chairman of the national baseball commission, for reinstatement. "Finding the call of baseball too strong to resist," Wagner's telegram said, "I desire to continue to play the game I love, and to which I owe all I possess, and I hereby petition the national commission to grant my request for reinstatement, so that I may play with my old club tomorrow."[6]

Herrmann gave immediate approval, and Wagner was in the Pittsburgh lineup the next day, playing first base[7]—he grounded to second his first three times up, then added an RBI single in his final at-bat—in a 5-3 loss to Brooklyn. The defeat left the Pirates in last place at 14-28. But Wagner's return accomplished at least one thing for Dreyfuss: some 2,000 fans showed up, by far the biggest mid-week crowd at Forbes Field for the season.

"Poor old Hans!" wrote Grantland Rice. "Just as he is well settled in retirement, with his first rest in 22 years, they lure him away from his hearthside by hanging up a baseball in front of his nose and showing him the picture of a bat. This is rougher stuff than holding a whiskey bottle under the nose of a drunkard who is trying to swear off."[8]

In reality, Wagner needed little coaxing. Despite his love for Bessie, his 43 years, and his dislike of the travel attached to being a ballplayer, he missed the game and wanted to return.

Wagner got a warm welcome back. On June 22, fans and friends sponsored "Honus Wagner Day" at Forbes Field. A parade of 150 cars and two dozen bands wound its way from Carnegie to the ballpark, where 12,000 fans saw Mayor Joseph G. Armstrong present Wagner with a loving cup, and where Wagner was given a lifetime membership in the Elks. The Pirates capped off the day with a 4-3, 10-inning victory over the Cubs.

Two days later, it was Chicago's turn to honor Wagner. He was presented with a large bouquet of roses and subjected to words of praise before the game, which the Pirates lost 2-1. Wagner accounted for Pittsburgh's only run, scoring from second on a Hinchman single to left in the fifth inning—knocking the ball out of catcher Art Wilson's glove to tally the run.

Wagner showed a few flashes of the old Honus in his first weeks back—a 2-for-4 day on June 12 against Boston, a 4-for-5 afternoon the next day against the Giants, and a 13-for-22 streak (.591) over the last week of the month that brought his average to an impressive .349.

By the end of June, the Pirates were 20-40, still buried in last place. Fans and the press were calling for Callahan's firing and the hiring of Wagner as manager. Wrote the *Pittsburgh Leader*: "The time has come when a change, and a decided one at that, must be made for the betterment of the Pirates. The team is all right, but the players have a millstone about their necks in the shape of one manager, Jimmy Callahan. Manager Callahan has not the confidence of his players. He has been after the men at every turn, and his ways are not the ways that bring out the best results in the players. They absolutely will not do their best work under him, and the Pirate team could be benefited if he were deposed as manager and Honus Wagner put in his place."[9]

On June 28, Dreyfuss denied there were plans to replace Callahan with Wagner. But two days later, that's exactly what he did.

The hard-driving and hard-drinking Callahan was fired on the morning of June 30, and Wagner was named temporary manager. He had one stipulation: that his duties be confined to on-the-field activities. Someone else would have to handle the business end of the job. Dreyfuss agreed, naming longtime Pirate scout Hugo Bezdek as Wagner's assistant.

Wagner's managerial regime was short and unhappy. The Pirates won in his debut on June 30—a victory over Cincinnati to which he contributed a single and a double—but lost the next four games: a double-header in Cincinnati on July 1, a 6-4 decision in St. Louis on July 2, and an 8-6 loss in St. Louis on July 3. The final loss was particularly ugly, featuring sloppy play and three throws by Pirate outfielders that missed cutoff men, something that was noted in the Pittsburgh papers.

"If Jimmy [Callahan] had been on the Pirate bench yesterday, he would have raved while his men placed opposing runners in a position to tally on a single," reported the *Gazette Times*. "Honus Wagner knows that his men played ragged baseball in this regard, but no manager should find it necessary to tell a major league ball player more than once about his mistakes."[10]

Wagner had had enough. He tendered his resignation on the morning of July 4, effective immediately, and was replaced as manager by Bezdek.

The rest of the season turned into a melancholy farewell tour for Wagner. Around the league, he was feted before games with speeches, gifts and the obligatory bouquet of roses. One of the more enjoyable tributes came in Boston on July 19, marking the 20th anniversary of his major-league debut. Before the game, which he missed because of injury, Braves' management presented him with an elaborate fishing outfit.

On the field, he was able to contribute little. A heel injury, suffered July 16 against Boston, had him in and out of the lineup for the rest of the month. When he did play, his fielding and hitting were both less than mediocre (in a July 25 double-header against Brooklyn, he was hitless in eight at-bats, and made an error that gave the Dodgers a victory in Game 1).

Wagner started August with a .278 average, but age and Bezdek's lineup shuffling did him in. He got into only 17 of the Pirates' 27 games in August; and in four of those games he appeared only as a pinch-hitter. When he did play, it was at first base, third base or shortstop; and he was dropped to seventh in the batting order. By the end of the month, he had been convinced it was time to go.

The Pirates had five games in the first three days of September, Wagner appearing in four of them. After that, he was relegated to the bench as Bezdek turned first base over to newly arrived Fritz Mollwitz[11]. Wagner pinch-hit on September 8, and he mopped up at second base on the 11th. What would be his final appearance came on September 17 as a late-inning replacement at second for Bill Webb.

After 21 years, 2,785 regular-season games, 3,418 hits, a lifetime .327 batting average and eight National League batting championships, Honus Wagner was finished.

# *Sixteen*

Honus and Bessie Wagner didn't have time to reflect on the end of his baseball career in the weeks following the conclusion of the 1917 season. Their lives were full of plans for the arrival of the baby and plans for the new house. The house was being built on Beechwood Avenue—the nicest part of Carnegie—in a section of large Victorian homes. It was a couple of blocks up a hill from the center of town, less than a five-minute walk to Wagner's beloved Elks Club and several of his other haunts. He had purchased a double lot and was having a roomy two-story, three-bedroom white brick home built.

As Bessie's due date approached, Honus busied himself with final preparations—he made sure work on the house was on schedule, he shopped for furniture for the home. He also decided he needed to hire someone to help Bessie run the house once the baby arrived.

Mabel Aston was the 18-year-old sister of George Aston, Honus' longtime friend whom Wagner had gotten hired as the Pirates' equipment man nearly 10 years earlier. When George learned that the Wagners were looking for domestic help, he suggested his sister. Mabel interviewed for the job—Honus' main concern was whether she could cook—and was hired.

Bessie went into the hospital in the first week of January to have the baby. The new house had been completed, and while his wife was away, Honus had the furnishings delivered. When it came time to set up the nursery, he and Mabel did it themselves, arranging the room in anticipation of the baby's arrival.

Elva Wagner was born on January 8, 1918. But her birth was difficult, and it was immediately obvious that the child was not going to survive. Little Elva died without ever leaving the hospital, cradled by her parents. Honus Wagner, who so loved children and who so wanted a family of his own, brought Bessie home alone from the hospital to the new house on Beechwood Avenue. The two of them were grief-stricken over Elva's death, often spending evenings talking about her in their parlor, evenings that usually ended with tears.

When his mother died late in the 1900 season, Wagner threw himself into baseball, almost carrying the Pirates to the National League championship. He found a different outlet as he mourned Elva: supporting the American war effort.

With World War I at its peak, Wagner went to work doing what he could—playing in exhibition baseball games to raise money for soldiers at boot camp, helping run charity events, selling Liberty Bonds and, most of all, giving speeches.

Honus Wagner, who only a few years earlier declined to speak even at banquets in his honor, was attracting crowds—and cheers—with his patriotic rhetoric. One such speech was on Flag Day at a ceremony at a Pittsburgh train yard.

"It is said to have been one of the best speeches of the local [Liberty Bond] campaign, and at its close there were given three cheers for Honus that could almost have been heard in Carnegie," reported the *Carnegie Union*.

"Honus took a baseball game as an illustration of the present war . . . In comparing the baseball game to the war, he took it up inning by inning, closing with the remarks that we had now reached the crisis of the game, with Uncle Sam at the bat and the Kaiser in the box for the opponents. Uncle Sam was standing erect, swinging his bat freely and confident that he had the pitcher's goat. The Kaiser was laboring under a mental strain, uncertain of his support and afraid of the battle, for he well knew if he ever grooved one over the plate it was 'good night' for him, as Uncle Sam had the punch and that he would hit the ball so hard that the cry would go up from the bleachers, yelling at the batter to 'touch all the bases,' and the game would be over."[1]

Wagner seemed to be giving speeches everywhere that summer, sometimes delivering addresses at three events in one day. He spoke at Carnegie's 4th of July celebration, helping dedicate a plaque honoring young men from the town who were in the service; that night he spoke from the stage of Carnegie's music hall; two days later he was helping sell Liberty Bonds in nearby Bridgeville, and a week later in the towns of McDonald and Oakdale; on Sunday, July

14 he addressed the brotherhood class of the United Presbyterian Church in Carnegie.

Wagner was also relishing his new status as a private citizen. He volunteered to be chairman for Carnegie's Chamber of Commerce July picnic, then also took on duties as head of the sports committee, setting up potato races, a three-legged race, the tug-of-war, and a baseball game between married and single men. In the fall, he agreed to coach Carnegie's high school football team; over the winter he coached the school's basketball team.

His first love, though, was still baseball. And when the Carnegie Institute of Technology in Pittsburgh came calling with a job offer in February 1919, he was ready to listen. The school, which had approached him several times before[2] and where he had been an informal coach-adviser in the past, was looking for someone to run its athletic program. Wagner, who wasn't interested in the money, accepted the offer, agreeing to be in charge of the program (his title was "general athletic trainer"). The most attractive part of the job was that it allowed him to coach Tech's baseball team.[3]

Spring of 1919 brought more big news to the Wagner household: Bessie was pregnant again, with a due date in early December. It was thrilling news for Wagner, who had adapted easily to the role of homebody after more than 20 years on the road as a professional athlete. Mabel had turned out to be an excellent cook who provided Honus with his favorite meals—simple fare such as ham and boiled cabbage, baked chicken, macaroni and cheese, and fish—as well as baked goods and homemade ice cream. When he wasn't occupied with his minimal duties at Carnegie Tech, he was content to hang around the house, downing cup after cup of Mabel's coffee and reading his newspapers, or visiting friends at the Elks Club.[4]

He was still a popular figure in Pittsburgh. And with that in mind, and with prompting from his old friend, adviser and Beechwood Avenue neighbor Jim Orris, Wagner decided to make a foray into the business world. On August 18, 1919, the Honus Wagner Sporting Goods Co. was incorporated,[5] with him as president, Pittsburgh businessman Henry Bakerman as secretary and treasurer, and Wagner, Bakerman, H.B. Miller, Dudley Reid and R.R. Zimmerman the directors. A total of $75,000 was raised to get the business off the ground—much of it put up by Wagner and Orris. In addition to putting his name and money into the project, Wagner also "worked" at the store, dropping by irregularly, greeting customers and swapping tales with the help.[6]

The stay-at-home Wagner was thrown a curve late in the year with a tempting offer: a chance to get back in professional baseball. The Akron ballclub of the International League wanted him as manager for the 1920 season. It would mean steady work in an atmosphere he loved; it would also mean being away from his home and wife and new baby. It was no contest. He turned down the job.

A healthy baby girl, christened Betty Blaine Wagner, was born on December 5, 1919. Her arrival was a proud moment for Honus, as thrilling to him as any he had ever had on the field. And he played the role of father perfectly, doting over his daughter, taking her to events such as town picnics, showing her off to his cronies. When he was honored at a 47th birthday celebration at the General Forbes Hotel in Pittsburgh in 1921, among the gifts presented by the 300-some guests was a large hand-colored photo of young Betty, holding a baseball. Wagner, in an unusual display of public emotion, was moved to tears.

Wagner was comfortable and happy in his role as family man and Carnegie's first citizen. As the latter, he became one of the town's points of interest. Babe Ruth, after a July 1921 visit to St. Paul's Orphanage in nearby Idlewood, asked for a quick motor tour of Wagner's hometown.[7] Rabbit Maranville, the Pirates' star shortstop, made a similar request a few weeks earlier after having met Wagner at a banquet and listening to his stories about Carnegie; he recruited *Pittsburgh Chronicle Telegraph* sportswriter Chester Conboy to drive him around town, showing him Wagner's old haunts.

Early in the fall of 1921, Honus and Bessie learned they would be parents again. Another beautiful daughter, Virginia, was born on May 3, 1922. The Wagners and their daughters—Honus referred to them as "my boys"—settled in to a comfortable home life at 605 Beechwood. Honus fussed over the children, humoring them and treating them as his most precious possessions. He left discipline to Bessie; his handling of problems seldom went beyond a disapproving glance, though the girls got the message.

Wagner was willing to let life come to him. His contract at Carnegie Tech had run out after the 1922 season; the sporting goods store was best left run by others (he made occasional visits, but often said he was no salesman); he had his barnstorming, four games a week sometimes, but that was seasonal. He was content with his simple life, happy to appear as the drawing card in charity baseball games either as a coach, umpire or player, to be guest speaker at various banquets and functions, to assume civic duties, such as acting as chairman of the board of the Carnegie Basketball League or helping put on a bicycle race, or to lend his name and expertise to a worthy cause.

On February 26, 1922, at the General Forbes Hotel in Pittsburgh, Wagner was elected president of the newly founded Greater Pittsburgh Baseball Association. The 100-plus managers of independent and amateur teams needed Wagner's help: The Pittsburgh City Council was debating whether to repeal Daylight Savings Time. Wagner, speaking on behalf of the association, appeared before the body on March 10 to ask that it be continued. In making his case, Wagner told council members that he couldn't throw a curveball until he was 14, and that young players now could do it at 8, which he attributed to the extra hour of daylight they had to practice. Four days later, whether swayed by Wagner's appeal or not, the council voted 5-4 to kill the bill to repeal Daylight Savings Time.

Wagner's life was low-key, comfortable and predictable, in keeping with his character. Spring, summer and fall were for barnstorming. The sporting goods store had become something of a Pittsburgh institution; not much of a money-maker, but it was getting by. For relaxation he had the Elks Club. For peace of mind, he had Bessie and "my boys."

This domestic tranquility was broken only rarely. One such occasion was the death of Honus' older brother Luke on February 16, 1923. Luke—a talented ballplayer in his younger days—lived with his sister Carrie in Carnegie and had made his living as a plasterer. He had come down with pneumonia a week earlier and died at St. Francis Hospital. He was 51.

But for Honus, the days, weeks and months, by and large, fell into a pleasant, almost monotonous pattern. That changed, however, in the summer of 1925.

# *Seventeen*

By 1925, the Wagner family had established a comfortable routine in the big house on Beechwood Avenue. Honus divided his time between the store, barnstorming, public appearances and occasional visits to Forbes Field. For relaxation, he went to the Elks Club. Bessie tended to the girls, and, with the help of Mabel Aston, kept the house running.

Financially, there were no serious worries. Honus hadn't saved a lot of money from his playing days, and much of what he had put aside went into his new home and getting the sporting goods business started. But his combined income from barnstorming,[1] investments and the store was enough so that finances weren't a pressing concern.

That changed on April 25, 1925, however, when the Carnegie Trust and First National Bank went into receivership and closed because of financial irregularities.[2] Wagner had a large portion of his savings in the bank. And when the institution shut its doors, he found himself if not exactly strapped, then at least in unfamiliar territory.[3]

The incident served as a wakeup call for Wagner, who realized that it might be a good idea to get into some steady line of work. He decided to try politics.

Wagner was no stranger to the political arena. He had learned to enjoy being a public speaker; more important, he had discovered that people would listen to what he had to say because he was Honus Wagner. And he was no stranger to quasi-governmental bodies. He had been appointed to the Pittsburgh Boxing Commission in March 1920; he had been made a member of the state fisheries commission by Gov. John Tener in 1914; and he had had the successful appearance before the Pittsburgh City Council in 1922 under his belt.

In the summer of 1925, Wagner allowed himself to be persuaded to run for Allegheny County Sheriff. He was a popular candidate—helped by the fact that baseball fever was raging in Pittsburgh as the Pirates were on their way to the National League pennant—and was well-received on the campaign trail. Wagner pledged "to purge our government of graft and corruption and to drive from public office men who are servile to political mastery and whose political records prove them unworthy of trust."[4]

His message was well-received; in the September 15 primary, Wagner led all candidates on the Labor ballot. (He also was second among Democrat and Republican voters and third on Socialist and Prohibition Party ballots.) In the November 3 general election, he ran under the Labor and Non-Partisan banner. The Citizens' Political Union, an independent civic organization, endorsed Wagner. "He is pledged to the Non-Partisan platform with especial [sic] emphasis upon law enforcement, particularly of the prohibition acts," the group said in a statement issued three days before the election. "We feel that his word can be relied upon when he promises vigorous and rigid law enforcement and elimination of discrimination in the conduct of the office."[5]

But the endorsement and his fame as a baseball player didn't translate into votes. He finished a distant second in the five-man race, some 90,000 votes behind winning Republican candidate Robert Braun. (Wagner, who didn't even carry Carnegie, did have the consolation of finishing ahead of the Democratic, Prohibition and Socialist candidates.)

None the worse for wear, Wagner brushed off the defeat and went back to an increasingly simple life in Carnegie. His family and baseball were still dearest to him. At times, the urge to get back in the game was great; but the girls were growing up quickly and he enjoyed spending time with them.

Eventually, he had to make a decision. In the spring of 1927, Wagner was offered a job as manager of the Twin City Twins of the Eastern Ohio League. The ballclub was based in the towns of Uhrichsville and Dennison, about 60 miles west of Carnegie, and played its games on weekends. Other teams in the league were Zanesville, Bellaire, Coshocton, New Philadelphia and Cambridge—a long way from the major leagues, a long way even from Wagner's old days in the Iron & Oil League. But it gave him a chance to manage a real team, not just a barnstorming squad. And, who knows, maybe it could get him started on a path back to the majors.

It was obvious early on that Wagner was no John McGraw. He got his first look at his whole team on Sunday, April 24—the day of its opener. Without having had the benefit of even one practice, the Twins lost to Coshocton 5-4. Wagner's managerial career was shortlived. The Twins flopped on the field and at the gate, losing their first six games and failing to attract enough fans to break even financially. On Monday, June 13, the directors of the team decided that expenses needed to be cut, and that they couldn't afford the luxury of a non-playing manager, even if it was Honus Wagner. So Wagner was let go, along with two players.

He returned to Carnegie, where bigger problems soon began wearing on him. His sporting goods store was foundering. Wagner had never devoted a lot of time or effort to running the business. He'd stop by often, mingle with employees and customers—maybe even help sell an item or two. But it wasn't a booming business. The situation worsened over the next year, and finally in mid-1928, it went bankrupt.

Wagner suffered an even more crushing blow late in 1928, one that affected him deeply. His brother Al, who had bladder and other physical ailments—most traceable to his years of drinking— died in his doctor's office in Pittsburgh on November 26. Al, who had been working as a hotel clerk, was 59.

The death of his older brother, who had been his hero as he grew up and his best friend all his life, and who had been so instrumental at the outset of his baseball career, marked the start of a turbulent year for Honus.

Wagner's many friends were aware of his worsening financial situation, and many were looking out for him. On January 15, 1929, he was one of 18 men to receive political appointments as assistant sergeants-at-arms in the Pennsylvania House of Representatives in Harrisburg. The position paid $7 a day.

A week later, Wagner found a way to bring home an additional $60 a week. On January 21, he signed over the use of his name and likeness—for $1—to E. Louis Braunstein, who had purchased the assets of the Honus Wagner Sporting Goods Co. in bankruptcy proceedings. In a separate agreement signed the same day, Braunstein hired Wagner as a salesman for a revived sporting goods concern, to be called the Honus Wagner Company. It was a three-year contract, giving Wagner $60 a week plus commissions.[6]

With a $60 salary assured—from a job only a few minutes from home, as opposed to the 200-some miles to the capital—Wagner decided to give up his job in Harrisburg. He had hardly been a dedicated state employee, making only a handful of appearances because of the travel involved, a persistent case of the flu and his general lack of interest in the position. On March 27, he handed in his resignation.

"I could not handle two jobs and do them both right," he told the *Pittsburgh Press*. "You know, they just reorganized the [sporting goods] company and made me president. ... [I]t's just a case of taking the better job."[7]

It may have been a better job, but it wasn't exactly as Wagner was painting it. He was, simply, window dressing for the owners of the sporting goods store. He tried to be a salesman, but his heart wasn't in it. He often ended his day by noon; at other times, hunting and fishing trips took precedence over schmoozing with customers, and he wouldn't show up at all.

The hefty sales commissions Wagner had hoped for never materialized, but at the outset, his salary, barnstorming proceeds[8] and money from several testimonials held in his honor were enough to ensure a pleasant home life. He could afford to take his family on a vacation to Conneaut Lake in northwest Pennsylvania in July, and later that month Bessie was able to travel to Chicago to visit her sister. But as the Great Depression deepened, Carnegie and the Wagner family found themselves in an ever-tightening financial situation.

In the first month of 1932, Carnegie's Salvation Army fed more than 6,000 people, a considerable number for a town of only about 12,500 residents. A free lunch program was established by Rev. Ercole Dominicis, a local Catholic priest, but it couldn't keep up with the number of needy and eventually went out of business; barbers reduced the price of haircuts from 60 cents to 50; the board of the Methodist Episcopal Church voted to stop passing the plate, and instead set up boxes at church entrances; the Carnegie Theater reduced admission prices; the town's other theaters ignored tradition and local blue laws and operated on Sundays to raise money for the Salvation Army fund drive; dances and card parties raised money; more came in from a musical revue at the Carnegie Free Library—one of the performers was 12-year-old Betty Wagner.

The Wagners were suffering too. When his three-year deal to work as a salesman with the Honus Wagner Company ended in

1932, he wasn't rehired. The loss of the $60 salary was a crippling blow to the family. Wagner knew he had few options. His attempts at business and politics had failed. Two people he had often turned to, James Orris and Barney Dreyfuss, couldn't help him any longer. Orris, Wagner's friend, neighbor, adviser and business partner, had died in December 1930. Fourteen months later, Dreyfuss, the man who had brought Wagner home to Pittsburgh in 1900, passed away.

All that was left for Wagner was baseball. One thing that never wavered during the lean times was his dedication to the game. He helped put together several teams and leagues in and around Carnegie—the Honus Wagner-Pie Traynor Chartiers Valley Mushball League, the Hans Wagner County League, the Wagner-Traynor Junior League, among them—often holding the organizational meetings at his home. Now it was time for baseball to help him.

Shortly before the end of the 1932 season, the last-place Cincinnati Reds relieved manager Dan Howley of his duties. After the season, Wagner got in touch with Reds management and applied for the job. He drove to Cincinnati on October 12, interviewing with team president Sidney Weil and getting a promise that his application would get full consideration. Eventually, though, the job went to Donie Bush, leaving Wagner back where he started.

The baseball establishment knew that Wagner was interested in a return to the game. In addition to applying for the Cincinnati job, he had sent letters to several other clubs, inquiring about coaching positions; and he had asked National League officials about possible employment as an umpire. But only a few people were aware of how badly he needed a job. Finally, all sides were brought together by *New York Evening Post* columnist Fred Lieb late in 1932. A Pittsburgh woman wrote to him, detailing the Wagner family's plight.

"The lady said they hardly had enough to eat," Lieb wrote in his memoir. "Because of the high rate of unemployment and scarcity of dollars to spend on anything beyond necessities, his sporting goods business in Pittsburgh had failed. He had other debts and couldn't get a job. The lady wrote, 'He is too proud to ask for charity from the Pittsburgh club, but surely the National League should do something now for this greatest of players, now that Honus is sorely in need.' "[9]

Lieb's column told of Wagner's problems and criticized the National League for forgetting about him and other past heroes of the game who were feeling the full effects of the Depression.

"Wagner isn't exactly reduced to the bread lines," Lieb wrote in his column. "However, things haven't gone too well with him. His little sporting goods store in Pittsburgh proved to be more of a liability than an asset. In Pittsburgh they said he was too generous for his own good. Like many old-time ball players, he was a poor business man.

"...With men and women dying in our midst from hunger and exhaustion, this perhaps is no time for a sob story about a former ball player, even a Hans Wagner. I suppose he gets his three meals a day and has a warm place to sleep. But it has been tight scratching.

"Wagner isn't the only player who is hard up. The mail of such a man as [Commissioner] Judge Landis, [NL President] Judge Heydler, [AL President] Will Harridge, John McGraw and Babe Ruth are full of letters from former ball players asking for help. All ask for jobs, but if no jobs are available, they ask for something to tide them over the winter.

"However, if there is one player that I believe the league should look after, it is Wagner. I know most of the clubs were hit pretty hard last season; the Cubs alone made money. ... Yet if the league created a job for Wagner as National League coach to young players at $5,000 a year, that would cost each club $625. I believe it would be well worth it in creating good will. And no doubt it would be a godsend to the greatest player developed by the league in its fifty-six years."[10]

The response to the column was almost immediate. National League President John Heydler sent a copy to Bill Benswanger, Dreyfuss' son-in-law, who had taken control of the Pirates after Dreyfuss' death. Benswanger said he had no idea of the situation. He helped Wagner clear up some outstanding bills. More importantly, he offered him a coaching job with the Pirates. Honus Wagner was back where he belonged.

# Eighteen

The last thing Pirates President Bill Benswanger needed for the 1933 season was another coach—manager George Gibson already had Otis Crandall and Grover Hartley as his two assistants. Other teams, hit hard by the Depression, were cutting back to one coach. But Benswanger knew that as a matter of decency—not to mention public relations—he had to bring Honus Wagner back.

Wagner visited the Pirates offices several times over the last two weeks of January 1933 to discuss his return. Finally, on February 2, he signed a one-year contract.

"Why shouldn't I be happy?" he told the *Pittsburgh Press*. "Baseball has been my life, there is nothing I like so well. To put on a Pittsburgh uniform again will be one of the happiest moments of my life."[1]

Simply being in uniform again wasn't enough for Wagner; he wanted something to do. 0Just having him in the dugout—during games, it was Wagner's habit to stand near the top step so he could be seen by fans—and signing autographs were the public relations pluses for the Pirates. But Gibson thought his old teammate might be able to help out around the team, so he was assigned some on-field duties. He pitched a little batting practice, he took charge of the bag of balls during infield warmups, and he was asked to help the team's young shortstop, Joseph Floyd "Arky" Vaughan.

Vaughan had broken in with Pittsburgh in 1932 in impressive fashion. He hit .318 for the Pirates, who had finished second, four games behind the pennant-winning Cubs. Vaughan's fielding, however, was hardly stellar. He led National League shortstops in errors with 46 (in 128 games), and his .934 fielding average was next to last among regulars at the position. Gibson asked Wagner to room with the 21-year-old Vaughan on the road, and hoped he could impart some pointers on playing shortstop. Wagner at first wasn't much of an instructor—his tips were often along the lines of the one he gave Vaughan when asked how to properly handle a slow-rolling grounder: ". . . run in, grab the ball and throw the guy out"[2]—but his presence and guidance helped Vaughan settle down. "They said if I couldn't make a shortstop out of Arky Vaughan, nobody could," Wagner recalled almost two decades later. "Of all the players I tried to help, he's the best and the one that went the farthest."[3, 4]

Wagner's return to baseball was big news not only in Pittsburgh but around the rest of the National League. He got the key to the city when the Pirates made their first 1933 trip to New York in May. The people of Brooklyn went several steps better, declaring May 4 Honus Wagner Day.

"Flatbush has playfully tossed pop bottles at defenseless umpires, whooped it up as it ran alien performers out of the park and generally made life miserable for visitors who dared take liberties with its baseball team," reported the *Pittsburgh Press,* "but never until yesterday had it honored a man who never did anything to it but dirt."[5]

Wagner was feted at Borough Hall, where thousands jammed the street and dignitaries from Borough President Henry Hesterberg to former heavyweight boxing champion Jack Dempsey turned out. Hands in pockets, chewing on the remnants of a cigar, he offered brief thanks, after which he was chauffeured to Ebbets Field, where some 9,000 fans awaited. And that evening he was honored yet again at a Coney Island banquet attended by 500 people.

The biggest welcome-back-to-baseball celebration, of course, was the one in Pittsburgh. The afternoon of June 9 was declared a holiday in Allegheny County, the city and surrounding boroughs. Wagner and his family, escorted by band buses and some four dozen cars, drove from Carnegie to Stockton Avenue and Federal Street on Pittsburgh's North Side, the staging area for a Wagner Day Parade. Heading the parade was a combined Carnegie and Bridgeville high school band, one of 20 bands that participated. More than 6,000 people and 800 vehicles made the two-mile-long march through the streets of Pittsburgh to Forbes Field.

There was a two-hour program at the ballpark, including a short oldtimers game (Fred Clarke, Cy Young, Claude Ritchey, Ed Abbaticchio and Deacon Phillipe among the participants)[6], field events featuring current Pirates Vaughan, Paul and Lloyd Waner, Gus

Suhr, Chick Hafey, Larry French and Woody Jensen, among others, and presentations to Wagner.

John Tener, former Pennsylvania governor and National League president, spoke first, praising Wagner for his achievements on the baseball diamond. He introduced Pittsburgh Mayor John Herron, who, after brief remarks, presented Wagner with a check for $1,500. Other gifts followed—floral tributes, three slabs of ham and bacon—before Wagner stepped to the microphone. Obviously overcome by the emotion of the day, he acknowledged the gifts, apologized for his oldtimers' team's loss, and then thanked the thousands of fans who filled Forbes Field.[7] Festivities continued that evening when nearly 1,000 friends and fans attended an Elks Club banquet, where Clarke and Young, among others, spoke in Wagner's honor.

Wagner was the center of attention in any city the Pirates visited. Fans turned out to see him at the ballparks, he was besieged for autographs, strangers greeted him on the streets, reporters came to him for his thoughts on the National League race. And he loved every minute of it.

Having a steady job and being on the road did have its drawbacks. Wagner was able to spend less time at home with his family and at his usual haunts in Carnegie. Still, Bessie was agreeable to the tradeoff. "I'm thrilled about the tributes he is getting," she told the *Pittsburgh Press*, "but there is something else that is so much a part of my dreams I don't even like to talk about it. That is having Jay back in baseball. It's his whole life. He never should have been out of the game."[8]

Wagner regularly brought his work home with him in the person of various Pirates he'd invite to dinner. The Waners and Suhr were among the most frequent visitors, sometimes as often as once a week. Mabel Aston looked forward to these visits. It gave her a chance to vary the menu of plain foods that Honus liked—she was an excellent cook and enjoyed preparing steak, standing rib roasts or stuffed baked chicken that the ballplayers were treated to. She also enjoyed the financial rewards. After dinner was finished, Honus and his guest or guests would go to the next room to visit while Mabel cleared the table. It was common for the ballplayers to leave her a tip under their plates. A kind of family joke evolved—Mabel would be picking up the dishes in the dining room, and Wagner would be in the next room, talking to his visitors but craning his neck to see how much money his guests had left.[9]

After 15 years with the Wagners, Mabel had become almost a member of the family. When there weren't guests, she would eat dinner with them, she helped plan the menus, she did the shopping, and she assisted Bessie with the girls. Not that Bessie needed a lot of help with Betty and Virginia; they were well-behaved, though different in dispositions and interests. Betty, 13, was the more artistic of the two, a straight-A student who was a member of the National Honor Society. She liked to write and dance. Ginny, 11, generally a B and C student, was the athlete who loved to play catch with her dad. (Before she was old enough to play ball, she and Honus would play another game around the house—she'd dress Bessie's cat in a baby bonnet and put it in a stroller, then have Honus push it around.)

With a steady job and a happy, peaceful home life, Wagner turned his attention to something that had been bothering him for years: the Honus Wagner Company. Wagner believed he had been taken advantage of when he signed over the use of his name for $1 in 1929, and he always thought that the company had shortchanged him on commissions. In June 1933, he filed suit in the Court of Common Pleas of Allegheny County against E. Louis Braunstein, who headed the Honus Wagner Company, and several other sporting goods businesses owned and/or controlled by Braunstein.

Wagner claimed that under terms of his contract with Braunstein, he was to be paid a commission on sales at the Honus Wagner Company, but that there was an intermingling of sales between the Wagner Company and two other Braunstein-controlled enterprises, the E.L. Braunstein Co. and United Sporting Goods, all of which were run from the same Liberty Avenue address. His lawsuit asked for a full accounting of sales by the defendants, that he receive any money that might be due to him after the accounting, and that the defendants be forbidden from using his name in conjunction with their businesses. Wagner's suit also claimed that he only signed over the use of his name in order to get the $60-a-week salesman's job that Braunstein offered.

The defendants denied shortchanging Wagner out of commissions by selling products labeled with his name in their other enterprises, and also denied his claim that he didn't receive proper credit for all sales he provided the companies. As for the use of Wagner's name, Braunstein pointed to the contract that Wagner had signed, and further offered as evidence on his behalf the fact that "the name 'Honus Wagner' was sold by the Trustee in Bankruptcy of Honus Wagner Sporting Goods Company to the defendant, E.L. Braunstein & Co., by Order of Court, at public sale"[10] in 1928.

It took more than a year for the case to be resolved—the defendants raised numerous objections to the original complaint, which was dismissed in October—and when the decision was rendered on August 21, 1934, Wagner was left empty-handed. In a two-page decree, the court found that "all commissions due, or alleged to be due, the plaintiff by any or all of the defendants by reason of any sales, or any cause or causes whatsoever, have been fully paid."

As for Wagner's efforts to stop the use of his name, the court found that "the right to the exclusive use of the name 'Honus Wagner' for all commercial and advertising purposes is vested in E.L. Braunstein & Co. Inc., . . . E.L. Braunstein and Honus Wagner Company ... their heirs, executors, administrators, successors and assigns ...."[11] The court based its decision on Braunstein's purchase of assets from the bankrupt Honus Wagner Sporting Goods Company, as well as the contract Wagner had signed in January 1929.

The ruling was a big disappointment for Wagner—he believed he had been cheated and he didn't like other people using his name—but he didn't pursue the case any further, although the situation would continue to bother him for years to come.

# *Nineteen*

Not only was Honus Wagner back in baseball, and with his beloved Pirates, but he found himself on a team involved in a pennant race in 1933. Led by Paul Waner (.309), Tony Piet (.323), Arky Vaughan (.314) and Larry French (18-13, 2.72), Pittsburgh challenged Bill Terry's New York Giants down the stretch before finally finishing second, five games back.

The following season, the Pirates stumbled early, and owner Bill Benswanger finally had enough of manager George Gibson. Gibson, who had been hired by Barney Dreyfuss shortly before Dreyfuss' death, had alienated his players with his frequent and often undeserved criticism. On June 19, with the team in fifth place at 27-24, Gibson was fired. Taking over was third baseman Pie Traynor, a Pittsburgh fan favorite who was known almost as much for his gentle disposition as for his baseball skills.[1]

Traynor never got the team into the race—the Pirates wound up fifth at 74-76—and the next two seasons brought a pair of fourth-place finishes.

Wagner's duties with the team remained much the same under Traynor, offering help as needed to Vaughan and other young players, taking charge of the bag of balls used in pregame warmups, and, most of all, serving as a goodwill ambassador for the Pirates and for baseball in general.

He was still a draw, whether at Forbes Field, at other ballparks around the league or at baseball functions. He was named commissioner of the National Semi-pro Baseball Congress in 1935, a position he would hold for six years, making appearances around the country and serving as the nominal head of semi-pro baseball in the United States. The job also allowed him to travel to Wichita, Kansas, each summer for the national tournament, where he would usually be reunited with Fred Clarke, who would make the trip from his home in Winfield, Kansas.

Yet another honor—one he was quite proud of—came Wagner's way in 1935. On August 21, the formation of the Baseball Hall of Fame was announced. That December, members of the Baseball Writers Association of America were asked to choose the first honorees from a list of 33 candidates. The inaugural class was announced on February 2—Ty Cobb, Babe Ruth, Walter Johnson, Christy Mathewson and Honus Wagner—and plans were made to enshrine them at a future ceremony in conjunction with baseball's centennial in 1939.

After their second straight fourth-place finish in 1936, the Pirates climbed to third the following year. With a talented ballclub—Paul Waner was third in the league with a .354 average in 1937, Arky Vaughan hit .322 and led the league in triples, and Lloyd Waner hit .330—the Pirates looked like the team to beat in 1938. And they played up to expectations, jumping into first place and holding a seemingly commanding seven-game lead on September 1. Pirate officials were so sure of the team that they had a World Series press box built atop the Forbes Field grandstand at a reported cost of $35,000.[2]

But as September wore on, the Pirates' lead shrank. By September 27, when they came to Chicago for a three-game series against the Cubs, it was only a game and a half. The Cubs won the opener 2-1 behind sore-armed Dizzy Dean to move within a half-game of first. The next day, September 28, was a day that would go down in Cubs history. The Pirates led 5-3 going into the bottom of the eighth, but the Cubs tied it. Then, with two outs in the bottom of the ninth and darkness settling in, Gabby Hartnett sent a Mace Brown fastball over the left-field wall, baseball's famed "Homer in the gloamin'," to give the Cubs a 6-5 victory, their ninth in a row, and put them in first place.

"You have seen them rush out to greet a hero after he touched the plate to terminate a great contest," wrote Edward Burns in the *Chicago Tribune*. "Well, you never saw nothin'. The mob started to gather around Gabby before he had reached first base. By the time he had rounded second he couldn't have been recognized in the mass of Cub players, frenzied fans and excited ushers but for that red face, which shone out even in the gray shadows."[3]

Chicago made it a sweep the next day, Bill Lee beating the dispirited Pirates 10-1, and the pennant race was all but over. Pittsburgh finished second to the Cubs, 2 games back.

The hangover from the collapse carried over to the 1939 season as the Pirates stumbled badly and ended up sixth, 28½ games out of first. The disappointing finish would cost Traynor his job, Benswanger turning to former St. Louis Cardinals manager Frankie Frisch.

While the Pirates were suffering through 1939, Wagner was being "rediscovered" yet again. All of baseball's eyes were on Cooperstown on June 12 for the dedication of the National Baseball Museum and Hall of Fame. Wagner, Babe Ruth, Ty Cobb, Connie Mack, Walter Johnson, Larry Lajoie, Grover Alexander, George Sisler, Cy Young, Eddie Collins ... all were present for the ceremonies. Each had his turn on the speaker's platform. It had all the makings of a solemn occasion, these dedication festivities for baseball's hallowed legends. But Wagner, the second speaker after the courtly Mack, broke the ice and put everyone at ease with his short, folksy acceptance speech.

"When I was just a kid I said I hope someday I'll be up there playing in this league," he told a crowd of some 4,000. "And by chance I did. Now, Connie Mack, the gentleman that preceded me here to the microphone, I remember walking 14 miles just to see him play ball for Pittsburgh. Walking and running or hitchhiking or riding on a buggy. Them days we had no automobiles. I certainly am pleased to be here at Cooperstown today. And this is just a wonderful little city, or town or village or whatever we call it. It puts me in mind of Sleepy Hollow. However, I want to thank you for being able to come here today."[4]

The Hall of Fame dedication had put Wagner back in the national spotlight. It also seemed to awaken the people of Carnegie to just how special a person he was, and how overdue recognition of that fact was.

Plans were made to honor Wagner at a huge banquet June 22 at the Carnegie Presbyterian Church. Among those on hand were Pennsylvania Attorney General James Duff, former teammates Deacon Phillippe and Tom McCreery, current Pirates Vaughan, Gus Suhr, Ray Berres and Bill Clemensen, Pirate owner Bill Benswanger and newspapermen Charles "Chilly" Doyle, Julius Levine and Harry Keck. Telegrams arrived from Baseball Commissioner Kennesaw Mountain Landis, former NL President John Tener, current NL President Ford Frick, and former players George Gibson, Tris Speaker, Fred Clarke, and Ginger Beaumont, among others. It was quite a display of affection and respect for the old man.

"He is the greatest advertising asset the town has ever known," reported Wagner's hometown paper, the *Carnegie Union*. "His name has been blazoned across the pages of every newspaper from Maine to California and from Canada to Mexico. And get this—he was always HONUS WAGNER OF CARNEGIE, PENNSYLVANIA.

"...He was, and still is, our A-No. 1 loyal citizen. He put Carnegie on the map as no other man has ever done. Citizens of our town, traveling far and wide over our country, have only to drop the casual remark in some public place that they are from Carnegie and they will be greeted with: 'How's Honus?' We have heard one or two instances where this happened in foreign lands. For forty years, Honus has been advertising Carnegie, while we as citizens simply took it for granted, but did nothing about it. We made no effort to honor him for so doing. That is, we never woke up to our duties until Tuesday evening of last week."[5]

More than 20 years after his last game in the major leagues, Honus Wagner was again a baseball star. He was sought as an after-dinner speaker, lending a big-league air to the smallest banquet; when traveling with the Pirates he couldn't walk down a street or into a hotel or tavern without being greeted; his barnstorming teams drew good crowds, not interested in seeing semi-pro baseball, but in seeing the great Honus; he often was the last of the Pirates to leave Forbes Field, staying around until every autograph request was satisfied.

"Here we take Honus too much for granted," reported the *Union*. "To appreciate just how well the Dutchman is thought of you need to see him lionized in other cities."[6]

At home, life remained largely unchanged. Despite his travels and other commitments, family came first. Dinner at the Wagner home was a serious proposition. No radio, no telephone calls, no interruptions of any kind. For Honus, this was Family Hour, when everyone ate together and spent time together. Each family member got an opportunity to speak, filling in the others on the latest news. It was a peaceful, pleasant daily break he could look forward to—Bessie's occasional protests about him slipping food to one of his dogs under the table notwithstanding.

Wagner, after all, considered his dogs family. From his days as a boy when he had several hunting dogs, Wagner always had one or more around. There was Jason Weatherby, the large mixed breed he owned during his playing days, a dog whose picture—shaking his master's hand—appeared in *The Sporting News* in 1911; Whitey, one of the mutts who'd mooch Mabel's cooking at the Wagner dinner table; Mickey, a cocker spaniel mix that was his companion in his later years; and there was Big Boy.

' Big Boy was a Great Dane Wagner owned in the 1940s. He had a habit of walking down the hill from the Wagner home on Beechwood and into a five-and-dime in town. He'd go to where the store had a display of rubber balls, lean into the bin and pick one out. Then he'd stand in the aisle, with the ball in his mouth. He'd drop the ball, then catch it on the bounce, trying to get the employees—or customers, Big Boy wasn't particular—to play. The clerks, reluctant to try to take the ball away from the frightening-looking hound, would then send someone up the hill to Wagner's house. He'd protest ("Well, just take the ball out of his mouth!"), but eventually he'd follow the clerk back down the hill and into the store, where he'd pay for the ball and collect Big Boy, and they'd both head over to the Elks Club before going home.

As always, Wagner also had a soft spot for kids as well as dogs. He was a favorite among the boys in the neighborhood, having turned his garage over to them for a clubhouse in the late '30s and early '40s, and was more than willing to share his expertise when they played softball out in front of his house. He also provided them with employment, handing out an autographed baseball and $1 for the group to share for cutting the grass in the vacant lot next to his home. Wagner also found the neighborhood boys to be an appreciative audience. They'd sit on his porch and listen to his stories, or stop by when one of the Pirates would be at the house for dinner, giving them a chance to meet one of their baseball heroes. Family, dogs, kids and baseball. Honus was never happier.

# Twenty

The Frankie Frisch years weren't much different from the regimes of George Gibson and Pie Traynor as far as Honus Wagner was concerned. His duties remained the same—serving as a goodwill ambassador for the Pirates, sometimes pitching batting practice, taking charge of the bag of balls used in infield practice, and always being there for the players who needed his help, whether it was giving hitting and fielding tips or bringing players home for dinner.

He cut back on his travel with the Pirates, a combination of wartime travel restrictions and his concession to age, and when the ballclub would go on the road he'd use the time to barnstorm. He more or less adopted a team from neighboring Dormont. When he was ready to go on tour, the ballclub would be rechristened the Honus Wagners, and they'd hit the road, playing everywhere from Buffalo to Cincinnati to West Virginia against Negro League, semi-pro or various towns' amateur teams.

Occasionally on fall trips he'd bring along members of the Pirates, once their season was over. He also made several tours with Dizzy Dean—Wagner hitting infield practice and Dean pitching an inning or two before both retired to the clubhouse, where they busied themselves icing down beer for the rest of the team.

These excursions were basically money-making ventures—games against the great Negro League teams like the Pittsburgh Crawfords drew huge crowds—but Wagner also used the trips as social occasions. A trip to Zanesville, Ohio, gave him a chance to spend a day with Cy Young; going through Emlenton, Pennsylvania, meant a visit with Claude Ritchey; and stops almost anywhere afforded him an opportunity to be the center of attention—Wagner had grown to love it—whether it was from autograph-seeking kids or from a bartender who'd give him the first beer on the house.

Wagner was also able to enjoy his popularity when he did travel with the Pirates. After games, it was his custom to go off for a meal and a few beers, and more often than not teammates—sometimes their families, too—would tag along. New York, Chicago, Cincinnati, Philadelphia . . . Wagner had his regular stops in each city, where the restaurateurs and barkeeps knew him and welcomed his visits.

Pittsburgh players also came to enjoy his company. His funny stories, his recollections of the old days, his insistence that modern-day players were far superior to those of his day, his sense of humor—even his quirks, like the limburger sandwiches on the train—all made him a favorite with players 40 or more years his junior.

The Pirates of 1940, '41, '42 and '43 were relegated to the middle of the pack in the National League. Frisch's record for those first four years was 305-304, the team never finishing higher than fourth. The 1944 season, though, was another story. The Pirates had their best year since 1938, winning 90 games. But that was the season Billy Southworth's Cardinals won 105 and cruised to the pennant over second-place Pittsburgh. More disappointments followed in 1945 (fourth) and '46 (seventh), the result being Frisch's resignation with three games left in the 1946 season.

A bigger change came for the Pirates in 1946. Bill Benswanger, whose family's ownership of the team dated to Barney Dreyfuss' days back in Louisville, announced in August that he was selling. The new owners were singer Bing Crosby, Indianapolis banker Frank E. McKinney, Ohio real estate developer John W. Galbreath and Pittsburgh attorney Thomas P. Johnson. Crosby, a minority owner, was a big fan of Wagner's, and the new owners had no intention of altering his arrangement with the team. It was one of the few things the new ownership didn't change.

Forbes Field was given a half-million-dollar facelift. Roy Hamey, president of the American Association, was named general manager and given permission to bring in as many new faces as he needed. Former Cub and Dodger great Billy Herman was named manager. The team's scouting staff and minor-league farm system were expanded. There were other changes, as well, including one that infuriated Wagner.

Clubhouse man George "Chauf" Aston, whom Wagner had gotten the Pirates to hire before the 1909 season, was let go. The company line was that it was just part of a general changing of the guard, but Aston, Wagner and others in the Pirate organization believed—and were probably correct—that his departure was racially motivated.[1]

The firing angered Wagner, a man who prized loyalty above all else. For days he moped around the house, alternately wondering aloud what he could do, then going for long walks that invariably ended at the Elks Club, where he had brought Chauf on occasion as his guest. But Wagner realized there was nothing he could do for his old friend. The new owners tried to soothe Wagner. They talked up spring training, what would be his first visit to Florida, making it sound as attractive as possible; Hamey and Herman came to Carnegie for the Elks Club's father and son night in early February. Eventually, Wagner's anger subsided, though the disappointment stayed with him for the rest of his life.

The first season under the new owners was a financial success, though an artistic disaster. Attendance was good—1,283,611, breaking the previous year's record by over 500,000—and even after the team tied for last place at 62-92, interest remained high. Before the start of the 1948 season, the team had already received more than $480,000 for season tickets.

The situation was similar in '48, '49 and '50. The Pirates never finished higher than fourth, but attendance and interest remained high.[2] Herman was let go after one season, succeeded by Billy Meyer. Ralph Kiner was the hitting star, leading the National League in home runs every year from his rookie season of 1946 until he was traded in 1953. Others who drew fans were Hank Greenberg, Rip Sewell and Johnny Hopp. But by and large, these Pirate teams weren't very good.

It didn't matter much to Wagner. He knew he was nearing the end of the line. The road trips were becoming less frequent. He went to spring training in California in 1948 but returned home ahead of the team, still feeling the effects of a long bout of the flu that had afflicted him over the winter. It was to be his last spring training.

Overall, his health remained good, his main complaints just the ravages of old age. The big house on Beechwood was still the center of his family life—and it was a family that had grown just after the war. Eleanor Howieson, who worked with the Wagners' daughter Virginia at the Union Trust Co. in Pittsburgh, had gone through a divorce and was looking for a place to live. Bessie and Honus had opened their doors to her, and she moved in and became part of the family, living with them for four years before eventually leaving to remarry in 1950.[3]

When he wasn't at home or at Forbes Field, Wagner spent his days and evenings at the Elks Club, visiting his favorite watering holes in Carnegie or hanging around Wilsher's barber shop in town.

"We see Honus every once in a while walking along Main Street," his hometown paper reported on the occasion of his 75th birthday. "The eyes are a little dim now behind the steel rimmed glasses which he takes off when you stop to talk to him. The steps are more measured now. The very young boys pass him by. They don't know who he is. But our particular generation will always remember the 'Flying Dutchman' club that was organized in his garage...

"Honus is a legend now. His feats have been told and retold so many times that they enter the realm of fable.

"Honus is content now, and not quite aware of his well-earned fame. Asked why he hadn't gone on to other sections of the country, he shrugged, 'I like it here in Carnegie.'

"As we said, there are many stories about Honus, some true, some half true, and others which have become legend. No one really cares. He's a great man to us."[4]

Wagner was twice honored in 1951 by having his name attached to local sites in Carnegie. In March, the Pennsylvania Railroad dedicated a new train tower and named it "Wagner Tower" (Wagner threw the first switch at the ceremonies). Later in the year, Carnegie's Little League organization was renamed the Honus Wagner Little League.

The Pirate failures of 1949 and '50 continued in 1951. As another disappointing season wore down, Wagner, increasingly bothered by various infirmities and feeling all of his 77 years, realized that he wouldn't be back for 1952. That fact was on his mind in the Pirates' Forbes Field clubhouse before a game late in the season, later recounted by *Pittsburgh Post-Gazette* columnist Al Abrams:

"There was Wagner standing in the middle of the room, his eyes staring first at one side of the dressing quarters, then slowly moving around as in search of memories deep in the recesses of his mind.

Always the Pirate, Wagner finds time for another of his favorite pastimes. *(Photo courtesy of Leslie Blair)*

The new Forbes Field, which would be the site of some of Wagner's and the Pirates' greatest moments. *(Photo courtesy of The Sporting News)*

Wagner and a salesman wait on a customer in 1930 in the sporting goods store that bore Wagner's name. *(Photo courtesy of Leslie Blair)*

Bessie Wagner relaxes with daughters Virginia (left) and Betty—Honus called them "my boys"—on the porch of the family home in 1933. *(Photo courtesy of Leslie Blair)*

With owner William Benswanger looking on, Wagner signs the contract that brought him back to the Pirates as a coach in 1933. *(Photo courtesy of the Pittsburgh Pirates)*

After a 15-year absence, Wagner returned to the Pirates as a coach in 1933. "Baseball has been my life," he said shortly before returning. "There is nothing I like so well." *(Photo courtesy of Leslie Blair)*

A studio portrait of Wagner in the 1930s. *(Photo courtesy of George Brace)*

When Pie Traynor became Pirates manager in 1934, one of the coaches he inherited was his old buddy. *(Photo courtesy of George Brace)*

Even from the back, there was no mistaking Wagner and his trademark bowed legs as he patrolled the Pirates dugout as a coach in the 1940s. *(Photo courtesy of Associated Press)*

Wagner keeps a close eye on batting practice during his tenure as a Pirate coach. He was always available to help the young players. *(Photo courtesy of Leslie Blair)*

Ten of the 11 living members of baseball's first Hall of Fame class met at Cooperstown on June 12, 1939, to celebrate the 100th anniversary of the invention of the game. Standing (left to right) are Honus Wagner, Grover Cleveland Alexander, Tris Speaker, Napoleon Lajoie, George Sisler and Walter Johnson; and seated (left to right) Eddie Collins, Babe Ruth, Connie Mack and Cy Young. The 11th member of that class, Ty Cobb, was delayed en route from California and arrived moments after the photo was taken. *(Photo courtesy of Associated Press/World Wide Photos)*

Frank Gustine, who played for the Pirates from 1939-48, was another of the young players Wagner took under his wing. He was a frequent dinner guest at the Wagner home. *(Photo courtesy of George Brace)*

The Waner brothers—Lloyd (left) and Paul—were Wagner favorites on and off the field. *(Photo courtesy of George Brace)*

After Bing Crosby became a part owner of the Pirates in 1946, he made a point of visiting Forbes Field—and Wagner—whenever he was in Pittsburgh. *(Photo courtesy of Leslie Blair)*

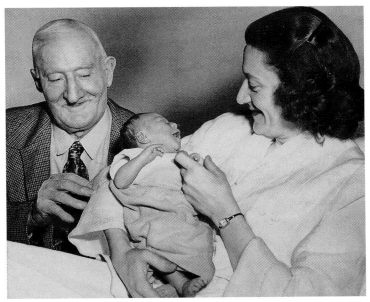

Honus Wagner, the proud grandfather, is introduced to his
new granddaughter, Leslie, by his daughter Betty in 1951.
*(Photo courtesy of Leslie Blair)*

On the eve of his 75th
birthday, Honus shares
a moment with the
family dog, Mickey.
*(Photo courtesy of the
Historical Society of
Carnegie)*

Wagner celebrates his
79th birthday with
Bessie and his grand-
daughter, Leslie Blair.
*(Photo courtesy of
Leslie Blair)*

A frail Wagner (in automobile) is honored at ceremonies unveiling his
statue outside Forbes Field on April 30, 1955. On the speakers' platform
are (left to right) Fred Clarke, George Gibson, Bill Benswanger, Rev.
N.R.H. Moor, Mrs. Benswanger, Baseball Commissioner Ford Frick,
National League President Warren Giles, Ben Fairless and John W.
Galbreath. It would be Wagner's last public appearance. *(Photo courtesy
of the Pittsburgh Pirates)*

"We, Ralph [Kiner] and I, watched Honus for a full ten minutes as he stood in one spot, motionless but for the swing of his watery eyes and the shaking of a hand gripped with palsy. The tentacles of illness had been wrapping themselves around Wagner for some time. This was to be his last visit to the Pirate clubhouse and he knew it."[5]

On February 16, 1952, the Pirates announced that Wagner, a week short of his 78th birthday, was being retired on a pension after 40 years in the National League. Branch Rickey, who had become the Pirates' general manager in 1950, had given Wagner the option of signing another contract or retiring at full pay on a lifetime pension. Wagner, who was increasingly having trouble getting around and who had missed the last three spring trainings because of health problems, mulled the offer over for a day before taking Rickey up on it.

"Guess old father time has caught up with me," he told reporters who gathered at his home.

"Never knew anybody to retire so young. Heck, the season is just about to get under way and here I am retiring. It sure took a long time."[6]

# Twenty-one

In February 1953, a group of former players approached Pittsburgh Mayor David Lawrence about one final honor for Wagner, then 79 and largely confined to his home by the infirmities of old age.

The players, members of the Pittsburgh Professional Baseball Association—Pie Traynor, Wilbur Cooper, Frank Gustine, Lee Handley and Moose Solters—originally wanted Forbes Field renamed "Honus Wagner Field." When that idea met with opposition, they proposed a statue honoring Wagner be erected at Pennant Place and Sennot Street, across from the press gate at Forbes Field.

The players got no argument from Lawrence, a big sports fan, or County Commissioner Harry Fowler, himself a onetime shortstop in the Federal League. With the city and county behind them, the PPBA began raising funds for the project.

The statue would be sculpted by Frank Vittor, an Italian-born artist who had come to the United States more than 40 years earlier and whose studio was on Fifth Avenue in Pittsburgh's Oakland section. The cost of the statue and its granite pedestal was $32,500. The piece—9 feet tall and a ton and a half—caught Wagner in his prime, following through on a swing; and on the side of the 9-foot pedestal would be his statistics. But the old man balked. No stats, he said; on the side of the pedestal he wanted carvings of children. Vittor didn't have to look far for models. Wagner's granddaughter, Leslie Blair, and three boys from the neighborhood were used.

Wagner may have been the most popular athlete ever to come out of Pittsburgh, but, surprisingly, the fundraising went slowly. Project backers sent 40,000 letters to Pirate season ticket-holders, statue subscribers and baseball fans in general. Donations trickled in, among them $100 from Bing Crosby, another $100 from the

Milwaukee Braves, $5 from the Pirates' Dick Groat (who was in the army at the time), and $25 from 84-year-old John Heydler, who had been president of the National League from 1916 to '34.

As of April 1954, only 729 of the 40,000 letters brought donations. But other fundraising methods were working: On Opening Day in 1954, a local modeling agency took up a collection in front of Forbes Field, raising $750; $75 was collected from fans at the West Penn Cup soccer tournament; South Park Speedway offered $500 or 50 percent of one night's gate, whichever was larger; money was collected at an oldtimers game at Forbes Field on August 9, 1954 between the "Has-Beens," including Traynor, Gustine, Cooper and others, and "Never-Wases," a team featuring local media members and celebrities.

What finally put the drive over the top was a dinner held by Benjamin F. Fairless, then a director of the Pirates and chairman of U.S. Steel Corp. It raised $18,000, bringing the fund's total to $40,000.

Wagner followed the fundraising efforts from his home in Carnegie, where he and Bessie spent almost all their time. Age had left him unable to go to the ballpark or virtually anywhere else for two years. The Wagners stayed out of the spotlight, emerging only for special occasions, such as his 80th birthday. Mayor Lawrence proclaimed February 24, 1954, "Honus Wagner Day" in Pittsburgh. He made the announcement at the Wagner home, during a ceremony attended by Cooper, Bill Benswanger and friends and family. And on his birthday, Wagner received a congratulatory letter from President Dwight Eisenhower, who years before had said that as a boy, he wanted to be a ballplayer like Wagner. Eisenhower wrote, ". . . your name and the records you established are as well known to the boy of today as they were to me, and that, I think, must prove that you are truly one of baseball's immortal heroes."[1]

As feeble as he had become, Wagner was still able to rise to the occasion, if needed. A calendar company wanted to feature him on a 1955 calendar. The idea was to pose him in uniform, signing a baseball for a young boy. Several boys were suggested, but Wagner himself selected the winner—7-year-old Gerry Sgro, who lived next door and was Wagner's favorite among the kids in the neighborhood.

Despite his 80 years, Wagner donned a uniform and posed for a photo on his porch during the summer of 1954; an artist painted a portrait from the photo, inserting Gerry Sgro, and the calendar was later printed from the portrait.

Wagner was also able to appear at the dedication of his statue on the morning of April 30, 1955, in Schenley Park Plaza. Among the guests were dozens of former players, including Fred Clarke, Max Carey, Traynor, George Sisler, Cy Young, Ginger Beaumont, Tommy Leach, Alex McCarthy, Cooper, George Gibson, Hans Lobert, Ed Abbaticchio, Jimmy Viox, Mike Simon and Lefty Leifield. Honus was driven out from Carnegie, and, never leaving the car parked in front of the speakers' platform, listened as a parade of guests extolled his virtues as a person and accomplishments as a ballplayer. When they were done, after Benswanger, Baseball Commissioner Ford Frick, Mayor Lawrence, National League President Warren Giles and the others finished their speeches, Honus' granddaughter Leslie pulled the cord that unveiled the statue.

Through the ceremonies, Wagner had sat impassively in the front passenger seat of the car. But as his monument was unveiled, his eyes widened, and a slight smile crossed his face. Minutes later, the car drove away, taking the exhausted Wagner back home. It was to be his final public appearance.

Honus Wagner didn't have much time left. On October 9, he fell in his living room, hurting his shoulder and hip. He never recovered from the injuries. He was confined to bed, and his already frail health began deteriorating. By late November he was growing steadily weaker and his blood pressure was dangerously low. He slipped in and out of consciousness, and only occasionally was he able to recognize visitors.

Sportswriter Charles "Chilly" Doyle of the *Pittsburgh Sun Telegraph* came by to visit. "I tried to talk to Wagner a few days before he died," he wrote after Wagner's death. "But he was unconscious. His faithful wife, with tears in her eyes, leaned close to his ear and said: 'Can you say hello to Chilly?'

"Then, when I mentioned Fred Clarke, he tried to smile. But death was hovering so close that the only thing I could do was hold that wonderful right hand and vow thereafter to remember a marvelous friend in my prayers."[2]

Toward the end, the only person Wagner recognized was his 4-year-old granddaughter, Leslie. She'd climb up on his bed, and he'd greet her with "Hello, Sweetheart," the name he always called her.

December 5 was the 36th birthday of Honus' daughter Betty. She had feared that he might die on her birthday. That day, a Monday, came, and Wagner had held on. Just after midnight, with family members around his bed, he stirred. He had made it past her birthday.

Then, at 12:56 a.m. on December 6, John Peter Wagner died.

More than 2,000 mourners paid tribute to Wagner at Beinhauer Mortuary on Liberty Avenue in Pittsburgh. The funeral was December 9, attended by another 200-some friends and luminaries from sports, business and politics. Pallbearers included Cooper, Traynor, Gustine and Benswanger.

Among the baseball players past and present in attendance were Hugh Mulcahy, Frank Thomas, Dick Groat, Moose Solters, Billy Southworth and Pete Castiglione. Some of Honus' old friends were also there—brothers Beggs and Buck Snyder, who played basketball on Wagner's barnstorming teams in the early 1900s; sportswriters Chilly Doyle and Les Biederman; and dozens of his neighbors from Carnegie.

Outside the funeral home, honorary pallbearers—among them National League President Warren Giles, Pirates President John Galbreath, Mayor Lawrence, State Supreme Court Justice Michael Musmanno and former player George Sisler—formed an honor guard on West Liberty Avenue, standing hatless in the swirling snow.

The family—Bessie, daughters Betty and Virginia, Honus' sister Carrie and brother Bill—led the procession to Jefferson Memorial Park. There, late on a cold, windswept December afternoon, Honus Wagner was laid to rest.

# *Epilogue*

After Honus Wagner's death, Bessie continued living in the house on Beechwood Avenue. When Three Rivers Stadium was built and the Pirates abandoned Forbes Field, Bessie was offered a chance to throw out a ceremonial first pitch at the inaugural game at the new ballpark or at the final day at Forbes Field. Knowing how much Forbes meant to Honus, she chose the latter. In ceremonies on June 28, 1970, she delivered a first pitch before the Pirates' final appearance at Forbes Field, a double-header against Chicago. Bessie died on June 30, 1971. The Wagners' daughters spent the rest of their lives in the Pittsburgh area. Betty and her husband, Harry Blair, had one child, Leslie. Betty died in October 1992. Virginia Wagner never married; she died in 1985. Eleanor Howieson, who moved into the Wagner home after World War II and was something of an "adopted" family member, remarried in 1950 and now lives in North Canton, Ohio.

# Honus Wagner's Career Statistics

| Year | Team | G | AB | H | R | HR | RBI | 2B | 3B | Avg. | SB |
|------|------|---|----|----|----|----|-----|----|----|------|----|
| 1897 | Louisville | 61 | 237 | 80 | 37 | 2 | 39 | 17 | 4 | .338 | 19 |
| 1898 | Louisville | 151 | 591 | 180 | 80 | 10 | 105 | 31 | 4 | .305 | 27 |
| 1899 | Louisville | 147 | 571 | 192 | 98 | 7 | 113 | 43 | 13 | .336 | 37 |
| 1900 | Pittsburgh | 135 | 527 | 201 | 107 | 4 | 100 | 45 | 22 | .381 | 38 |
| 1901 | Pittsburgh | 141 | 556 | 196 | 100 | 6 | 126 | 37 | 11 | .353 | 49 |
| 1902 | Pittsburgh | 137 | 538 | 177 | 105 | 3 | 91 | 33 | 16 | .329 | 42 |
| 1903 | Pittsburgh | 129 | 512 | 182 | 97 | 5 | 101 | 30 | 19 | .355 | 46 |
| 1904 | Pittsburgh | 132 | 490 | 171 | 97 | 4 | 75 | 44 | 14 | .349 | 53 |
| 1905 | Pittsburgh | 147 | 548 | 199 | 114 | 6 | 101 | 32 | 14 | .363 | 57 |
| 1906 | Pittsburgh | 142 | 516 | 175 | 103 | 2 | 71 | 38 | 9 | .339 | 53 |
| 1907 | Pittsburgh | 142 | 515 | 180 | 98 | 6 | 82 | 38 | 14 | .359 | 61 |
| 1908 | Pittsburgh | 51 | 568 | 201 | 100 | 10 | 109 | 39 | 19 | .354 | 53 |
| 1909 | Pittsburgh | 137 | 495 | 168 | 92 | 5 | 100 | 39 | 10 | .339 | 35 |
| 1910 | Pittsburgh | 150 | 556 | 178 | 90 | 4 | 81 | 34 | 8 | .320 | 24 |
| 1911 | Pittsburgh | 130 | 473 | 158 | 87 | 9 | 89 | 23 | 16 | .334 | 20 |
| 1912 | Pittsburgh | 145 | 558 | 181 | 91 | 7 | 102 | 35 | 20 | .324 | 26 |
| 1913 | Pittsburgh | 114 | 413 | 124 | 51 | 3 | 56 | 18 | 4 | .300 | 21 |
| 1914 | Pittsburgh | 150 | 552 | 139 | 60 | 1 | 50 | 15 | 9 | .252 | 23 |
| 1915 | Pittsburgh | 151 | 566 | 155 | 68 | 6 | 78 | 32 | 17 | .274 | 22 |
| 1916 | Pittsburgh | 123 | 432 | 124 | 45 | 1 | 39 | 15 | 9 | .287 | 11 |
| 1917 | Pittsburgh | 74 | 230 | 61 | 15 | 0 | 24 | 7 | 1 | .265 | 5 |
| **21 Years** | | 2789 | 10449 | 3430 | 1740 | 101 | 1732 | 651 | 252 | .327 | 722 |

# Appendices

*"Here I am standing up to make a speech, but I don't know what I am going to say. Well, I can't see any use in standing here, so I guess I might just as well sit down."*
— Honus Wagner, addressing
a banquet in his honor in
St. Joseph, Missouri, in 1914[1]

*"He'd tell you more damned stories. And half of 'em were rather ridiculous. But he loved to talk and he loved to tell stories. ...He was such a nice man. Everyone loved him."*
— Dr. Harold "Jack" Snyder,
who barnstormed with
Wagner in the 1940s

During his playing career, Honus Wagner was as inconspicuous off the field as he was dazzling on it. A shy individual, he did his best to stay out of the public eye.

He went to great lengths to avoid talking to reporters. Once, the *New York Times'* Harry Cross showed up at Wagner's room at the Ansonia Hotel, where the Pirates stayed when they were in New York. Years later, Pittsburgh sportswriter Fred Lieb recounted the visit. "When Harry knocked at his door, Wagner, dressed only in his shorts (it was long before any hotel had air conditioning), greeted him in a friendly spirit. 'I'm from the *New York Times* and I would like to do a story on you,' said Harry. Wagner showed him into his bathroom. His tub was filled with cracked ice and bottles of beer. 'Drink all the beer you want, but no story,' said Honus."[2]

It was only years later, after his playing career had ended and he was back in uniform as a coach for the Pirates, that he became a popular figure on the banquet circuit.

To entertain his audiences, he had a repertoire of baseball stories. Some were based on fact; but most were the products of his imagination, stories he had told his daughters at bedtime when they were young, instead of fairy tales.

Following are some of the stories Honus Wagner liked to tell.

\* \* \*

There were train tracks that ran behind Forbes Field, and an opposing batter hit a ball over the fence and into the smokestack of a train. I was playing in the outfield, and I ran to the fence. The train engineer pulled a lever and a giant puff of steam came out of the smokestack, blowing the ball out. It came back over the fence, and I caught it for the out.

\* \* \*

It was the bottom of the ninth, the score was 2-2, there were two outs, and I was up. All of our bats were broken, so the batboy brought me a hatchet to use. The first ball was a strike; the second one, a strike. On the next pitch, I hit the ball, slicing it in half. One half was caught by one of the outfielders, but the other half went over the fence ... so the Pirates won 2 ½ -2.

\* \* \*

Once, I decided to have myself chased from a game early in order to go fishing. The game was played in Boston and Bill Klem was the judge at the plate. I told him, before the game, that I would crab at called strikes and would appreciate it if he threw me out of the game. I described that great fishing spot near Boston.

On my first appearance at bat the pitcher threw some beautiful strikes. I turned to Klem and insisted that they were outside. But he remained silent.

In the fourth inning I also protested but he didn't say a word. Finally I came to bat in the seventh with two on base and the Pirates behind. Now I wanted to hit and win the ballgame. Well, the first one was at least six inches outside and Klem called it a strike. I turned to Klem and seriously protested his decision. Finally he spoke. "You're out of the game, Honus; now go fishing."

\* \* \*

I had a pointer once that was the best in the world. He loved to hunt. We went out in the hills for quail one morning, and this dog picked up the scent and took off. I spent the whole day looking for him, but I never found him. So I finally went home. Two years later I was out in those same hills and I found him. There was nothing left but his skeleton, but he was still right on point. The dog died right there waiting for me to come up and shoot those quail.

\* \* \*

Although the spitter and shineball have been used for some time, Jack Miller, our second baseman, had never faced such pitching. In his first three trips to the plate, Jack failed to even foul the ball.

As we took our positions in the field, Jack insisted that the beer of the night before was the cause of his failure to hit. He swore off night life. I told him it wasn't the liquor—it was the shineball. Then I told him to watch the flight of the ball to see it hook.

On his next appearance to bat, Miller watched the shineball hook twice, and then finally fouled the third strike.

Overjoyed, he turned to me and yelled, "I fouled it, Hans! I fouled it! Now I can continue drinking."

* * *

When I broke into organized ball with Paterson, I was stationed at first base. I chewed tobacco continuously while playing, always having a pocketful of the best scrap. One afternoon as I reached for a chew, my hand became caught in the lining of my uniform. As I tried to get my hand free, the batter hit sharply to short. The ball was handled cleverly and I managed to make the catch by a one-hand stab. And to boot, my manager thought I was grandstanding. I was suspended for three days.

* * *

When I was playing with the Pirates, we had a rookie, Everett Booe. One day, we were giving home plate umpire Bill Klem a hard time, and his temper was short. Fred Clarke sent Booe up to pinch hit, and Klem asked him his name. He said, "Booe." Klem said, "What did you say?" And the rookie replied, "Booe." Well, Klem got infuriated, and was going to throw Booe out of the game until Clarke came out and showed him the scorecard, and told him that the kid's name really was Booe.

* * *

I had a lot of good hunting dogs, but Arky Vaughan had one that was pretty good too. Arky would tie a piece of liver to the dog's tail when he went fishing. He'd put the dog's tail in the water, and when the fish came up and latched onto the dog's tail, he'd turn around and smack the fish silly on the bank.

* * *

Aside from being a good pitcher, Claude Hendrix could outeat any player in the National League. Claude and I decided upon a deep-water fishing trip one day. He hired a large motor boat while

I obtained the fishing tackle and bait. I questioned some old fishermen around the dock and they told me to use clams for bait. So I
got about three dozen of them and placed them in a sack. Hendrix
had the motor going and we traveled for nearly an hour before we
decided to cast the anchor. I set the poles and asked Claude to
pass the bait. He didn't understand me, so I told him, "The clams."
"Oh, the bait," he said. "If it's the clams you want, I ate them. I was so
hungry."

\* \* \*

I've got a riddle. The bases are loaded, and the batter hits the
ball over the fence for a home run. Yet not a man scores. How can
that be? Give up? It was a ladies' game!

\* \* \*

We were playing St. Louis, during the 1909 season. The Cardinals had a young pitcher, a real sensation. The kid had us beaten 4-
0, in the last of the seventh, and he seemed to be getting stronger.
In desperation, Fred Clarke asked me to do something, anything, to
break the youngster's concentration. I went to the plate and begged
him to throw his fastball. He did, a strike that sizzled over the plate.
Even though I had trouble seeing it, I asked him to throw another
one. It came in, even faster than the first. Once more I asked for his
fastball, and he threw an even faster pitch. As it crossed the plate, I
stuck out my bare hand and caught it, looked the ball over care-
fully, then tossed it back to him and said that he should quit throwing slow balls. It worked. The poor rookie was so upset that he
walked the next six batters. We won the game, but my hand was
sore for a week.

\* \* \*

We were playing at Forbes Field. It was late in the day and it was getting dark. The batter hit a ground ball toward me. Just at that time, a rabbit ran onto the field. By mistake I grabbed the rabbit  instead of the ball and threw it to first. The batter was out by a hare.

# List of Sources

## Publications

The Baseball Encyclopedia

Baseball Magazine

Burlington (Wisconsin) Press

Carnegie Magazine

Carnegie Signal-Item

Carnegie Union

Chicago Daily Inter Ocean

Chicago Herald American

Chicago Tribune

Christian Science Monitor

Collier's

Dawson Springs (Kentucky) Progress

The De Molay Councilor

Kansas City Star

Louisville Courier-Journal

Mansfield (Pennsylvania) Item

Marion (Indiana) Chronicle

The National Pastime

New York Evening Telegram

New York Evening Post

New York Herald

New York Times

Paterson (New Jersey) Evening News

Philadelphia Bulletin

Philadelphia Public Ledger

Pittsburgh Chronicle Telegraph

Pittsburgh Leader

Pittsburgh Gazette-Times

Pittsburgh Press

Pittsburgh Post

Pittsburgh Post-Gazette

Pittsburgh Sun-Telegraph

Reach's Official Baseball Guides

The Referee

Spalding's Official Baseball Guides

Sport Magazine

Sporting Life

The Sporting News

Sports Collectors Digest

Sports Illustrated

Uniontown (Pennsylvania) Morning Herald

Warren Times Observer

Warren Ledger

Wheeling Register

Wilmington Morning News


### *Organizations and Institutions*

Akron-Summit Co. Public Library, Akron, Ohio

Allegheny County (Pennsylvania) Prothonotary's Office

Alexandria (Louisiana) Public Library

Aurora (Illinois) Public Library

Brown University

Burlington (Wisconsin) Public Library

The Carnegie, Pittsburgh, Pennsylvania

Carnegie (Pennsylvania) Free Library

Carnegie-Mellon University

Center for Research Libraries, Chicago

Clerk of the U.S. Bankruptcy Court, Pittsburgh

Cleveland Public Library

Comptroller of the Currency, Washington

Danforth Library, Paterson, New Jersey

Dawson Springs (Kentucky) Museum and Art Center

Deland (Florida) Public Library

Delaware Secretary of State's Division of Corporations

Dennison (Ohio) Public Library

Enoch Pratt Free Library, Baltimore

Haines City (Florida) Public Library

Harold Washington Library, Chicago

Hillman Library, University of Pittsburgh

Historical Society of Carnegie, Pennsylvania

Honus Wagner Co., Pittsburgh

Library of Congress

Mansfield (Ohio) Public Library

Margaret I. King Library, University of Kentucky

Museum of Tobacco Art and History

National Archives and Record Service, Washington

National Baseball Museum and Hall of Fame

Ohio County (West Virginia) Library

Paterson (New Jersey) Historical Society

Paterson (New Jersey) Sports Hall of Fame

Pennsylvania State Department of Education

Pennsylvania State Department of Vital Records

Philadelphia Free Library

The Pittsburgh Pirates

Pittsburgh Chamber of Commerce

St. John's Lutheran Church, Carnegie, Pennsylvania

St. Louis Public Library

Saranac Lake (New York) Public Library

Society for American Baseball Research

Thomasville (Georgia) Public Library

University of Pittsburgh

U.S. Census Bureau

U.S. Department of Justice

Western Pennsylvania Historical Society

Wicomico Co. (Maryland) Public Library

Wilmington (Delaware) Institute Library

## *Books*

*The Genealogical and Personal History of Western Pennsylvania,* Lewis Historical Publishing Co., 1915

*A Baseball Album,* Lippincott & Crowell Publishers, 1980

*The Pittsburgh Pirates,* Frederick Lieb, G.P. Putnam's Sons, 1948

*The Story of the World Series, An Informal History,* Frederick Lieb, G.P. Putnam's Sons, 1949

*Sport Magazine's All-Time All Stars,* Edited by Tom Murray, Atheneum, 1977

*Baseball, The Golden Age,* Harold Seymour, New York-Oxford University Press, 1971

*Baseball Personalities,* Jimmy Powers, Rudolph Field Publisher, 1949

*The Baseball Story,* Frederick Lieb, G.P. Putnam's Sons, 1950

*Baseball's Hall of Fame*, Ken Smith, A.S. Barnes and Company, 1952

*Baseball Grins,* Honus Wagner, Laurel House, 1933

*Baseball,* Robert Smith, Simon and Schuster, 1947

*The Umpire Story*, James M. Kahn, G.P. Putnam's Sons, 1953

*Kings of the Diamond,* Lee Allen and Tom Meany, G.P. Putnam's Sons, 1965

*The Story of Ty Cobb*, Gene Schoor, Simon and Schuster, 1952

*Baseball's Greatest Lineup,* Christy Walsh, A.S. Barnes and Company, 1952

*Baseball's Greatest Teams*, Tom Meany, A.S. Barnes and Company, 1949

*My Life in Baseball, The True Record,* Ty Cobb with Al Stump, Doubleday & Co., 1961

*The Story of Baseball In Words and Pictures,* John Durant, Hastings House, 1947

*The Best of Baseball,* Edited by Sidney Offit, G.P. Putnam's Sons, 1956

*Christy Mathewson, Baseball's Greatest Pitcher,* Gene Schoor, Julian Messner Inc., 1953

*The National League*, Edited by Ed Fitzgerald, A.S. Barnes and Company, 1952

*100 Years of Baseball,* Lee Allen, Bartholomew House, 1950

*Baseball As I Have Known It,* Fred Lieb, Coward, McCann and Geoghegan, 1952

*The Tumult and the Shouting*, Grantland Rice, A.S. Barnes and Company, 1954

*Baseball and Mr. Spalding,* Arthur Bartlett, Farrar, Straus and Young, Inc., 1951

*My Fifty Years in Baseball,* Edward Grant Barrow with James M. Kahn, Coward-McCann, 1951

# *Footnotes*

### Chapter One Footnotes

1.  U.S. Census, 1880, 1900

2.  The house was later razed and the Carnegie jail was built on the site. Chartiers Street itself no longer exists, having been closed off and converted into a walkway when downtown Carnegie was turned into a pedestrian mall in the 1960s, and the jail was later demolished. A funeral home now stands on the property that had been the site of Wagner's birthplace.

3.  Wagner was referred to as "Hannis" in the press at the start of his minor-league career. That evolved into "Honus" and "Hans." Teammates called him "Dutch" early in his career; in his later years, they called him "Jay." Some teammates, near the end of his playing career, accorded him a respectful "Mr. Wagner." He was also "Jay" to his wife, Bessie.

4.  Rev. Dittmer came to the Carnegie-Mansfield area from Farley, Missouri, in November 1882, and became one of the town's religious leaders. He formed a lifelong acquaintance with Wagner, later performing his wedding ceremony.

5.  *The Sporting News*, Nov. 22, 1950.

6.  *The Mansfield Item*, May 19, 1882.

7.  In an interview with the *Carnegie Signal-Item* for a story marking his 75th birthday (Feb. 24, 1949), Wagner recalled that he had survived several close calls in the mines, including two gas explosions in one day. He said he finally got disgusted with the work, and after a long, tedious day of loading two coal cars threw down his tools and walked off. "Grant Mine still owes me for those two cars," he said.

8.  *Pittsburgh Gazette Times*, Jan. 15, 1924.

9.   Mansfield and Chartiers combined in 1894; the new city was named Carnegie.

10.  *Collier's*, April 12, 1930.

11.  Like many events in his life, Wagner's recollection of his signing with Steubenville was greatly embellished as the years wore on. The story he told in the 1930s and '40s went something like this: Al had already signed with Steubenville for 1895. When he arrived in Ohio, he learned that the team was looking for players to fill out its roster, and he convinced Moreland to sign John. The team sent him an offer of $35 a month. He thought he deserved $40, and asked for it. Moreland wired back, telling Wagner to take it or leave it. He accepted the $35 salary, and hopped the next freight—in some versions he stowed away in a coal car—to Steubenville. This tale was told and retold by Wagner on the banquet circuit and after he returned to the Pirates as a coach. It appeared in print in more than a dozen newspapers and magazines during that time.

12.  Statistics from 1895 are from A.D. Suehsdorf, who documented the Wagners' season in the Winter 1987 edition of *The National Pastime* in an article entitled "Honus Wagner's Rookie Season."

13.  *Warren* (Ohio) *Ledger*, July 30, 1895.

14.  *Pittsburgh Gazette Times*, Jan. 18, 1924.


Chapter Two Footnotes


1.   Barrow's early reminiscences of that meeting with Wagner had it set in back of a Carnegie pool room, where Honus was pitching horseshoes. As the years went on, that story evolved into the rock-throwing contest in the train yard outside of town. Wagner, for his part, also went with the second, more dramatic version in his later years.

2.   *My Fifty Years in Baseball*, by Edward Grant Barrow with James M. Kahn (Coward-McCann)

3.   *The Sporting News*, Nov. 22, 1950.

4.   The *Paterson Evening News* referred to him as both "Hannis" and "Hannes."

5.    The player Dreyfuss and Pulliam were scouting was Dave Fultz,
      then playing for Brown University. Fultz later had a seven-year
      major-league career in Philadelphia, Baltimore and New York.
      McFarlan, for his part, later became a Pittsburgh sportswriter.

6.    *The Sporting News*, April 14, 1904.

7.    *The Sporting News*, Dec. 26, 1907.

8.    *Washington* (Pennsylvania) *Observer*, June 15, 1897.

9.    The six-hit, 20-total base day was reported on Page 1 of the Aug.
      28, 1897 edition of *The Sporting News*, complete with a large
      sketch of Wagner.

### Chapter Three Footnotes

1.    Instead of accepting a spot as a utilityman, Rogers asked for, and
      got, his release. The next day, Rogers was offered a contract by Pitts-
      burgh. He declined the offer to join the Pirates immediately, saying
      he had to tend to his sick wife. By the time he was ready to join
      Pittsburgh, the Pirates had found help elsewhere. He never made it
      back to the majors, and eventually caught on with Springfield of
      the Eastern League. In August in Wilkes-Barre, Pennsylvania, he got
      involved in a fight with a fan, breaking the man's leg and cutting his
      face. Rogers was saved from an angry crowd by teammates who
      got him out of town. By the end of the season, he had sunk to Class
      B ball.

2.    *The Sporting News*, Nov. 22, 1950.

3.    Third baseman Collins had batted .346 for first-place Boston in 1897.
      His .917 fielding percentage was fourth among regulars. Clingman
      was the best at his position with a .947 percentage, though he bat-
      ted just .228.

4.    *Louisville Courier-Journal*, March 8, 1898.

5.    Wagner had failed to return a contract sent him in January. It called
      for a salary of $1,500 a year. His delay in signing was more a matter
      of his indifference to legal matters than a holdout. He eventually
      signed for the $1,500.

6.    *The Sporting News*, Feb. 19, 1898.

## Chapter Four Footnotes

1.  Despite the team's late rush, Pulliam wasn't standing pat. He made two key additions in September, obtaining pitcher Deacon Phillippe from Minneapolis of the Western League and third baseman Tommy Leach from Auburn of the New York State League. Both were important players in the championship Pittsburgh teams of the early 1900s. Of the 24 players who started the 1898 season with the Colonels, only nine were left by season's end.

2.  *Louisville Courier-Journal*, Sept. 4, 1898.

3.  *Louisville Courier-Journal*, Sept. 15, 1898.

4.  Editions of the *Chicago Tribune* and *Louisville Courier-Journal* of Oct. 17, 1898 both referred to Wagner's throw as a record. The *Tribune* said the old record was 400 feet, 7 ½ inches, set in 1872 by John Hatfield, who had a one-game career with New York that year. The *Courier-Journal* listed the record as 399 feet, and said it was set by former Chicago infielder Ned Williamson "years ago."

5.  *The Sporting News,* March 30, 1900. Interestingly, a few years later Dexter would be a hero in a much more tragic event. He was in the audience at the Iroquois Theater in Chicago on Dec. 30, 1903 when a fire broke out. He rushed his family to safety, then pulled people out of the crush of frantic theatergoers who were trying to escape. More than 600 people died in the fire and subsequent panic.

6.  In a few months, the story had been embellished to include Clarke greeting Wagner at home plate after the winning blast and announcing a $25 fine for ignoring the bunt sign. Wagner kept the tale alive in his later years on the banquet circuit. After Wagner died in 1955, Clarke was reflecting on the life of his old friend. He acknowledged that "the bunt story" was fiction.

7.  *Chicago Inter Ocean,* May 15, 1899.

8.  *Louisville Courier-Journal,* June 19, 1899.

9.  *Louisville Courier-Journal,* July 17, 1899.

10. *Washington Post,* July 17, 1899.

11. *The Sporting News*, Sept. 2, 1899.

12.   *Louisville Courier-Journal,* Aug, 23, 1899.

13.   In addition to being brought to Paterson and Louisville—and later Pittsburgh—thanks to Wagner, Flaherty was present when Wagner signed his first professional contract in 1895. Flaherty, in fact, signed it too, as a witness.

14.   *The Sporting News,* Dec. 15, 1900.


Chapter Five Footnotes

1.   *Pittsburgh Commercial Appeal,* March 14, 1900.

2.   *Sport Magazine's All-time All Stars,* edited by Tom Murray (Atheneum).

3.   *The Sporting News,* March 31, 1900.

4.   *A Baseball Century: The First 100 Years of the National League* (Macmillan Publishing Co. Inc).

5.   In addition to his one appearance on the mound in 1900, Wagner was at third base in nine games, at second base in seven, and at first base in three. He had 118 games in the outfield, playing all three positions.

6.   Wagner gave his slightly inaccurate account of winning the 1900 batting championship in numerous interviews after his playing career, and often told the story on the banquet circuit during his days as a Pirates coach. Several of his obituaries also repeated the story as fact.

7.   The players' shares from the postseason series were fattened by the fact that they refused to give Pittsburgh baseball writers a portion of the proceeds. The writers had assumed they'd get a cut because the trophy that they played for was donated by the *Pittsburgh Chronicle Telegraph,* which helped hype the series. But Wagner and his teammates vetoed sharing the profits with the writers.

8.   *The Sporting News,* Nov. 22, 1950.

9.   *The Sporting News,* April 4, 1901.

10.    A similar incident occurred about six weeks later. The Pittsburgh
       crowd was stirred up by umpire Bob Emslie's ejection of Wagner
       during a game against Philadelphia. The mob surrounded the ump
       after the game, but he was able to escape Exposition Park on his
       own.

11.    *The Sporting News*, July 6, 1901.

12.    Carr was also released in August after playing in only nine games
       with the Pirates. He never returned to the majors.


## Chapter Six Footnotes


1.    As quoted in *Sporting Life*, May 31, 1902.

2.    As quoted in *Sporting Life*, June 28, 1902.

3.    *Chicago Tribune*, July 25, 1902.

4.    *Chicago Tribune*, Aug. 16, 1902.

5.    *Pittsburgh Press*, Aug. 16, 1902.

6.    Dexter had broken his ankle early in the season and was slow to
      recover. One night, Dreyfuss and president Harry Pulliam were
      checking out a report that American League president Ban Johnson
      had come to Pittsburgh to try to lure their players to the AL. They
      went out looking for him; instead, they found the supposedly in-
      jured Dexter enjoying a night on the town. Tannehill was declared
      ineligible in August when the Pirates discovered he had taken a
      $1,000 advance from the American League, even though he had
      already signed a Pittsburgh contract for 1903.

7.    Seymour, who had broken in as a pitcher, played nine more years
      without ever taking the mound again; it was also the last of only
      four pitching appearances in Donlin's 12-year career. Beckley's four
      innings of work that day was the only time he pitched in his 20-
      year career.

8.    The Pirates had an opportunity to win a 104th game; their season
      was scheduled to end Oct. 5, but the field was unplayable.

9.    *Sport Magazine's All-Time All-Stars*, edited by Tom Murray (Ath-
      eneum)

10.  Tommy Leach and Harry Smith also signed with the AL for 1903, but both had already agreed to terms with the Pirates. Dreyfuss protested their AL contracts, and a joint AL-NL committee ordered both players returned to Pittsburgh.


### Chapter Seven Footnotes

1.  A month later Pulliam made another disciplinary move, asking for and receiving the resignation of umpire Holliday, whose competence had been questioned by other teams before the incident with Wagner.

2.  *Sporting Life,* Oct. 3, 1903.

3.  *Cincinnati Enquirer,* quoted in *The Sporting News*, June 20, 1903.

4.  Wagner was being booed not only in Chicago, but in several National League cities. He was getting a reputation as a dirty player and "kicker," or ump-baiter (*Sporting Life*, Aug. 1, 1903).

5.  Wilhelm's dedication was admirable, but he never made it to the 1903 World Series, having been released by the Pirates in early September.

6.  *Chicago Tribune*, Aug. 6, 1903.

7.  Dreyfuss' negotiations with the American League further infuriated some of the National League's old-guard owners, who believed that a postseason series would further legitimize the new league. The first World Series, then, was set up solely through the two owners, who bypassed the National Commission.

8.  *Pittsburgh Press*, Sept. 19, 1903.

9.  Doheny, who had gone 16-4 in 1902 and 16-8 in 1903, had been acting strangely over the course of the season before finally being hospitalized. Twice during the 1903 campaign he left the team, once for three days, the second time for two weeks after telling teammates "detectives" were following him. While his teammates were playing in the World Series, he attacked and severely injured a faith cure doctor, Oberlin Horwarth, with a poker and was committed to the Danvers (Massachusetts) Insane Asylum. He never recovered from the breakdown and died in 1916, at age 32.

10.  Wagner and many of his teammates became regular patients of Reese over the years. "That fellow has something," Fred Clarke was quoted in the Sept. 26, 1903 edition of *Sporting Life*. "I don't know what, but he manages to make a sore man feel good."

11.  Young was one of the pitchers Wagner mastered during his career, hitting .343 against him.

12.  *The Story of the World Series: An Informal History*, by Frederick G. Lieb (G.P. Putnam's Sons).

13.  The 1903 season was Murphy's last with the Pirates. He became groundskeeper for the New York Giants for the 1904 season, replaced in Pittsburgh by James O'Malley. He got a baptism by fire in late January, 1904, when floods swamped Exposition Park. O'Malley, new to the job, went to the outfield in a boat to assess damage. While sitting there, a large chunk of ice floated by; sitting on it was a rabbit.

Chapter Eight Footnotes

1.  Interview with Harold Snyder, Oct. 22, 1993.

2  Dreyfuss' cautions weren't aimed only at Wagner. Tommy Leach usually played in indoor baseball leagues in Cleveland during the off-season, something else Dreyfuss tried to discourage.

3.  *The Sporting News*, Jan. 2, 1904.

4  Toward the end of the 1903 season, National League President Harry Pulliam had asked Wagner for a photo to hang in his New York office. All winter, Wagner declined, citing his disappointing World Series performance.

5.  At the National League meeting in New York on Dec. 14, 1904, owners unanimously approved the idea of an annual World Series.

6.  *The Sporting News*, Nov. 5, 1904.

7.  The Jan. 21, 1905 edition of *The Sporting News* quoted a letter from Bransfield to Wagner, in which the former Pirate wrote: "It breaks me all up to think of separating from the best crowd of fellows possible to get together on a ball team. Still, it may all be for

the best, and will probably be of benefit to me." And both Wagner and Bransfield wrote to the *Pittsburgh Dispatch* to deny there had been trouble between them.

8.  *The Sporting News*, Nov. 19, 1904.

9.  Pulliam fined McGraw $150 and suspended him for 15 games for his behavior in the series. He planned further punishment for Muggsy's verbal abuse of Dreyfuss, but McGraw got an injunction from Superior Court in Boston. On June 1, the NL Board of Directors found McGraw innocent of wrongdoing, and further, censured Dreyfuss for engaging in a public altercation with the Giants manager. The courts later blocked Pulliam from disciplining McGraw because the Giants manager hadn't been given a hearing on Dreyfuss' charges.

10. *Pittsburgh Press*, Aug. 2, 1905.

11. *Pittsburgh Press*, Aug. 3, 1905.

12. Cobb was called up late in the season by Detroit, and played in 41 games for the Tigers that year.


Chapter Nine Footnotes


1.  *The Sporting News*, July 4, 1907.

2   *Pittsburgh Press*, Sept. 23, 1906.

3.  *The Sporting News*, Oct. 20, 1906.

4   Flaherty was still property of the Pirates, although he spent the 1906 season with Columbus, where he went 23-9.

5.  *The Sporting News*, Dec. 22, 1906.


Chapter Ten Footnotes


1.  *The Sporting News*, March 19, 1908.

2   *The New York Times*, Dec. 10, 1907.

3.    *The Sporting News,* Dec. 26, 1907.

4.    *The Sporting News,* March 5, 1908.

5.    The Pirates' original offer to Wagner for 1908 called for a $6,000 salary. While the team was at spring training, Dreyfuss twice came to Carnegie—meeting secretly with Wagner and his representatives in the home of Wagner's friend John S. Robb—to increase the offer, first to $7,500, then to $10,000.

6.    *Carnegie Union,* Feb. 21, 1908.

7.    *The Sporting News,* March 19, 1908.

8.    *Carnegie Union,* March 13, 1908.

9.    *Carnegie Union,* March 20, 1908.

10.   *The Pittsburgh Pirates,* by Frederick Lieb (G. P. Putnam's Sons).

11.   *Carnegie Union,* April 3, 1908.

12.   *Pittsburgh Gazette Times,* April 3, 1908.

13.   *Pittsburgh Gazette Times,* April 14, 1908.

14.   *The Sporting News,* April 16, 1908.

15.   *The Sporting News,* June 25, 1908.

16.   *Pittsburgh Gazette Times,* July 18, 1908.

17.   *The Sporting News,* July 16, 1908.

18.   *The Sporting News,* Aug. 6, 1908.

19.   *Chicago Tribune,* Oct. 6, 1908.

## Chapter Eleven Footnotes

1.    *The Sporting News,* Nov. 12, 1908.

2. The new park was to be named Forbes Field after British Gen. John Forbes, who played a major role in the founding of Pittsburgh. His name was chosen from some 100,000 suggestions received by Dreyfuss, who solicited fans' ideas.

3. *The Sporting News,* June 17, 1909.

4. *Pittsburgh Press,* May 30, 1909.

5. *Spalding's Official Baseball Guide for 1910.*

6. *Chicago Tribune,* July 1, 1909.

7. The Southern League teams, ignoring the request of President W.M. Kavanaugh, played a full schedule of games, although flags at all ballparks were lowered to half staff. In all, 30 professional leagues did not play in Pulliam's memory.

8. One of Pulliam's pallbearers was Claude McFarlan, who years earlier, as a pitcher for Norfolk of the Atlantic League, had tipped Pulliam off about a hotshot infielder playing for Paterson, Honus Wagner.

9. *My Life In Baseball—The True Record,* by Ty Cobb with Al Stump (Doubleday and Company Inc.).

10. *The Sporting News,* Oct. 14, 1909.

11. *My Life In Baseball—The True Record,* by Ty Cobb with Al Stump (Doubleday and Company Inc.).

12. *Chicago Tribune,* Oct. 12, 1909.

13. *The Sporting News,* Nov. 4, 1909.

14. *Carnegie Union,* Oct. 21, 1909.

15. *The Sporting News,* Dec. 16, 1909.

16. Wagner allowed his likeness to be used on other tobacco products—including cards put out by Kotton Cigarettes, manufactured by the Peoples Tobacco Co. Ltd. of Louisiana; and Toledo's Pinkerton Tobacco Co. cabinet cards. He also had a brand of cigar named in his honor, and the cigar bands carried his photo. And during the 1909 World Series, his photo appeared in half-page ads

for Murad cigarettes that ran in Pittsburgh newspapers. As for the idea that Wagner didn't want children exposed to tobacco, it should be noted that in Wagner's later years, several teenage boys in his hometown of Carnegie got their first lessons in chewing tobacco from Wagner himself. What Wagner did object to was the youngsters spending their money on tobacco.

17.   *The Sporting News*, Oct. 24, 1912.

18.   About 50 of the Wagner cards survive. Although not the rarest of tobacco cards, they are considered the Holy Grail of the card-collecting hobby. One sold at auction in March 1991 for $451,000.

19.   *The Sporting News*, Feb. 9, 1911.

20.   *Sporting Life*, May 21, 1910.


Chapter Twelve Footnotes

1.   *The Pittsburgh Pirates*, by Frederick Lieb (G.P. Putnam's Sons).

2   *The Sporting News*, July 14, 1910.

3.   *Sporting Life*, July 2, 1910.

4.   *Pittsburgh Press*, July 1, 1910.

5.   *Sporting Life,* July 23, 1910.

6.   First base had been a problem for the Pirates since Kitty Bransfield was traded before the 1905 season. Flynn had been their 13th first baseman in the last seven years.

7.   Before the 1910 season, he had played 97 games at first base, although he hadn't played the position since 1907.

8.   *Sporting Life*, Oct. 22, 1910.

9.   *The Sporting News*, Nov. 3, 1910.

10.   *The Sporting News*, Oct. 20, 1910.

11.   *The Sporting News,* Dec. 8, 1910.

12.     *The Sporting News*, Dec. 15, 1910.

13.     *The Sporting News*, Feb. 12, 1911.

14.     *Pittsburgh Press*, Aug. 17, 1911.

15.     *Pittsburgh Press*, Aug. 18, 1911.

16.     O'Toole turned out to be one of the worst investments Dreyfuss ever made, going 25-35 in a Pirate career that covered two full seasons and parts of two others. He finished his career going 1-1 in 10 games with the Giants at the end of the 1914 season. He was returned to the Pirates by New York for the 1915 campaign, but was released before the season.

17.     *Pittsburgh Gazette Times*, May 31, 1912.

18.     Donlin's wife died of cancer shortly after the season ended.

19.     *The Sporting News*, Oct. 24, 1912.

20.     The deal that sent Leach and Leifield to Chicago turned out, like the purchase of Marty O'Toole, to be a major disappointment. Artie Hofman left the Pirates in early September to go home to recover from "acute nervousness," and King Cole didn't last the season, having been sent to the minors. He was cut after the season. Hofman hit .283 in 17 games; Cole had a 2-2 record in 12 games. Leifield went 7-2 for the Cubs, while Leach hit .242 as a regular.

21.     *The Sporting News*, Oct. 31, 1912.

Chapter Thirteen Footnotes

1.     *Sporting Life*, Aug. 30, 1913.

2.     *Sporting Life*, Aug. 9, 1913.

3.     *Pittsburgh Gazette Times*, Oct. 5, 1913.

4.     In addition to finding a job for his father with the Pirates, Wagner was able to get his brother Al occasional work at the ballpark.

5.    *The Sporting News*, Dec. 20, 1913.

6.    *The Sporting News*, March 2, 1949.

7.    The $10,000 had been Wagner's salary every year since his short-lived "retirement" of 1908. By comparison, Detroit Tiger star Ty Cobb was earning $16,000 at this time.

8.    *Sporting Life*, March 21, 1914.

9.    *Sporting Life*, May 2, 1914.

10.    *Sporting Life*, July 18, 1914.

11.    *Philadelphia Public Ledger*, May 9, 1915.

12.    Gerber appeared at shortstop in 17 games for the 1914 Pirates, hitting just .241. The Pirates gave up on him after the 1915 season, and he eventually went to the St. Louis Browns and Boston Red Sox, for whom he appeared in more than 1,400 games in a career that lasted until 1929.

13.    *Sporting Life*, Dec. 19, 1914.

14.    He was hitting .273 at the time. At the end of the next two weeks, he was down to .261.

15.    *Sporting Life*, Aug. 22, 1914.


### Chapter Fourteen Footnotes

1.    *The Sporting News*, Dec. 17, 1914.

2    *The Sporting News*, Jan. 14, 1915.

3.    *The Sporting News*, Nov. 29, 1950.

4.    Interestingly, Wagner handled more than 50 chances at second flawlessly. He made an error on his first chance at shortstop, fielding Roger Bresnahan's grounder cleanly but unleashing his throw to first into the seats, allowing a run to score for Chicago.

5.    *Pittsburgh Press*, Sept. 9, 1915.

6. *Pittsburgh Press*, Sept. 9, 1915.

7. *Marion (Indiana) Chronicle*, Sept. 30, 1915.

8. The *Marion Chronicle* devoted more than half of its front page the next day to the "trial," complete with photos of Wagner, Condo, Browne and Stricler. Leading the coverage was a huge headline: "EXTRA! HANS WAGNER CONVICTED OF TERRIBLE, HORRIBLE, AWFUL CRIME"

9. *The Sporting News,* Dec. 30, 1915.

10. *Pittsburgh Gazette Times*, Feb. 25, 1916.

11. *The Sporting News*, March 2, 1916.

12. *The Sporting News*, Sept. 7, 1916.


Chapter Fifteen Footnotes

1. "*Sport Magazine*'s All-Time All Stars," edited by Tom Murray (Atheneum).

2. *The Sporting News* of November 28, 1912, reported that stories were circulating in Pittsburgh that Wagner was engaged. He denied the rumor. Periodically over the years, news would surface that he was about to marry, but each had always been a false alarm.

3. *The Pittsburgh Pirates*, by Frederick Lieb (G.P. Putnam's Sons).

4. *The Sporting News*, March 22, 1917.

5. *The Sporting News*, May 31, 1917.

6. *Chicago Tribune*, June 7, 1917.

7. Bill Hinchman, like Warren Adams, had failed to make the grade as a first baseman. He was returned to the outfield, and Bunny Brief was purchased from Salt Lake of the Pacific Coast League. Shortly after Wagner signed, Brief was sent back to Utah.

8. *Pittsburgh Gazette Times*, June 12, 1917.

9.    *Pittsburgh Leader,* June 15, 1917.

10.    *Pittsburgh Gazette Times,* July 4, 1917.

11.    Mollwitz, who had spent parts of four undistinguished seasons in the National League, was obtained from Kansas City of the American Association on August 30. In a bit of irony, as part of the payment for Mollwitz, Alex McCarthy, one of Wagner's close buddies on the team, was sent to Kansas City.


Chapter Sixteen Footnotes


1.    *Carnegie Union,* June 21, 1918.

2    During Wagner's "retirement"/holdout before the 1908 season, Carnegie Tech offered him a similar position.

3.    In a season shortened by numerous rainouts and cancellations, Wagner's team won its first two games, then lost its next eight.

4.    Wagner also became a Mason. On May 19, 1919, more than 700 Masons—the largest gathering ever for the Masons in Carnegie— met for the conferring of degrees on Wagner by the Centennial Lodge, No. 544, F & AM.

5.    In March 1924, the corporate name of the company was changed to Honus Wagner Inc., but papers were filed later that year to change the name back to Honus Wagner Sporting Goods Co.

6.    Wagner also sent business to the store through his various baseball enterprises in Carnegie. The town's high school team, for example, bought its uniforms from the Honus Wagner Sporting Goods Co., as did teams from other city leagues Wagner was involved with through the years.

7.    Later that year, Wagner invited Ruth to attend an Elks fundraiser in Carnegie. On December 29, Ruth was the guest of honor at the Elks Club for an evening of speeches, music and boxing exhibitions.

## Chapter Seventeen Footnotes

1.   Wagner's main reason for barnstorming was to play ball, not to make money. He was the main attraction, obviously, and the fans came out to see him, but he didn't exploit that fact to take a larger cut of the gate. One thing Wagner insisted upon when he took his various teams on the road was an equal split. No matter the opponent, no matter the situation, Wagner saw to it that both ballclubs—and all members of his team—shared receipts equally.

2.   John A. Bell, the president of Carnegie Trust, was later convicted on 12 counts of embezzlement over the disappearance of more than $800,000.

3.   People who had money in the bank when it closed eventually got most of it back, starting with a 40 percent payment issued on August 13, 1925. Three 10 percent payments followed over the next 14 months, with a 13.9 percent payment coming in August 1929.

4.   *Pittsburgh Gazette Times,* Nov. 1, 1925.

5.   Statement issued by the Citizens' Political Union of Pittsburgh, Oct. 31, 1925.

6.   Wagner was to receive 1 percent net annually on sales made by salesmen (other than Wagner) through outside solicitation, 3 percent on sales he himself made through outside solicitations, and another 1 percent on gross sales over $50,000.

7.   *Pittsburgh Press,* March 27, 1929.

8.   The Homestead Grays and Pittsburgh Crawfords, two of the top Negro League teams, were frequent visitors for games against Wagner's ballclubs, drawing sizeable crowds. But Wagner's teams' road games weren't big money-makers, and his insistence on keeping the teams operating sometimes ended up costing him money.

9.   *Baseball As I Have Known It,* by Fred Lieb (Coward, McCann and Geoghegan Inc.).

10.   *New York Evening Post,* Nov. 29, 1932.

Chapter Eighteen Footnotes

1.    *Pittsburgh Press,* Feb. 3, 1933.

2.    *Pittsburgh Gazette Times,* June 9, 1933.

3.    *Pittsburgh Press,* Feb. 17, 1952.

4.    Vaughan also led the league in errors in 1933 before turning into one of baseball's top fielders, and leading NL shortstops in putouts and assists for three years. Vaughan's Pirate career lasted until December 12, 1941, when he was traded to Brooklyn. He finally retired in 1948, and he was elected to the Baseball Hall of Fame in 1985, 33 years after his death in a boating accident in Eagleville, California.

5.    *Pittsburgh Press,* May 5, 1933.

6.    For the record, Wagner's team lost 7-0. He popped up to Jewel Ens at third in his only at-bat, but handled seven chances flawlessly at short.

7.    Some 60 years after the event, the Historical Society of Carnegie (PA) came into possession of a home movie of the celebration, which it had duplicated and sold to raise funds. The silent film included several minutes of the parade, some shots from the oldtimers game and field day activities, and presentations to Wagner.

8.    *Pittsburgh Press,* June 9, 1933.

9.    The Waner brothers were Mabel's favorite visitors. Not only were they fun, polite and appreciative of her cooking, Paul regularly slipped $5 under his plate. Lloyd, "Little Poison," usually left $2.

10.    Answer of Defendants, Case No. 3326, July Term, 1933, in the Court of Common Pleas of Allegheny County, Pennsylvania.

11.    Decree, Case No. 3326, July Term, 1933, in the Court of Common Pleas of Allegheny County, Pennsylvania.

## Chapter Nineteen Footnotes

1.  Traynor and Wagner's friendship went back more than a decade; he invested in Wagner's sporting goods store and the two of them lent their names to numerous Pittsburgh-area baseball leagues in the 1920s and '30s.

2.  *Chicago Tribune*, Oct. 12, 1938.

3.  *Chicago Tribune*, Sept. 29, 1938.

4.  Courtesy of the National Baseball Museum and Hall of Fame.

5.  *Carnegie Union*, June 29, 1939.

6.  *Carnegie Union*, Feb. 22, 1940.

## Chapter Twenty Footnotes

1 .  Aston didn't find another job after the Pirates let him go. His health began failing, he developed heart trouble, and he died the following September. He was just 60.

2.  In 1948, the Pirates drew more than 1.5 million fans, and went over the half-million-dollar mark in advance sales for the 1949 season by mid-January of that year.

3.  Honus relished playing the role of father for Eleanor. Once she brought home a boyfriend and introduced him to her adopted family. Wagner gave him the once-over, then asked: "Well, son, what are your intentions?" He and Eleanor eventually married.

4.  *Carnegie Signal-Item*, Feb. 24, 1949.

5.  *Pittsburgh Post-Gazette*, Dec. 7, 1955.

6.  *Chicago Herald American*, Feb. 17, 1952.

## Chapter Twenty-one Footnotes

1.  *Pittsburgh Press,* Feb. 21, 1954.

2.  *Pittsburgh Sun-Telegraph*, Dec. 7, 1955.

### Appendices footnotes

1.    *Sporting Life*, Nov. 7, 1914.

2.    *Baseball As I Have Known It*, by Fred Lieb (Coward, McCann and Geoghegan).